Wild Policy

Anthropology of Policy

Cris Shore and Susan Wright, editors

Wild Policy

Indigeneity and the Unruly Logics of Intervention

Tess Lea

Stanford University Press
Stanford, California

Stanford University Press
Stanford, California

Printed in the United States of America on acid-free, archival-quality paper

Library of Congress Cataloging-in-Publication Data

Names: Lea, Tess, author.
Title: Wild policy : indigeneity and the unruly logics of intervention / Tess Lea.
Other titles: Anthropology of policy (Stanford, Calif.)
Description: Stanford, California : Stanford University Press, 2020. | Series: Anthropology of policy | Includes bibliographical references and index.
Identifiers: LCCN 2020008438 (print) | LCCN 2020008439 (ebook) | ISBN 9781503612655 (cloth) | ISBN 9781503612662 (paperback) | ISBN 9781503612679 (ebook)
Subjects: LCSH: Aboriginal Australians—Government relations. | Aboriginal Australians—Government policy. | Aboriginal Australians—Social conditions. | Australia—Social policy.
Classification: LCC DU124.G68 L43 2020 (print) | LCC DU124.G68 (ebook) | DDC 323.1199/159—dc23
LC record available at https://lccn.loc.gov/2020008438
LC ebook record available at https://lccn.loc.gov/2020008439

Cover design: Rob Ehle

Contents

Figures

Acknowledgments

I have everyone's problem with acknowledgments: how to condense all the obligations racked up in the years of thinking, talking, listening, reading, and gleaning, that this—that any—book gathers into itself.

First and foremost, I am in debt to John Singer. When I first stammered out my rough proposal based vaguely on what I did not want to do, having no more precise an outline, he took a punt. Every year since, I've learned something new. Most of all, I have learned about perseverance and courage where there could so easily be defeat or rage. With all my heart, John, thank you for trusting me.

John does not work alone. To the people at Nganampa Health, and especially Paul Torzillo and Stephan Rainow, my profound appreciation for your support through thick and thin. The inspirational architect and policy critic Paul Pholeros died before I could get this book into a form he might have approved of. With others, I miss him daily. Early on at Groote Eylandt, Andy Irvine and Jeff Green, Richard Preece and Tony Wurramarrba, separately permitted my attention on the tumultuous SIHIP times; Ben Hall hosted me and checked details; and before I was evicted, David Ritchie and Jim Davidson enabled brief glimpses into bureaucratic backrooms. Justin O'Brien, Yvonne Margarula, and the Gundjeihmi Aboriginal Corporation have been fundamental to my re-seeing the everyday militarism infusing our lifeworlds and the tolls being paid. I hope our collaborative journey continues through the challenges ahead.

The Karrabing Film Collective tolerated my bad catering, even that time when we ran out of meat and I pretended couscous was a substitute (well, Moonbill had something to say about that rubbish). May the work of Trevor Bianamu, Gavin Bianamu, Sheree Bianamu, Telish Bianamu, Cameron Bianamu, Natasha Bigfoot, Katrina Bigfoot, Kelvin Bigfoot, Marcia Bigfoot, Rex Edmunds, Chloe Gordon, Claudette Gordon, Miles Gordon, Claude Holtze, Reggie Jorrock, Marcus Jorrock, Ethan Jorrock, Arthur Jorrock, Melissa Jorrock, Patsy-Ann Jorrock, Alethia Jorrock, Roblin Lane, Danielle Lane, Darryll Lane, Loraine Lane,

Sharon Lane, Serena Lane, Paul Lane, Akaydia Lee, Angela Lewis, Cecilia Lewis, Elizabeth Povinelli, Quinton Shields, Rex Sing, Shannon Sing, Aiden Sing, Kieran Sing, Cassie Sing, Alice Wainbirri, Joslyn McDonald, Daphne Yarrowin, Sandra Yarrowin, Claudia Yarrowin, Roy Yarrowin, Georgia Yarrowin, Linda Yarrowin, and Roger Yarrowin continue to change hearts and minds the world over. To Bush Beth, aka Elizabeth Povinelli: if I could be half as true as you, I'd be a genius. I am up for more years of your high expectations and potty-mouthed debate. You in?

My work has been supported by the intellectual generosity and inspiration of past and present colleagues in the Department of Gender and Cultural Studies at the University of Sydney. Being among you is a privilege. And to all the behind-the-scenes professionals who support academics and students, my profound gratitude for your being so good at what you do, even as your roles get harder and more precarious.

Christen Cornell, Kirsty Howey, Thomas Michel, Stuart Rollo, and Liam Grealy—thank you for reading choked drafts, for your own inspiring scholarship, and for encouragement. (I love my sachet samples.) Barbara Caine, Danielle Celermajer, Glenda Sluga, Julia Klindt, Katherine Biber, Claire Monagle, Moira Gatens, and Helen Groth, for deadlines, feedback, and unstinting support; Sascha Callaghan, Ian Buchanan, Jodi Frawley, and Jennifer Biddle, for lacking doubt and offering always-needed prompts; Allan McConnell, for sharpening my sense of policy's natural incoherence; Melinda Barbagallo, for maps; Joel Tarling, for figures, and Sean Fuller, for attentive eyes; and I cannot forget Jesse Boag, who treats my books as gay décor and demanded a refresh.

To Cris Shore and Susan Wright, editors of the Anthropology of Policy book series, my deepest appreciation for your vision and trail making; Don Brenneis, for a career's worth of encouragement; and Michelle Lipinski, for the kind of stewardship I wish all writers may experience. My thanks also to my unknown reviewers for your acute and generous readings.

There are many more people I should thank (all the Indigenous analysts; the post- and undergraduate students, the lawyers, engineers, architects, and tradespeople; the Infrastructural Inequalities reading group, café operators, dog walkers, and gym friends; inspiring academics; folk who invited my talks and forced gossamer thoughts to cohere . . .), but time and a strict character limit compel a stop. A Queen Elizabeth II Fellowship from the Australian Research Council (DP1094139) and support from the Henry Halloran Trust to establish the Housing for Health Incubator proved critical. A collaboration with Astrida Neimanis, Caren Kaplan, and Jennifer Terry exploring Everyday Militarisms as an intersectional feminist project has reoriented my analysis profoundly, as did the book that precedes this, *Darwin* (Lea 2014), which forced me to properly focus on the military underpinnings of continuing settler occupation.

My final thanks go to all the dogs who have ever hounded me to walk, snuggle, and play, and my nonfur family, Elise, Daniel, and Greg Moo, for their continuing love. They build planes, cook stir-fries, fix electrical systems, speak Spanish. They are clever and kind. They are the best part of me.

Wild Policy

Interlude I

When John Singer remembers his childhood on the Siassi Islands, a volcanic archipelago off the northern coast of Papua New Guinea, his thoughts fly first to the men's headdresses, with their spires of feathers stripped from forest birds, and on to the thrum of male dancing. He remembers bouncing quills, valuable shells sewn into splayed necklaces, wooden shields warded with spirit figures; the dung and grunt of pigs; meals of fish, pork, sweet potato, taro; and the thick, sweet taste of coconut milk. His fragmented memories are those of a young child's: all sounds, colors, smells, and tastes. But talk of the whys and wherefores of his being there, a young boy from the Aṉangu Pitjantjatjara Yankunytjatjara (APY) Lands of South Australia, is tactfully evaded. Hoping to learn more about his time with the two Lutheran missionaries he occasionally refers to as his other parents, I have asked a few times about the period when he was taken, age two, far from the desert country of his kin. He shrugs when I ask if it shaped his current politics, to have been pulled so far from home at such a young age, and subtly redirects the conversation.

He speaks more easily of the troubles facing the APY Lands today, some 10 percent of South Australia's land mass and home to around three thousand people, mostly Aṉangu, but the ease of reverting to this topic does not make it an easy one to discuss.

Now in his middle age, with the somber, carefully worded manner of a chief executive officer managing an intensely busy remote-area health center, John Singer's burdens are many. But in his own way, he is a risk taker, a man who still shows signs of the keen teenager who learned how to muster across the desert lands for "that old camel man," Roger Kayipipi, who lived at Fregon. The camels had originally come from India, Arabia, and Afghanistan, dying in vast numbers across treacherous shipping routes as they were forced to follow the continent's new colonial invaders to serve as live vehicles hauling trading goods, survey tools, rifles, and other land-grab technologies across the arid hinterland.

The enslaved camels exacted their revenge by finally escaping their human drivers and thriving in the harsh new environment they'd been dragooned into. For a while, such camel plenitude was a good thing. Before trains, trucks, and cars supplanted their utility, camels shipped everything imaginable across the deserts, including touring Italian violin players. But today, people are paid to round up the camels for slaughter, for according to hominid indexes of invasive species, the Australian hinterland cannot hold such camel kin. As Harriet Ritvo reports (2014, 25), citing Australian government camel data, as of 2009, "their feral descendants numbered close to one million—by far the largest herd of free-living camels in the world."

And that's why a younger John was rounding them up, learning through silent instructions from the *tjilpi* [senior people] who were leading the musters.

"So, we used to go out, mustering, out west, and spend two, three months out bush, just mustering camel, mustering camel."

Each day, that mustering, mustering, broke into other tasks: for slow cooking, selecting firewood corralled from a country that offers the unwary softwoods that explode into ash, and hardwoods that blunt your axe and refuse to burn at all. There was preparing meat for camp stews and rolling dough for crusty dampers to soak up the edges of remaining hunger, washing the cooking gear and packing it all down again for the next day's muster. In the morning, fresh routines: another fire, a billy of tea, an audit of supplies; saddling up for another long trek chasing camel signs, soft cleft sand tracks and broken infrastructure, fences pushed over, water tanks trampled down. Through miles and miles of back country, past saltbush plains, weeping trees, rocky ochre hills, and crumbling purple crevices, wordlessly trekking past the landings of ancestor spirits, the eternal creation marks of the makers.

"Certain areas we were going. But nothing was said. We'd just go certain areas. Oh, we'd be shown a certain rockhole here and there, get to know that country, whatever, but nothing said."

It wasn't until years later, after John had become *wati* [initiated] and had returned for more senior law, that the cryptic mysteries of the mustering were revealed.

"Hello! We in *that* country, where I been running around as a teenager," he says, clicking his middle finger and thumb to emphasize the moment of revelation.

"Suddenly this clicks into me: oh yeah, *that's* why we been running round."

For this long wisdom, there was no learning plan; no curriculum; no time-table, desk, paper, books, or examinations; no PowerPoint projection; no verbal briefings.

"It's not 'Oh right, let's make an appointment and we will go and look out bush.' As the *tjilpi* are taking you around, they're not telling you what you're there for. Years later you're sitting in that spot, in the ceremony, you realize 'Ah, that's what this thing [is]' and then—only then—out come the story."

As he meditates on the deep learning impacts of lessons taught to him by the *tjilpi*, who cadged occasions for going on country[1] out of the fractures created by policies past and present, John wonders why today no one seems to have much energy left to fight the "big picture" issues. People used to speak strong for their land, for the future, about care for young and old, about negotiating how to deal with crises or big decisions, he says. They held strong for their legal and moral rights, fighting with conviction and direction. Now it seems few can be bothered with meetings, and fighting has turned inward. Navigating the endlessly partitioned local organizations and their internecine squabbles drains what is left of people's political energy. Where once old people would hijack the policy problems created by settler colonists to hold on to their country, now they are more likely to sit and watch cars.

It is not simply that people are physically exhausted, although that is part of it. John struggles with describing the ineffable, nameless forces that steal people's outward vitality. He wants to capture an erosion of dignity, of author-ity, that has taken place without the fanfare of a particular event, out of the slow corrosions wrought by ever-moving policy interferences with their long-lasting residual effects. Their hauntology.

"The environment they in has made them useless in one way, and made them … lose their soul," he says.

"They become like a robot. Just go shop, get some food, come home, get a cup of tea. When you look at a lot of policy and a lot of young people—like in health, social and emotional well-being, or mental health—and the problems those young kids are having, well, we have a lot of country out there, that we never access. And so, you've got a bunch of old people who are really knowl-edgeable about the bush, but you've got policies that are centralized around that community where they've got no skills.

"They don't know how to run [a] shop; they don't have office skills. For them, that was all ours," he says, pointing to himself.

"That was for young people growing up. The old people thought, 'Young people can work in the office, they can work in the school, they can run the clinic. We can just do the bush, teaching the young fellas culture side.' That's the way they thought.

"They old people had a good philosophy, *tjungu*, working together, they seen it when they put the land rights act together.

"But then all the policies went, got rid of the homelands, all these other programs that government just decided to centralize, get rid of the small homeland projects happening around and threw everyone into one community, and that's not where the old people's skills are.

"So they just sit there, watching cars go past, kids driving up and down. It makes them sad, watching all that. They haven't taught their next generation like their old ones taught them. So, they get depressed sitting there. And they might think, 'Well, why am I gonna teach that kid, when he's running around drinking and smoking?' They might give up. They think he's too silly with drink and smoke. 'What do I got to teach him main stories for? He might come and tell everyone stuff he shouldn't, and I will get in trouble. Better I just leave it, keep it to myself, and I'll die with that story.' Some older people feel like that."

One day fades into another. But some periods stand out.

By necessity, as chief executive officer of Nganampa Health Council, Australia's oldest remote-area community-controlled health service, John's policy antennae tune in to a wide and noisy spectrum of possibilities and threats, beyond attending to issues specifically marked "health" or "Indigenous." He is aware that policy particles from decisions made by other people, for other people, bioaccumulate in the present. Policies that did not target Indigenous people specifically (for example, the importation of animals for transport and fences for containment; and later, roads, railway lines, crush machinery, mining pits, electricity lines, dams, roads, towns, and a mass system of penalties, fees, and fines) forced dispossession as effectively as Martini–Henry rifles, diseases, and crucifixes once did. These ghostly particles aggregate within human bodies and surround services with habits, systems, and histories, enabling some actions, making others more difficult or even impossible to conceptualize. They are part of the ambient conditions of life under continuing occupation. They form the ambient conditions of policy too. As the leader of Nganampa, John Singer manages the health and well-being impacts of policies past and present, and he must stay on the alert for what's around the corner. What new, soon-could-be-disasters lurk in the policy wings? What benefits might he wrest from the latest poorly thought-out announcements? What new policy ignorance must he patiently try to reeducate and redirect?

Such permanent vigilance holds its own exhaustions; and like most busy professionals caught in the webs of institutional demands, he has ebb times when the point and purpose of his career come into question. For John, one such time was 2014, "a year to forget."

In 2014, fifty-four-year-old Ian Hunter, the first openly gay cabinet minister to marry his same-sex partner while still a cabinet minister (the couple had to head to Granada, Spain, for the official ceremony), amended the Anangu Pitjantjatjara Yankunytjatjara Land Rights Act 1981 (the APY Act). The amendment gave the minister the power to suspend the locally elected APY executive board and appoint an external administrator, a power that is exercisable on any ground and at any time that a minister thinks fit.

Originally granted under the self-determination ethic streaming into Indigenous policymaking in the 1970s, the 1981 APY Act had given the Anangu inalienable freehold title to their ancestral country, and with it, an elected APY council as their overarching body.[2] For a short time, the act was hailed as the best in its class. It is a context thing. The act replaced the Aboriginal Affairs Act 1962, itself ostensibly an improvement on the more draconian powers of the 1930s that were instituted when, earlier extermination efforts having failed, the authorities moved to severely confine Aboriginal groups within centralized sites such as missions, compounds, and stations, clearing the land so that other developments might plough through. The APY Act represented a new means to direct affairs on the Lands, and its governance structure was created, like all such organizations birthed from the 1970s on, to replace the pastoral stationmasters, policemen, administrators, and missionaries of former times as key intermediaries for dealing with settler colonial policy and funding decisions. Under the act, the APY council oversaw the granting and denial of visitor entry permits to the Lands, covering some 102,360 square kilometers: 400 kilometers east to west, 240 kilometers north to south. The permit rituals symbolized a form of sovereignty, even if the legislation creating APY territory lacked matching funds and freighted in too many controls and constraints for truly autonomous administration. Its symbolism also explains why the APY legislation has been amended four times in its short history, including Minister Hunter's amendments of late 2014, when he made self-management a matter of a ministerial thumbs-up, thumbs-down.

In that year to forget, 2014, the Australian federal government also announced its Indigenous Advancement Strategy. The detail was scant. In lieu of any actual strategy, the national government proposed cuts of AUD$534.4 million[3] from Indigenous affairs at large, including $165 million from Indigenous health, arguing that state governments would have to shoulder more of the responsibility for financing remote communities into the future. Housing and infrastructure services received the same message.

Minister Hunter warned that the APY communities would be disbanded altogether if the South Australian, and not the federal, government now had to pick up the tab for such citizen services as water supply, the maintenance of landing strips, or power generation. (Hunter's Wikipedia profile mentions none of this.)

In 2014, with these threats of defunding hovering over Anangu communities, other forms of death had come visiting, too close to home to ignore. John's fifteen-year-old nephew was killed, driving along the poorly tended APY roads. A niece was murdered, unnoticed by the media. And John's biological mother, having survived for years with her blood pulled through one tube, filtered of its toxins, and returned via a separate catheter, also suddenly died. She had not given any prior sign that anything beyond her chronic condition was awry, so the family had missed her final moments, despite their years of vigil. He wonders now: What had she thought in those long years, as she lay against the familiar cushions, looking at the same floors, the same walls; sniffed the same antiseptic wash lingering on the linoleum; listened to the same whooshing sound as her blood was siphoned?

When John talks of end-stage renal dialysis, he talks of his ongoing fight to stop the march of these "death machines" onto the APY Lands. It pits him against those who want dialysis available on country, closer to where people are from, and it is a hard stance to take. He wants the causes of the disease itself to be eradicated, and an end to this cyborgian prolongation of dying, withering slowly, tethered to a machine; but this isn't the reason that, under his watch,

Nganampa Health Council initially resisted the introduction of a dialysis service on the Lands.

John knows it would be kinder for families to be kept together, rather than having people see out the end of their lives in towns like Alice Springs in the center of Australia, or Port Augusta and Adelaide to the country's south, unlikely to return outside a coffin. Urban dialysis clinics are dingy places to eke out a life—with their fluorescent lights, linoleum floors, the smell of disinfectant, the groans of patients with skin bruised and sore from the fistula connecting machines to veins to organs and back again, and always the whir and click of the mechanical kidney as toxins are cleared from blood—thus there is acute pressure to have this process take place closer to home and with the care of extended kin, in remote-area communities.

But for dialysis to work, in the netherworld of prolonging death, there are essential ingredients such as skilled labor, machine maintenance, purified water, and reliable power supply that must be held constant by caring human effort and permanently secured funding—the two things Indigenous people across Australia cannot rely on. Other questions tumble from him, as I prod and poke at his concerns. Where will people stay when they are not being dialyzed? Who will provide the transport? What happens when things go wrong? If the government defunds air strips, how can emergency evacuations take place? Without such guarantees, the borrowed time offered by dialysis becomes even more precarious. For dialysis to prolong life and not hasten death, the wider ecology of policy delivery needs to be attended to. Otherwise, as John says, "Things get a bit crazy when government acts wild."

So when, in 2014, amid talk of cutting funding for remote-area communities to make them disappear altogether, the Australian government arbitrarily pledged a grant for the capital works to house four renal dialysis machines at Ernabella, the largest of the APY communities, John was skeptical, not celebratory. The estimate of all the costs involved for the dialysis clinic first came in a three-page proposal, their brevity a vast contrast to the painful detail normally demanded from community organizations come grant application or acquittal time, and their verity was hard to determine. Savings would apparently come from replacing the mobile dialysis van currently in use, and it seemed there were dollars to be recouped from not having to pay the cross-border charges whenever patients left South Australia for Alice Springs in the Northern Territory.

But there was no detail to show how new costs would be met by such repatriated outlays, just a gestural reassurance that failed to reassure. On the Lands, people must cover extreme distances to travel the network of Nganampa clinics spread across an expanse the size of Cuba. On the Lands, power is routinely disrupted. The hard water, full of minerals leached from the desert, instantly calcifies machine fittings and cannot be used, but neither can rainwater, for it contaminates too quickly at slow replenishment rates in arid regions. Specialist nurses arrive in the form of locum staff who fly in and fly out again; and an aerial medical evacuation, should anything go wrong, as it inevitably will, takes long, anxious hours to organize, on a potholed landing strip whose recurrent funding is not guaranteed, given the threat of closures still hanging over remote-community heads. How could it be "cheaper, safer and more reliable" to operate dialysis under such uncertain macro- and microenvironmental conditions? John asks.

Reversing the usual descriptions of how Aboriginal people are thwarted by policy rationalities and the enumerative impulse, it is the irrationality and anarchic nature of policy that makes John wary of wasting his time with pursuits that don't yield an evidenced outcome. On the one hand, he is fighting the threat of all-out community closures by appealing to the fears of mayors and councilors in the non-Indigenous regional towns most likely to receive an influx of Anangu refugees should closures occur. Perhaps, given their invasion fears, the good town burghers could join their voices to those of Aboriginal people fighting to stay on country? On the other hand, he is trying to reduce the number of Anangu who are held hostage by preventable disease, without making them victims of the greater unpredictability of wild policy.

As John Singer ponders how to keep motivating himself to continue the task of organizational leadership, given how very hard it has all become, it is the arbitrariness of policy initiatives, and the superficial knowledge of rotating government messengers, that fatigue him the most. Although he is not yet resigned to watching from the sidelines as visitors come and go, he long ago stopped listening hard to anyone proposing a new salvation for Aboriginal affairs, a new committee, a new project or trial, a research project, or even new funding. If these suggestions lack a sound business case, long-term commitment of deep expertise, attention to recurrent staffing costs, and a clear plan for local benefit within fractured places, he listens with respectful, mostly silent, rejection. Especially when brief policy visits and too-loud bonhomie are meant to substitute for familiarity with the issues and well-earned community trust. He is especially silent then.

Chapter 1

Can there be good policy?

If you leave the town of Timber Creek in the Victoria River Downs of the Northern Territory of Australia, and head north along the Victoria Highway, you will reach a Spartan cement bridge spanning the mighty Victoria River, full of crocodiles, broken trees from floods gone by, and sex-changing barramundi. A short drive will do it. You can take photographs of the bridge and even walk along it for a wee while, though this is no place for ordinary travelers. Here the wild river is a moat, and the bridge a span to a military citadel, accessible only to the present-day legions with authorization to train there, weaponizing themselves for conflicts to the north, east, and west of the continent.

Trespass signs warn against touching anything ("It may explode and kill you"), and metal barricades, CCTV, and guard posts reinforce the message. These signs are soon forgotten as you bypass the bridge and continue along the highway, a long way from other distractions, barring termite mounds, meager woodlands, and red scoria, the air undulating with humid heat over broiling bitumen. The weary eye sees nothing more outstanding. The scrubby country inside the protected weapons range is so unremarkably like the scrubby country outside it, its relevance to the story of Indigenous social policy also slips from view. A military field occupying land the size of Cyprus can have that effect—as can attending too closely to the normative terms for anthropological and social policy analysis. Familiar tools of scrutiny can blind us to what might also be there, hidden in plain sight, if we care to look askance.

This book is an ethnography of interventions that were visited upon Aboriginal people in regional and remote Australia as the country entered the twenty-first century. The bulk of the ethnographic research took place between 2007 and 2017, spanning three changes of national government in Australia and multiple prime ministers. The US announced an intensified military presence in the Asia Pacific and changed presidencies, Australia entertained the rise and fall of a mining boom led by industrial and property developments in China and India, and catastrophic climate change shifted from the forebodings of a few to the center of international policy debate. This was also the time when a National Emergency Response was called to intervene into the plight of Aboriginal living conditions in the Northern Territory; and, later, social policy announcements included new threats of abandonment, as entire swathes of Aboriginal occupied lands face the abrupt withdrawal of any service supports whatsoever.

Each of these events feed into Aboriginal policy determinations, but their interconnectivity is seldom made clear. Mining often takes place on Aboriginal land, but the relations between mining, Euro-American military expansionism, and the conditions set for the delivery or denial of services for Indigenous Australians tend not to be described together. For that matter, my own dependency on extractivism and militarized trade relations and how this too shapes what is made available for Indigenous people is not something I am routinely made to think about either. The embedded infrastructures of militarily enabled extractive relations that saturate our surroundings and make us possible are so omnipresent, they have become imperceptible.

Wild Policy attempts to bring these adjacencies back into view, arguing they are at the heart of the tensions, engagements, and arbitrariness of Indigenous social policy. It contends that the militarized global political economy that most urbanized liberal settler populations depend on drives key domestic policy. The resulting chaos for many Indigenous groups is simply collateral damage. At the same time, prolonged attention to such "structural determinants" of policy can pose two equally problematic methodological dangers. First, analysis rebounds into a structure-versus-agency binary, while attention is distracted from the everyday transactions and dramas within organizations, contracted businesses and bureaucracies, and families and individuals, as policies percolate within and through these locations too. Yet, if instead we shift focus to these more everyday transactions, a second methodological danger presents itself. When we foreground the minutiae of individual resistances, or the exquisite detail of organizational practices—by making visible the micropolitics of discretionary transactions within a welfare office, let's say—what these are simultaneously part of can disappear.

Wild Policy seeks different landing points. Focusing on macro- and micropolicy conditions and the activation potential of the meso in between (Stengers 2009), it explores the inconsistency of policy effects, the multiplicity of human and nonhuman actors, the complexity of interactions, and the absence of any master controller, beyond that of a globalized military political economy, with the hope that, rewoven into ethnographic narratives, settler colonial policy ramifications under late liberalism can be more properly explained.

It pulls in material from what many see as the still wild parts of Australia. It visits Groote Eylandt to the northeast of Arnhem Land in the Northern Territory of Australia, site of the world's largest sea-borne manganese operation. It refers to the cattle country and defense force training grounds of the Victoria River Downs region and to country either side of Anson River at the mouth of the Daly River, both to the southwest of Darwin, capital of the Northern Territory.[1] It repeatedly returns to the Anangu Pitjantjatjara Yankunytjatjara (APY) Lands of northern South Australia, where fallout from nuclear tests at Maralinga once blinded Yami Lester, the first leader of Nganampa Health Council, now Australia's oldest remote-area community-controlled health center. And it zigzags in and out of cities, from offices in Darwin, Adelaide, Sydney, and Canberra, to homes in suburbs on the fringes of towns.

The sites are not irrelevant, and the place-specific issues they present are real. But this geographic outline is not a claim for multisited ethnography; rather, it traces the contours of a deliberately erratic fieldwork approach. *Wild Policy* is the product of a purposely fragmented ethnographic gleaning technique, a methodological process and framing that I call *policy ecology*, by which I mean both the ecology of policy environments themselves and the variegated connections that stem from and flow through the alive, inhabited worlds that policy emanates from and enters into, the coalescences between humans and multiple other forces, and the stretches of time and hauntings that help shape the capacious policy category known as "Indigenous circumstances."

As a combined method and conceptual framing, policy ecology ducks around the analytical grappling hooks that gouge thought whenever such topics as social policy, Indigenous Australians, or development under continuing occupation are brought into view. By refusing the closure and holism suggested by bounded fieldwork, whether of a community or from a "follow a project to its conclusion" approach, I try to escape the paradigmatic enclosure of Aboriginal policy within normative, juridico-political policy frameworks.

By way of an alternative approach, in this book, policy is approached as a wild force, with all the meanings the word *wild* invokes. Synonyms include primitive, natural, free, savage, barbarous, deserted, fierce, neglected, rampant, overgrown, undomesticated, tangled, verdant, rude, uncivilized, uncontrolled, vicious, feral, female, and indigenous. By claiming the word to better describe the unruliness of policy unfurlings, the title of this book embraces and inverts the target of state-centered settler colonial policy (the putatively wild or dysfunctional Aboriginal people who must be tamed) to suggest a more accurate description of policy's natural incoherence, its steady-state irrationality. When policy is considered as wild to begin with, it is no longer a stable body of rational thought whose deviations in practice might be traced as "unintended consequences." It loses its conventional political science demarcation between policy and program, with its convenient separation of the intended from the unintended. It becomes instead what I believe it always is: an ambient saturation that works its way into and out of human and nonhuman lives, affected by forces beyond those formally acknowledged as sovereign policy agents; and a fetishized state-effect impacting lives in fragmented, inchoate, cumulative, and highly individualized ways. As a growing body of scholarship within the anthropology of policy has shown, policies have multiple genealogies and chronologies. They have dispersed and fitful starting points and becomings. They operate more organically than centrist analyses tend to allow. They are *wilder*.

In March 2015, as yet another searing summer was breaking climate records in Australia, former prime minister Tony Abbott declared his full support of a campaign to shut down more than half the remote Aboriginal communities of Western Australia (WA), stating that taxpayers should not be expected to finance Indigenous people's "lifestyle choices." The (also former) WA premier, Colin Barnett, had made it clear that approximately 150 Aboriginal communities—precise locations deliberately unspecified—were no longer viable. "I have no choice," said Premier Barnett, joining his voice with that of his Labor Party rival, South Australian minister Ian Hunter.

It will cause great distress to Aboriginal people who will [have to] move, it will cause issues in regional towns as Aboriginal people move into them. But high rates of suicide, poor education, poor health, no jobs . . . it's a huge economic, social and health issue. They [the communities] are not viable and the social outcomes, the abuse and neglect of young children, is [sic] a disgrace to this state.[2]

This was the exact same rationale that authorized the Northern Territory National Emergency Response (NTNER) of 2007, the now-notorious legislative fiat whereby the Australian government suspended its own Racial Discrimination Act to impose racially targeted restrictions on welfare access, land tenure, household tenancy, school attendance, medical scrutiny, alcohol consumption, and internet freedom. The NTNER, more commonly known by its military moniker as "the Intervention," was imposed to deal with alleged child sexual abuse in Aboriginal communities and town camps, through projects of "normalization" (Altman and Hinkson 2007). The sociological, let alone statistical, verity of these deviance claims was never clear. They did not need to be clear. An ideal standard—a righteous, non-Indigenous, urbanized, house-owning, able-bodied, male citizen—was already in place as the unmarked baseline to measure the gross abnormalities now being routed out. The allegedly wide-scale and out-of-control perversion in Aboriginal communities would be stabilized through stricter policing and data management of everything, from school attendance to property relations, all made vaguely "relative to liberal market norms" (Povinelli 2015a, 176).

At the time of its announcement, the Intervention received bipartisan support, releasing funds to flow along already well-routed service provision furrows. In key sites, the Intervention meant more services—or at least more of a particular sort: more police, more truancy officers, more teachers, more departmental data collectors, and, in a suite of projects to be discussed in the following chapters, more training for imagined jobs, more enforced school attendance, more housing, and more jailings. A decade on, the same assumed pathologies that legitimated interventionary overload became a reason to cease funding and threaten community closures instead.

How to explain the apparent opposition in policy responses to identical portraits of Aboriginal deficit and pathology—the vacillation between withdrawal and intervention, provision and denial—beyond the colonial state's long-standing assumption of authority to create harm to offset harm? Why does improving Indigenous social conditions remain such an elusive goal for those committing themselves to this pursuit? These knots are picked at in this book.

Can there be good policy?

Wild Policy pursues a beguilingly simple question: Can there be good Indigenous social policy under late liberal settler occupation? Drawing on case studies from infrastructure, health, housing, mining rehabilitation, and vernacular multimedia initiatives across regional and remote Australia, it argues *yes* there can be, and *no* there can't be, for deeply connected reasons.

Of course, yes. With skillful policy brokerage and detailed acts of project translation, different policy schemes can be made to work. The "can be made to" clause is crucial. Many skeletons lie in the graveyard of trying to secure high-fidelity project results for disadvantaged beneficiaries. The difficulty of policy realization is not something to be taken for granted or expected: this difficulty needs to be treated as strange. The hard toil of it all requires a theorized response. If, as many Foucauldian scholars of Indigenous–state relations have claimed, state interventions are aimed at disciplining the subject (Lattas and Morris 2010), why are the mechanisms of the disciplinary apparatus so contemptible? Why do people have to fight to receive the very tools—the schooling, the health services, the secure housing, the rule of law—that are meant to be reshaping them as normed and settled subjects? Why do they have to demand that which would domesticate? Whether it is classroom teaching that refuses racialized pedagogy, a construction program that delivers well-designed and robustly built housing, or a road that resists subsidence with the first season's rains, why do policy benefits have to be *willfully and doggedly* extracted? Why must skillful players *battle* to shape whatever was intended into locally productive effects?

Wild Policy tracks the work of differently situated protagonists operating within, through, and against policy to *extract* some of the benefits that policies claim to automatically provide. It probes the problem of why realizing policy benefit is so hard; or, to position this focus differently, why the people stubbornly chasing ethical results so often end up becoming what I call, borrowing from Sara Ahmed, institutional killjoys.

Ahmed (2012, 62) was talking of feminist killjoys, who, when contesting the expected raced, classed, and sexed social order every time it is casually reasserted, pose a problem because they keep exposing problems. Under conditions of settler colonial policy intervention in Aboriginal Australia, *institutional killjoys* are those who, working hard to pull benefits from policy opportunities, insist that contracts be honored, promises be kept, accounts be held, corruptions be resisted, projects have fidelity, and people be respectfully supported. Thus insisting, they call into question the compromised, belittling, or discriminatory ways that things are ordinarily done. Ordinarily—say, when there is evidence of a state-funded, state-run project not being implemented properly in an Aboriginal community—the official policy response begins with denial or demands for more evidence and a rush behind the scenes to discredit the claims. The business of taming the outbreak also requires respective players to perform their parts, colluding to "solve" the issue, which is to say, to make signs of trouble disappear.[3] We might call this "glamouring" the trouble (cf. Haraway 2016).

But institutional killjoys tend to become obsessed with the lack of clarity in vague reassurances. They demand tricky detail. So doing, their stubborn insistence that policy commitments must have specificity and be adhered to meets a more densely populated institutional obduracy. By speaking up or out, in holding a line, killjoys often become out of line with their affective community. They can reach a point where, worn down by butting into institutional walls, they find their jobs untenable. Over my years of studying policy, such battle-scarred actors were often my interlocutors, and although career obituaries are not my main focus, I want to note these sacrifices. Institutional killjoys are not necessarily settler colonial killjoys, or decolonists, to use David Garneau's definition (2014, 5), which would see non-Indigenous people seeking to Indigenize their institutions and cultural practices. They are not, as per Eve Tuck's and K. Wayne Yang's account of what *non-metaphorical* decolonization requires, seeking to repatriate all of the land they have taken and still rely on (Tuck and Wayne Yang 2017).

Even so, people fighting to extract benefits from policy openings and who risk becoming killjoys in the process are essential to the "yes" of possible good from policy. Dragging some good out of Indigenous social policy is not for the fainthearted. As following chapters elaborate, the pulling of good out of different policy assemblages can be a labor of resistance against a more normative investment in crafting the appearance of omnimeritorious and necessary policy.

All the same, killjoys should not be understood as the noble grass roots fighting from the bottom against an all-powerful center. Such topographic metaphors ignore the complexity of policy translations across multiple nodes and formations as they shape-shift between and through written artifactual and ambient cultural practices. Besides, "It's the system" doesn't get us far analytically, and effective killjoys operate within established orders too. Policy is in no way a hermetic, integrated, and smoothly operating interventionary apparatus coming down from on high to "impact" "communities" (where, similarly, no such complete entity exists) in some totalizing way, but more often unfurls as a series of project stutters, misdirects, and meanderings; as lost objects and insensible procedures; and as ghostly residues from past practices and sunk capital—out of which benefits as well as harms arise. Mostly the benefits flow to the already benefited, but redirects are possible too. As Stephen Ball confessed some time ago, it is impossible to define policy, because policies are not just things but also processes and outcomes:

[T]he complexity and scope of policy analysis—from an interest in the workings of the state to a concern with contexts of practice and the distributional outcomes of policy— preclude the possibility of successful single theory explanations. (Ball 1993, 10)

To cope, he argued, we need a toolbox, not one approach but many, to span the macro of policy, the micro of it, and the meso in between; from structural concerns to issues of embodiment and perception. And we need to remember that at every level, even when polices are formulated in their most black-letter artifactual form, policy intentions keep company with compromises, struggles, and ad hockery. Policy translations are capricious, and to make them work requires creative interpretations and clever evasions.

Reflecting on this relationship between policy announcements and the inventive, discretionary ways in which policies might be put into action, the political scientist Michael Lipsky famously argued that policy materializes within embodied relationships between enforcers and supplicants. Lipsky called this "street-level bureaucracy," arguing that policy does not exist simply as a legislative artifact but belongs to a field of discretion, where police, social workers, nurses, teachers, or, now, perhaps an electronic "customer service operator" at the end of a digital connection reveal policy's true interactive relation (Lipsky 1980). How street-level bureaucrats interpret a problem or request and choose to act is mightily consequential for how policy is relayed and experienced.

The point is taken up in a different way by the development anthropologist David Mosse (2004), who, in attending to issues of policy translation and brokerage, asks a provocative question that has clearly inspired my own analysis. Mosse asks, 'Is good policy unimplementable?" and casts his answer as a cautionary tale. Good policy is unimplementable, he argues, because the ingredients needed to secure policy proposals at one level, the features that make it "good" for alliance building among policy cognoscenti, must be translated into practical terms. Compromises, mutations, and deformations are invariably necessary to policy instantiation. Following Mosse's model, an argument that favors, say, increased employment, improved education, and a reduction of child sexual abuse as outcomes from a housing and infrastructure program might be initially heralded as urgent and necessary "good policy" if its generalizing, horoscope-style wording enables multiple allies to commit their respective energies to realizing it as a visibly launched, proper-noun initiative. (As we will see, I refer to policy words and documents as the artifactual face of policy). But the task of securing said housing and infrastructure in three-dimensional material form necessarily relies on many other messy translations.

In turn, the task of converting what ends up being done in policy's name through such messy translations to appear *as if* it all matches the original heroic ambitions falls to "policy brokers" who skillfully re-represent the chaos of implementation into more orderly accounts, as they acquit funds, simplify outcome reports, and seek renewed support and funding for future actions. Translators make the more chaotic arena of actual practice better align with often highly unrealistic policy ideals. For Mosse, the frequently bemoaned "gaps" between policy and practice are not a failure of policy's compass (which critical analysis of policy's omissions will therefore fix) but are highly productive lacunae. Policy is made to "work," for good and ill purposes, through a density of interpersonal microinteractions, translations, and clever representational footwork. Folk on the ground get more money to do more things, and official, or artifactual, policy gets to retain its normative premises through this co-opting dance.

In settler colonial countries like Australia, such interactive fields of policy translation and re-representation might sit outside metropolitan areas altogether, in places where dusty roads and low-ceilinged offices take the place of streets and skyscrapers. The different policy landing points explored in this book include a remote-area health clinic, an Indigenous-controlled civil and civic engineering company, a land council, a royalty administering body, and a grassroots mixed-media corporation made up of relatives and friends.[4] Sometimes policy translators do not work within organizations, nor do they even see themselves as occupying policy roles at all. They might be independently funded anthropologists working over decades with family descendants, for instance; but their work in fielding institutional assaults, fronting magistrates as character witnesses, or brokering project opportunities to and for their friends and allies is unavoidably also policy inflected.

More often, however, the policy brokers working to materially improve conditions for Indigenous people are organization based, holding grant-dependent contract positions and working against the limits of wit and energy to achieve the purported goals of precariously funded programs. Paradoxically, if they are doing more than taking a salary and masquerading usefulness, they will almost certainly be operating within the breach of stated rules and conventions. Theirs are domains where resources will never meet demands, where long hours cannot meet limitless reporting loads, and where performance targets can only be approximated, offering services that are—can only be—partial, if they exist at all. I will argue that settler occupation offers additional factors, such as the paternalism of governing a people whose labor is no longer needed for profiteering requirements. Pointing any of this out, beyond strictly time-limited formulas of acceptable complaint, will risk such brokers becoming institutional killjoys who must be managed, silenced, or off-loaded. Again, the question remains: Why is this so?

Policy in the wild

By now it should be clear that the answer "Yes, there can be good policy" emphasizes the people who make policy work, rather than any particular policy. This is not policy understood as an epochal transition (as in "colonization" or "self-determination") or singular event (as in "the Intervention"), though *Wild Policy* still describes such events and provides various backstories for different "artifactual" declarations of program intent. When we pause to look closely at how policies spread out and change conditions of possibility and hope, they're anything but neat, anything but complete and fully presenting. Policy can go feral. It acts in strange ways. It mutates and shape-shifts. Making it work requires herculean tasks of translation. Considering what brokers must do to translate policies in favor of highly volatile practical interests, we could paraphrase Mosse afresh: Why is implementing social policy so that it is good for at least some of its intended beneficiaries so inordinately hard for the people who attempt it?

Asked this way around, the same productive gaps that allow skillful players and institutional killjoys to bend the (mis)directions of policy in the direction of local visions are also what make a sustained realization of good policy an impossible pursuit. For at the macro scale, *no*, there cannot be "good social policy." Even those laborious extractions of good depend on whose idea of "good" gains prominence; what ideas of life, nonlife, knowledge, sentience, sociality, ecology, and economy are included, and who stands to benefit. "Good" is contingent on how things are done, measured over what kinds of scale or metrics, using what kind of cultural values or ethics—and much more besides. The combination of "good" and "social policy" raises the issues of who is the "we" that is doing the asking or supplying the advice, of what kinds of living or inanimate matter this "we" instinctively takes into consideration or excludes, and—most fundamental of all—of whether social policy is really aiming to "fix" the founding conditions of social stratification in the first place.

This book argues that *no*, policy is not trying to eradicate foundational inequalities. Stated as caricature, policy's first-order job is aiding and abetting the interests of extractive capital, pushing profit upward in the name of economic development, financial debt, and corporate wealth.[5] Ameliorating or softening the harsher collateral effects of inequality, rather than overturning the socioeconomic system that relies on serial exploitations to thrive, is the actual (albeit disavowed) task of social policy within most democratic nation-states. In settler colonial nations, this hidden relation between profiteering and impoverishment is becoming more apparent. Evidence of continuing dispossession insistently leaks past nationalist attempts to cauterize dispossessive acts as part of a done-and-dusted invasion episode. The late historian Patrick Wolfe (2007) usefully qualified settler colonialism as a "structure and not an event," referring to the ongoing domestication of seized territories via shifting technologies of dispossession. As Audra Simpson (2014) also shows, for the *Kahnawá:ke* Mohawk tribe, ongoing settler colonial incursions are continually encountered, even as lands and bodies have been ostensibly "settled."

According to Ghassan Hage (2016), this leaking out of contained history and geographies is happening everywhere. Neocolonial nations were once able to shield their privileged citizens from the ongoing colonial conditions of their good life. One could be happily privileged and have the extractions taking place somewhere else, in other countries, in hinterlands, in hidden dens, among people who appeared as ghostly remnants of something prior, shrouded from awareness. But the veiled plunder that feeds the privileges of the settler good life is shifting closer to the worlds of those who formerly could be blind to what they drew on. As capital seeks new sources of wealth, the world is becoming smaller, Hage argues, shrinking the insulating fabrics that hid the sources and costs of colonial privileging (see also Hage 2017). Today, mining threatens wealthy vintners, while ash and lead can pollute the water catchments of cosmopolitan cities. Decolonial Indigenous scholars would additionally point out that settler colonial nations never entirely restricted their exploitations to other places. They operate abroad and at home at the same time. "Decolonization in a settler context is fraught because empire, settlement, and internal colony have no spatial separation," write Eve Tuck and K. Wayne Yang (2017, 7). Settler colonists extract for domestic and world profit and enact ongoing internal subjection "because there is no spatial separation between metropole and colony" (5).

To confront this embeddedness, consider how Australia's stock markets are heavily weighted in two sectors, finance and resources. Each sector has differentiated interests in (former and current Indigenous) land as (nonsentient) divisible property. Among other things, Australian middle-class lifestyles survive on the affordances of the country's resource extraction and property development industries (with housing now assetized for financial returns, not shelter [Nethercote 2019]). Mining activities—an industry at the heart of most forms of civic infrastructure—sit within contemporary forms of Indigenous dispossession, ineluctably and inevitably. The principal country where mining takes place is occupied by those enduring Indigenous populations who, having survived original dispossessions by being on property of such low commercial interest that it was eventually reserved for Aboriginal occupation, now find themselves at the heart of the "race for what is left" (Klare 2012). This phrase is borrowed from Michael Klare's survey of increasing energy scarcity in his book *The Race for What's Left: The Global Scramble for the World's Last Resources*, but it also distills the intensified attention given to (allocated or reclaimed) Aboriginal land holdings.

In Australia, land repossession under different land rights and native title laws "has by and large been limited to unalienated Crown land in an inverse relationship to the colonial settlement pattern" (Altman 2009, 27). That is, claimable land was where settlers weren't. Land reclamation legislation differs from state to state, but uniformly denies Aboriginal people mineral or other resource rights in favor of exploration and extraction industries (17). Mining companies might be nefarious, but they are not the main culprits. I depend on their extraction activities for my lifeworld: the car, the shower head, the quinoa shipped from South America, come to me through extraction-dependent tributaries. Ironically, mining also supplies the material means for surviving in reduced and displaced circumstances for Indigenous people too. Resources dragged raw from Aboriginal lands are returned as construction materials, road-sealing aggregates, and bodies and engines of the freight trucks delivering infrastructural materials and food supplies, or as dialysis machines, or in the form of the word processor an ethnographer might use to capture field data, bringing minerals, oils, and their rich synthetic products through elaborate and immeasurable circuits of dispossession and species depletion to the tips of her agile fingers.

Aboriginal people must yield to forms of extraction to receive infrastructural services, just as they must cede to pathological portraits of their population for health, education, and other social programs. The coincidence of mining, the supply of essential services, and the ongoing forfeit of survival in autonomy is obscured by demands that Aboriginal people be assisted by whatever means necessary to reach their full potential (that is, to be socialized as wealth-accumulating, debt-servicing individuals through various mechanisms of moral tutelage, such as compulsory schooling, tightly defined forms of paid employment, and a constant threat of incarceration). With serial domestic and community policy intrusions demanding front-stage attention, further extinguishment of rights to negotiate access to the subsurface resources of large parts of traditional territories can take place, without this ever needing to be fully articulated as the underbelly of the policy benefits on offer. At the same time, everyone knows, deep in their bones, that policy insistences can be enforced by state-sanctioned violence (Graeber 2012).

This political-economic extractive formation is the most pertinent backdrop for the all-too-often disorderly, chaotic, inept, corrupt, underconceptualized, and badly implemented social policy efforts offered to close settler colonial gaps. For here's the sting in the tail of liberal settler remediation: given that the state has more or less secured the legal means to pull what it wants from remnant Indigenous estates, it can afford to be hit or miss with its increasingly fragmented policy and service provision arms, limping as administrations now are from bouts of outsourcing, cost-cutting, ethical emptying, and relentlessly punitive attacks on welfare. Thus both withdrawal and provision can be justified using the same humanitarian logic. When Indigenous programs are occasionally generously funded (at least in terms of the casual metrics of general media scrutiny, relative to their usual parsimony), they are frequently timed to buttress military, extraction industry, property development, construction, and freight sector requirements (cf. Bear 2015).

Anthropologist Gerald Sider (2014, 179) provides a searing account of analogous "epidemics of collective self-destruction which make people into the authors of their own and each other's misery" among Canada's Innu and Inuit peoples, together with the forced resettlements and cruelly pathetic service offerings that aid and abet this process in the name of modernization and development. Sider argues that Innu and Inuit moved from being exploitable peoples (labor that could be used ruthlessly) to being disposable peoples (unneeded for capital), and accordingly are now under pressure to either assimilate fully and disappear into the neoliberal economy or suffer the remedial humiliations dealt to those whose form of endurance and resistance is to live even "harder lives in harder places" (2014, 182; see also Mignolo and Escobar 2010).

This, in a nutshell, is the predicament of Indigenous people under continuing occupation, and the ultimate reason why the getting of good from social policy is so embattled.[6] The forces of dispossession that have Indigenous people living harder lives in even harder places are the same (well-defended) forces that accumulate benefit for many others, this being the cunning pact of settler colonial social policy (Dombrowski 2010). Although Indigenous people have refused to be eliminated, the state already has what it needs (including the creation of a cadre of legislated landowners through whom ongoing extractive interests can be negotiated or wrested), and so can afford the extravagances of its hit-and-miss social policies. Indigenous people can be supported, abandoned, sacrificed, and enabled. Even if we knew what we meant by the terms *good* or *policy*, there are no vital dependencies on getting social policy consistently "right."

Of course, reconciling the rights of those whose interests in land might conflict with those who hunger for the minerals below the surface is the source of ongoing dispute and arbitration; and the relationship between mining, Aboriginal welfare, and the wealth of others is endlessly complicated. All this to say, contemporary social policy is not setting out to overturn foundational conditions of inequality but, at best, to make it easier for people to slot themselves in to those conditions and, in the now familiar liberal pact, to make such compliance a lifetime self-improvement project. State interventions under liberal capitalism still follow long-used techniques of colonial rule, in which westernized housing, schooling, and the reorienting of labor away from care for human and other kin, toward waged work and forms of collateralized debt servicing are deemed necessary for contemporary existence. Note that David Graeber (2011) and David Harvey (2005b) have both insisted that the demonization of alternate ways of being in the world has always and ever been a requirement of markets. Indigenous people the world over have said the same, for a long, long time, over and again (Moreton-Robinson 2015, Whyte 2018a).

I am pointing out nothing new. The capitalist state still seeks to alienate Aboriginal people from themselves and to enforce the models of atomized social reproduction that assume the features of Euro-America—complete with legitimate habits of dangerous overconsumption—but herein lies the rub. With access to key resources assured, and Aboriginal labor irrelevant to the requirements of global capital, the state can also be extremely haphazard and wasteful with its interferences and inculcation attempts. It can be erratic with its elimination and its incorporation attempts too. This is also what makes policy emanations a wild kind of force, conceived as they are within nested interests that their "makers" cannot admit their subservience to, whether these are the profiteering interests of the extractive industries or more impersonal climatological, biological, and geographical agencies. And why wresting better, not worse, from policy openings and closings is so hard, so necessary, and so inadequate.

On concepts and methods

In what follows, *Wild Policy* offers four overlapping propositions. First, it insists that policies are nested compositions of human and other-than-human formations that are best approached ecologically. If we update Lipsky's instructions to look at the "street-level" sites where policy discretion and intersubjectivity reign supreme, recruiting feminist, queer, and ecocritical scholarship to make our analysis more ecological in both method and frame, other agents of policy effect come into view. There are human formulators and brokers, and more besides. Viewed ecologically, even such policy citadels as public service bureaus are more mucky, primal, libidinal, and organic than studies of governmentality ordinarily imply.

Second, *Wild Policy* interrupts the settler colonial habit of accounting for Indigenous issues in isolation, foregrounding select Indigenous and non-Indigenous policy dealings but not the wider political-economic and militarized global circulations these remain part of. The entire assembly of forces and flows that help explain haphazard Indigenous social policy is too often removed from analysis by those most genuinely seeking answers. The fact that Indigenous building programs mesh with the desires of building companies during downturns in metropolitan construction, for example, or that land tenure changes annexed to service delivery promises also meet the needs of mining and global capital, is not incidental to Indigenous inequality but constitutively part of it.

Third, this book joins interventions made by the policy anthropology community to subvert the power of policy teleology. Like metaphors for the state and claims of scientific fact, policy discourses have a centering effect.[7] Buttressed by the stories of necessity and purpose that surround a given policy announcement, policies are readily assumed to have intentions, the fulfillment or thwarting of which can be analyzed using (policy-familiar) theories of cause and effect. Thus reified, failed interventions lead to an insistence on more interventions of the same kind; perceived failures of coordination feed demands for more coordination efforts; and expectations of government policy and service delivery assume an ultimate rationality despite rampant inconsistencies in actual practice. The pioneers of policy anthropology, Cris Shore and Susan Wright, recommend highlighting "the actor's frame of reference" to resist such circularity (1997, 7). When we add lived detail, abstract policy claims are forced into reckoning with the intricacies of translation and the situated compromises and serendipities of implementation, inevitably drawing more complicated pictures.

This task of complicating the force of policy teleology is a difficult and ongoing challenge, for ethnographic narrative conventions can inadvertently feed the problem. It is hard to resist giving different policies a biography—a beginning, a rationale, a field of problems to act within, and a verdict—in establishing case examples. Even the simple act of providing background and context neatens and stabilizes processes that are more fragmented and unreachably immured in distributed sites, inside people's bodies, and in spectral and material forces, here, before, and beyond. Especially when we are describing policies that went awry, an evaluative tone (one that mimics the circular omniscience of interventionary ontologies) creeps into the account. But this evaluative disposition cannot help but imply and reaffirm a certain unidirectionality to policy entailments—there was an inception, followed by an outcome—and thus it cannot help but reinstate policy teleology. Evaluations reinforce myths of original policy coherency that this book is attempting to dislodge.

Anthropological resistance requires multiple tactics, from narrative experiments to conceptual and methodological ones. To this end, the ethnographic research for *Wild Policy* comprised an experiment worked along two axes: fieldwork and communication. Field exposures were deliberately fragmented, not to be fashionably multisited but to resist the lure of closure promised by disciplinary recommendations that we harness ethnographic details to the point of pattern redundancy. Patterns suggest an ordering; orderings suggest policy-aligned modes of seeing. Although I have tracked multiple policies from inception to implementation, I've barely entertained fulsome policy biographies.

I learned an important lesson from my inaugural work on the anthropology of social policy, *Bureaucrats and Bleeding Hearts: Indigenous Health in North-*

ern Australia. This applied classical anthropological techniques to a less-than-classical field, a government health bureaucracy. I immersed in the languages, bodily gestures, and grammars of sociopolitical exchange within one community in one jurisdiction, an intimate soaking that generated conditions of familiarity with the everyday lives of health professionals tasked with worrying about Indigenous health. But *Bureaucrats and Bleeding Hearts* also reproduced one of the major problems identified with classical anthropological ethnographies: it treated the "culture" of Territory Health Services as if it was a self-sustaining and bounded entity. And although I suggested that the bureaucracy was an organism that would fight for its own survival, I also described policy events in the form of enclosed case studies, returning coherence to events that by their nature are more fragmented, more historically laminated, more viral, than exemplifying vignettes otherwise suggest.

The research for *Wild Policy* was not simply multiscalar and multisited but as vertiginous and incoherent as I could manage, given the ordering devices of social scientific research that ethnographers rely on and readers require. Whenever I felt myself delving too far toward a policy's biography, amassing its teleological story at the expense of its wily shrapnel, I pulled myself away or let myself be pushed elsewhere. I moved between multiple sites, not to chase threads in the cause of holism, but to circumvent the pursuit of holism. Above all, I experimented with forms of communication throughout, for, presuming one can find things to say after the conventions of holistic capture are forfeited, the question of transmission remains. How might we convey ethnographic complexity to reach differently literate, differentially capacitated audiences?

To experiment with that challenge, I first wrote a social history of Darwin (Lea 2014a), where, for historical, constitutional, and budget-loading reasons, much Indigenous policy experimentation is focused; I experimented in turn with personal memoir, political critique, and lyrical nonfiction writing to create populist ethnography, hard theory softened in the warm honey of yarns. And I contributed to films directed by fellow anthropologist Elizabeth Povinelli in collaboration with the Karrabing Film Collective, showing the impacts of different policy unwindings in family lives through the visual vehicle of hyperrealist fiction (Lea and Povinelli 2018).[8] The work of these experiments comes into closer view in later chapters, but they were each in its way an attempt to crack the issue of showing policy's wild workings beyond narrative conventions and out of the confines of epochal policy chronologies.

Finally, as the fourth proposition, *Wild Policy* stakes a claim for a new method and conceptual model for tracking the shape-shifting trickster that is social policy—namely, policy ecology—using a figurative framing of policy artifacts and policy ambience. These distinctions will thicken in subsequent chapters, but for now, artifactual policy refers to policy in its official, black-letter, or statecraft modalities, a genre that is often recognized by unfriendly formats and technocratic or banally inoffensive writing. The idealizing language of artifactual policy is seldom gritty or surprising. Even when circulating images of depravity, of ill-health and social suffering, the words assume a moral torpor: think "low socioeconomic status" or "disadvantaged." This is policy as legislation, regulation, rule, or funded program, formulated within citadels that we call the government, bureaucracy, or sometimes "the state." However, when viewed ethnographically, policy leaks; it travels; it is porous. Policy citadels exist, but they do not contain policy worlds. (The Vatican exists with scripture, hierarchy, ceremony, political influence, and rule-setting powers too, but still does not contain all there is to know about Catholicism in the world.)

Policy is part of our everyday surroundings, even when it is not officially in play. Over time and across space, it soaks into our everyday strata and sediments unequal accruals of privilege and disadvantage, obstacle and conduit. Just as there is never a single human existing and enacting entirely unto herself, so too policy belongs to multiple configurations. It is never simply a one-off event, although it is pronounced this way, with proper nouns to mark out a given policy identity. Nor is its formulation restricted to official sites of governance. To better capture policy's everywhereness, in my work, I contrast the normative or artifactual idea of policy with what I call policy ambience. Methodologically and conceptually, seeing the artifactual in the ambient and vice versa calls for an ecological approach.

Like the word wild, *ecology* is also a multivalent term, a word that, for biologists, describes the relations between organisms and their environments; for political scientists, the relations between people and institutions; and for this anthropologist, the relations between all of these and the purpose of ethnography. Policy, whether understood as narrative, artifact, embodiment, surround sound, or state effect, is a mobile assemblage, composed of different forces, materials, and actors, wending through time and space. These forces can be human (an infinite variety of factions and alliances, from influential power brokers, lobbyists, and contractors to someone holding the keys to the only working vehicle in a community), and non-, or more than, human. Even restricting ourselves to more usual understandings of policy as a legislated or "black-letter" product, the artifacts that attract the noun *policy* are created by "symbiogenetic"[9] humans who spend the majority of their waking hours inside spaces with controlled temperatures and recycled air, facing monitors nested on laminated desks or held in hands, kitchens with dictatorial rules about the treatment of dirty dishes and fridge waste, and emergency stairwells that repel any but vermin and microbial life from their bare concrete and stale aromas. Each of these are relationally enmeshed with other substances and circulations, microbial, local, and global.

Inevitably, there are sociobiological and psychosexual effects associated with being quarantined in these ways. Close screen work and a life dictated by the time intrusions of multiple digital platforms help create professionals with desk-bound bodily morphologies. The French surely recognized this when they coined the neologism *bureaucracy* to describe the newly empowered cadre of paperworkers who emerged out of the revolutionary period: the men becoming "a piece of writing furniture" (Kafka 2012, 77–81, 87). Beset by backaches and acquired myopia, their muscularity at risk of atrophying without lunchtime yoga and gym memberships, policy formulators in "carpet worlds" imagine what is needed for the subjects and objects within their current administrative purview, subliminally influenced by their own inhabited and disciplined contexts, dreams, and longings. This term, by the way, *carpet worlds*, is a real vernacular description, and I use it throughout to draw attention to a bureaucratic lifeworld that otherwise renders itself transcendent, as if the work conducted in such places takes place outside of any biophysical contexts. Among other effects, these industrialized, administrative, bio-ontologies cannot countenance life as having meaning outside the parameters of paid work or personal gain through financial indebtedness, along with the educational scaffolding and domestic reproductions required to service these pursuits over a life course.

Another way of putting this is to say that just as world markets are actors in Indigenous social policy, so too the environments within which Indigenous social policies are fashioned are not indifferent to, but actively condition, what can be seen as desirable destinations for fashioning a life (no matter how abstracted this might be from the worlds of the people whose lives are being reconfigured by policy projections, or indeed, how abstracted the individuals are, lumped as "welfare" or "Indigenous"). As David Graeber has put it, with characteristic efficiency,

[I]f one gives sufficient social power to a class of people holding even the most outlandish ideas, they will, consciously or not, eventually contrive to produce a world organized in such a way that living in it will, in a thousand subtle ways, reinforce the impression that those ideas are self-evidently true. (Graeber 2015, 37)

Policy not only materializes within compositions of technical and virtual infrastructures, from computers and databases to parliaments and office spaces, but also is compositionally organic. Human policy actors are never discretely human, acting alone. They cohabit. They are always interdependent with other things, human and nonhuman, animate and inanimate, here and now, from deep within their porous bodies all the way to outer space, back through time and into the future. Humans come into being with, absorb, and become other matter, not prior to it or separate from it, but in and of it. We intra-act.[10] And what policy enters into is also always in companionship with other matter, organic and not. Rust eats steel, water corrodes pipes, rats chew wiring, toxins destroy organs. There may even be ghosts, hauntings, and ensorcelling. Deaths repeatedly enter these pages; the past is always in the present, the future in yesterday. *Wild Policy* happens to call upon Australian examples. The sad truth is, what it describes could also be anywhere. The book's arguments speak to issues that like as not will speak loudly elsewhere, in Canada, the US, and South Asia, among other places.

What to expect

In what follows, each chapter focuses on different characters taking up policy unfurlings and fighting for their benefits, drawn from housing, infrastructure, health, and family-driven-enterprise examples. In line with its commitment to avoiding policy teleology, *Wild Policy* is not organized in a strictly chronological format but follows different characters, as housing interventions and other policies addressed to Australian Indigenous people come in and out of view. Interludes between chapters return to the Anangu leader John Singer, CEO of Nganampa Health Council, as one of the few people I have encountered in the field who has stayed the course. As an Indigenous man, he doesn't get to exit the issues when professional burnout sears the will to proceed; and his ongoing commentary is a salutary reminder that the policy effects captured here do not reduce to a jurisdiction (national or state), to a particular policy or program, to personalities, or to particular dates and events, even as all may play a part.

The year in which any particular thing happens could also be any place, any program, any day.

After Singer's next intercession, chapter 2 returns to a moment of policy crisis, when the Strategic Indigenous Housing and Infrastructure Program, SIHIP, the largest such program attempted in Indigenous Australia to date, brought the Northern Territory government to an electoral precipice. It explores the mechanics, processes, and architectures of record keeping, including spectral decision points and missing files lost in impenetrable archives, the mundane drifts and the preoccupying scandals, that make carpet-world policy "hard." I zoom in on the work needed to stabilize SIHIP so that the projected instabilities of Indigenous communities could return as the proper object of public critique, and how these cauterizing efforts created new forms of chaos for the multiple brokers and translators trying to actualize the houses, civic infrastructure, profitable land tenures, local community input, and jobs and training programs that SIHIP promised on the ground.

Chapter 3 shifts from the political machinations of SIHIP to Groote Eylandt, a manganese-rich island in the Gulf of Carpentaria, and the battles faced by Groote's institutional killjoys—the people who had to fight to wrest promised policy benefits into material form. Groote also symbolizes the entangled history of military expansion, mining, and Indigenous dispossession within Australia's global-to-local settler colonial relations. And it briefly shows the other companions occupying the poor living conditions that are used to justify interventions and their withdrawal in the name of health and well-being: the rats, salts, winds, fungi, and insects whose material entropy makes sustained repair and maintenance regimes one of the few policy prescriptions I explicitly wish for.[11] Houses took a long time to emerge on Groote, and although the housing debacle experienced there could easily be read and forgotten as a discrete fiasco, the chapter argues that such forms of corruption and elision are more endemic to social policy enactments, at least while policy acts to camouflage the larger extractive interests that connect individual everyday consumption with militarized trade pacts and profiteering.

The previous chapters having illustrated some of what a policy ecology approach generates, chapters 4 and 5 go to different nodes of policy interface, from film shoots to manganese and uranium mines. Each is explored for what it might reveal about what policy does—never alone, always in relationship with other forces and entities. Chapter 4 introduces the Karrabing Film Collective, a coalition of Indigenous friends and family who deploy neorealist films to speak about, among other things, the lingering effects of policy's saturation in our surroundings, or, as I prefer, its ambient presence, in the anything-but-simple business of navigating ordinary life. As I account for it, Karrabing abilities to narrate policy hauntings out of the stickiness of policy's permeating conditions also propel social transformations. On the back of their filmmaking, now most often shot using stabilized smartphones, members have become seasoned international travelers able to enter into dialogue with master curators at elite creative institutions, such as the Tate London or the German Berlinale. A retrospective of the collective's work was held in spring 2019 in New York City, at no less a venue than the Museum of Modern Art. Young and old members alike have reinvigorated their connections to each other and to country, finding meaningful work in the process, as rangers or aged-care workers. All have become stronger speakers in front of inquisitive, well-meaning, and sometimes blundering white people, as they share their probative analytics about their worlds.

This chapter goes behind the scenes of the glossy catalogues. It is not cast as a policy success story, even though what the Karrabing have put in place, and what social policy pronouncements repeatedly say is desired for Indigenous people, are polemically aligned. Policy as it appears in chapter 4 is hauntological. Policy hovers in the margins of daily events, manifesting as the experience of past and present violations and assistance, as both presence and absence. It is simultaneously subject matter to represent creatively in films and a series of obstacles and enablers to live through in the ordeals and mundane rituals of any given day. Here I expand what I mean by the notion of policy hauntology, a concept I deploy to explain the deeply saturated effects of past policies, enduring and shaping conditions in the present, soaking into ambient surroundings (sometimes felt as static) and carried psychically. It helps explain why privilege and impoverishment are enabled, affecting possible futures. This is not hauntology as it was expounded by Jacques Derrida (1994) in *Specters of Marx: The State of the Debt, the Work of Mourning and the New International*. Rather, it borrows from feminist and decolonial theorists, who recruit the term to better understand the depth of settler colonial injustice. Avery Gordon's work is a key influence. In *Ghostly Matters*, Gordon (2008) gives haunting a more mobile range, from the active memory of those who have been disappeared under violent regimes in Argentina, to the lingering impact of racial slavery in the furniture of a sitting room in suburban America, to the resistant refusal of a grieving mother to let her stolen child be forgotten. I lift these ideas to understand policy phenomena as likewise being absent presences, scarrings, and potential mechanisms for resistance. To understand policy possibilities, one must come to grips with their invisibilized prior residues. Ghost policies can be hidden in plain sight, structuring everyday worlds, without having a named location or a proper-noun identity. That privatized property relations govern human and nonhuman spatiality is one such policy inheritance, no longer heralded, but fully met when, for example, an unauthorized being is found occupying a vacant building or park. "[A]t some point, we're going to have to talk about returning stolen land," write decolonial critics Eve Tuck and C. Ree, writing as a single author: "My guess is that people are going to be really reluctant to give up that ghost" (2013, 647).

My recasting of policy hauntology also draws from Ann Stoler's account of imperial debris as "the less perceptible effects of imperial interventions and their settling into the social and material ecologies in which people live and survive" (2013, 4); and again, as "the more protracted imperial processes that saturate the subsoil of people's lives and persist, sometimes subjacently, over a longer durée" (5). I prefer the concept of hauntology over that of debris or ruination, for relatively simple reasons. I share Stoler's desire to capture the psychological scarring and saturated effects of past policies within current conditions, but I also want to capture the truly ghostly, otherworldly dimensions that also pulse through the putatively rational domain of policy, from ghosts in institutional headquarters to ancestral forces making claims through all time—a resilience that concepts of "rot" or despoiling potentially occlude. For Tuck and Ree (2013), there is a relationship between "psychic-paranormal knowledge [and] state-official knowledge" (650). Haunting can also be about "the relentless remembering and reminding that will not be appeased by settler society's assurances of innocence and reconciliation" (642). To summarize, policy hauntology lets us consider spirits as well as structuring inheritances, survival and memory alongside denial and evasion, as part of a wider policy ecology. It reminds us that policies do not exist in singular form, nor are their effects over when the policy itself might be considered something done and dusted.

Questions of resilience matter beyond a semantic point about metaphorical inferences. There are many examples in this book showing how people make policy "work," or how they pull out some good, through determined efforts and creative analytics. To capture this ever-present potentiality, even within conditions where the odds are negatively stacked (in part because of the lingering policies delimiting what appears to be inevitable in the present), I explore what might be leveraged from Isabelle Stengers's concept of the mesopolitical. This is the space in between micro and macro layers of analysis, where forces that bind and stick might also be prized apart and new energies released (Stengers 2017). Policy hauntings may represent an ongoing social bias in the way things are presented—ordaining the ease of some paths, thickening the obstacles of others—but there is always the promise that worlds can be ordered differently. This is not a saccharine hope. The scarring implied by the notion of policy haunting offers a real precaution about what it takes.

That mesopolitics operate within a micro-macro relation that is also always a militarized relation is the focus of chapter 5. It shifts between the geographies referenced thus far (Groote Eylandt in the Cape of Carpentaria in Australia's northeast, the Anangu Pitjantjatjara Yankunytjatjara Lands south of the center, Anson Bay at the mouth of the Daly River in the northwest, and the towns of Darwin, Alice Springs, Adelaide, and Canberra) to include the efforts of the Gundjheimi Aboriginal Corporation, representing the Mirarr clan within Kakadu National Park. The Mirarr Gundjeihmi's battle to rid their country of uranium mining takes us closer to the entangled histories of military expansion, trade, and industry that haunt Indigenous dispossession under continuing occupation—and to my/your/our interests in all this staying in place.

Taken together, these intermissions and examples offer the truthful hope that people's initiatives *do matter* for policy effect, without being falsely anodyne about that hope. The military and economic drivers behind the growing rapaciousness of the extraction industry in the "race for what is left" as climate change reconfigures new profits and losses, and the conditions of Indigenous peoples in regional and remote Australia, are deeply interconnected. In turn, my own well-being and survival are dependent on both of these configurations. I cannot easily extract from my extractivist life supports. Understanding this ecology is key to returning greater nuance to the question "Can there be good policy?" This directly links to the conclusion, which addresses the perennial liberal humanist question, "What can be done?" Gathering together the themes of the book, the final chapter operates as something of a wild policy primer, exploring visions of alternate ways of conceptualizing nested and always entangled actions, and highlighting paths through thickets without promising magical transportation out of the settler colonial mire, for hope lies in dirty realism as much as it flies with visionary metaphors.

Interlude II

They found her body in a shallow grave, hastily dug, and not as far from her house as the search parties had originally anticipated. She had left her bed in the middle of the night, Thursday, March 24, 2016, possibly to answer a knock at the door. (There is no way of knowing.) Her sleeping husband, perhaps over-familiar with on-call disruptions, had no immediate cause to worry. It was Gayle's dedication as a nurse that had brought the couple to Kaltjiti, also known as Fregon, in the first place. He had fitted his life into hers out on the remote Aṉangu Pitjantjatjara Yankunytjatjara (APY) Lands, finding work as a handyman and teaching support at the local school. Gayle was not home when he woke on Friday morning, but she was mature, diligent, well liked, and reliable. He would check with the clinic later. Such is the life of a bush nurse in a remote community, summoned for everything from talking down suicide attempts to helping someone get acetaminophen. When he went to say hello later that morning at the clinic, however, she wasn't there either.

She had last been seen in the community "bush ambulance"—a retrofitted Toyota four-wheel drive, made clinical by its strapped-in oxygen tank and first-aid kit—with at least one other Aṉangu adult in the vehicle. When the ambulance had next come into view, it was carrying at least three people, perhaps with Gayle, perhaps not; the witness reports were as contradictory as the vehicle's erratic journey, recorded by its GPS transmitter. The vehicle had paused in Kaltjiti, careened through Mimili, on to Indulkana. By daybreak, it had reached the small roadside town of Marla, population seventy, a meagerly supplied service stop on the long, continent-splitting Stuart Highway, vending overpriced goods for travelers, professionals, and mining workers heading north, south, or perhaps westward, back toward the APY Lands. There the ambulance enjoyed another interlude, an hour this time, perchance for its passengers to take a toilet break. The ambulance was finally abandoned in

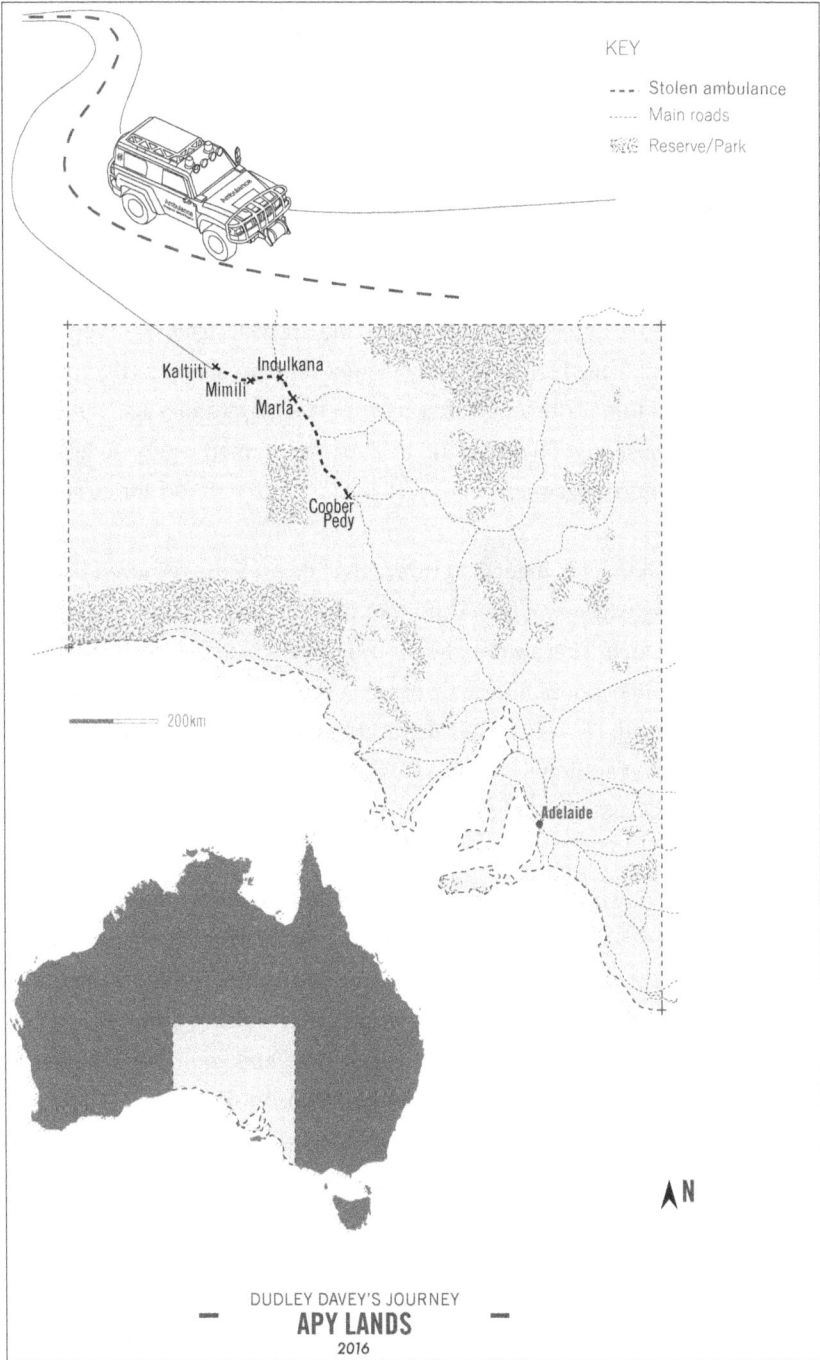

KEY

- - - Stolen ambulance
.... Main roads
Reserve/Park

Kaltjiti
Indulkana
Mimili
Marla
Coober Pedy
Adelaide

200km

N

DUDLEY DAVEY'S JOURNEY
APY LANDS
2016

Figure 1. Stolen ambulance journey, APY Lands. Map by M. Barbagallo.

Cooper Pedy, opal capital of the world, 370 kilometers from Gayle's house in Kaltjiti.

Gayle Woodford was still nowhere to be found. The driver, thirty-six-year-old Dudley David Davey, when arrested for stealing the ambulance, had nothing to say.

It was a huge arc of country to conduct a search, over a landscape of weathered layered rocks and fine-textured red soils, rich with nickel, cobalt, and copper deposits. As search parties combed through the tough shrubs and thorny grasses binding the red sands surrounding Kaltjiti, John Singer and managers at Nganampa Health Council began taking and making calls. This was their nurse who was missing. They had to urgently extract the ambulance's GPS tracking data before its automatic deletion after seventy-two hours and place it in police hands. But in those first few days, the local police seemed less panicked. The GPS data was not so essential. People get waylaid in the desert for all sorts of reasons.

By Monday, homicide detectives from Adelaide used the retrieved tracking logs and the long pause around Kaltjiti that the data revealed to urgently concentrate their search. That's when they found Gayle's battered body, a mere 1.5 kilometers from her house. Cause of death: a massive skull-crushing blow to the side of her head. There had been no recent rains to churn the red sands into mud slurries—an additional crime scene near the grave stayed preserved. She had been sexually assaulted, perhaps had escaped and been caught again.[1]

To see him, Dudley has the definite look of a central desert man, thick hair sprouting in all directions, refusing rule by comb. He also has what some see as an inevitable profile for unviable life in remote communities: in and out of custody, sometimes jailed, sometimes let go for assaulting different women and driving them into the ground, released time and again for supervised parole in desolate places with minimal supervision. He was a dangerous, disturbed man who appeared to take pleasure in assaulting women, young or old, white or black. Almost a year after Gayle's corpse had been found in its shallow pit, her neck twice smashed from his boot, Dudley pled guilty at his committal hearing at the Port Augusta Magistrates Court, with no interpreter, for none were willing to assist. He confessed to stealing Nganampa's ambulance and to raping and murdering Gayle. How he says he lured Gayle to cross the threshold, without her clinic keys or medical kit, is untrustworthy, Justice Ann Vanstone declared.[2]

Dudley is permanently banned from the APY Lands too, elders pronounced at his final court session, as a life sentence and nonparole period of thirty-two years was handed down. Upon appeal, the sentence was upheld.

It has undoubtedly been a time of unspeakable grief for Gayle's family; and she was mourned at Nganampa Health Council too, for she was one of theirs, a remote-area nurse of high regard. For John Singer, with the depressingly familiar figure of death now visiting in acutely public form, the nurse-safety campaign that was immediately galvanized with news of Gayle's murder opened an opportunity to wrest long-wanted funds for better staff security. From May 2016 on, no nurse was to attend a night call without an escort. And the murder gave his health council license to be even more resolute about the proposal for a renal dialysis facility at Pukatja (formerly Ernabella), the one that had first appeared with an inadequate business case, despite growing external outrage at Nganampa Health's apparent blocking of vitally necessary on-site renal dialysis services. The business case was retrospective because, or so Nganampa understood the backstory, the service was never meant to come to South Australia in the first place. They learned that Pukatja had been accidentally listed as part of a roll call of Northern Territory communities in line for dialysis, during a ministerial press conference. If so, it was a mistake, or perhaps an inclusion to appease those pressing for services to be closer to patients. Either way, Pukatja is not even in the Northern Territory.

"We won't stop you," John told representatives from the South Australian health department, when discussing Nganampa's continuing concerns about the overall viability of dialysis.

"Simply show us how the service will be staffed and maintained, where patients would stay in between being on dialysis, how people from other communities will be able to travel safely to access the facility, what will happen in wintertime when the unsealed air strip can't be used and we've got an emergency on our hands.

"And show us that there is recurrent funding for maintaining the facility and funding and protecting its nursing staff. Until then, we got little more to discuss."

In the wake of Gayle's murder, Nganampa was promised seven "real" ambulances. John's vigilance shifted to making sure these ambulances were not souvenired from former fleet vehicles retired because of unreliability or age. And he has had to organize, then postpone; organize, postpone; and organize again a visit from the federal minister for aged care and Indigenous health, Ken Wyatt. Each time, a date would be set, schedules adjusted to make sure continuing staff and Aɳangu elders were on notice to make themselves available, travel arrangements put in place to drive *tjilpi* (elders) in from outlying communities, visitor itineraries plotted, quotes from airline charter companies secured, ground transport and scant accommodation cleared for use—and the event would be cancelled. The first time, Nganampa was advised by way of telephoned apology that the minister had a diary clash. Then the facility was advised that he needed to make way for a sudden half-day visit to the Lands by (former) prime minister Turnbull, who seemed keen to offset media criticism of his underengagement with Indigenous affairs by quickly establishing his bona fides on the ground. Third time around, it seemed an election taking place in a separate organization altogether—the local council—rendered Wyatt's visit to Nganampa untimely.

Each postponement catalyzed administrative gear shifting, spurring new email flurries, cancellations, trashed calendars, and revised budgets. What may have been just another day in a well-staffed bureaucracy was, is, a pulverizing cost for a remote-area NGO, where the roles of personal assistant, business manager, courier, information officer, store supplier, travel coordinator, and information technology expert can be occupied by just the one person. Stop-start ministerial visits don't amount to much in themselves. Looked at from the dusty field, it can take a lot of work to not get very far, dealing with dignitaries and policy by press briefings.

Meanwhile, the administrative wear and tear through such serial nonevents as cancelled visits joins the distraction of withstanding what appear as arbitrary policy interventions and funding through short grants in diluting the organization's abilities to concentrate on its core business: promoting well-being and preventing premature death. These small but constant disruptions join emergency interventions and abandonments as an array of state mechanisms for letting lives wither, suspended between grievances and grief, even as the state claims to act in the name of people's betterment. These corrosive effects are so embedded within ambient policy surroundings, they cannot compete against dominant fields of interpretation that shout "Indigenous dysfunction."

Chapter 2

Policy specters

Entering the field

The first day I began fieldwork in the bureaucratic headquarters managing the Strategic Indigenous Housing and Infrastructure Program (SIHIP), in July 2009, Jim Davidson welcomed me with outstretched arms and a vigorous hand-shake. He had once been a ministerial advisor for an Australian Labor Party cabinet minister, then returned to the private sector, only to land a role heading Australia's largest-ever delivery program for remote Indigenous housing and infrastructure, as a lead consultant from the engineering company Parsons Brinkerhoff. Jim's star was on the rise, and he was exhilarated with the ascent.

"You are entering this complex housing program at just the right time," he told me, maintaining his opening bonhomie.

"We've had our first year. Much of the difficult work of selecting staff and in-stalling systems is done. We've been consulting communities. Employing locals. Working on designs. Things are now getting really interesting, and I want you to record it all—watch how we go from zero to hero!

"Make yourself known to my administrative assistant and let her know what meetings you'd like to sit in on."

Jim was overseeing a labyrinthine infrastructure operation, and I was mak-ing the most of the rare opportunity to observe a live policy unfolding from the inside. SIHIP was the most expensive part of the infamous Northern Territory National Emergency Response, aka the Intervention. The dramatic declaration of a national emergency in Northern Territory (NT) Indigenous communities in June 2007 was ostensibly triggered by the release of *Ampe Akelyernemane Meke Mekarle: "Little Children Are Sacred": Report of the Northern Territory Board of Inquiry into the Protection of Aboriginal Children from Sexual Abuse* (Wild and Anderson 2007). According to the report's authors, "rivers of grog [alcohol]," rampant child sexual abuse, and organized pedophilia rings were destroying any capacity of Indigenous people to exercise normal function. The veteran Indigenous affairs commentator Nicolas Rothwell (2017) reflects that it was this phrase, "rivers of grog," that set journalist hounds onto their hunt. Now that's a story.

Wild and Anderson's inquiry into sexual abuse had been commissioned by the NT government one year earlier, based on public outrage following a different kind of reporting, a late-night television interview. In May 2006, Nanette Rogers, an experienced Crown prosecutor based in Alice Springs, a small service town of some twenty-five thousand people in the middle of Australia, appeared on the Australian Broadcasting Commission's *Lateline* show.[1] Rogers detailed sickening cases of children suffering at the hands of their drunken and depraved family members. She provided graphic details of babies raped so badly that their genitals needed surgical repair and described a paralyzing malaise among all the groups that could possibly intervene, including a worrying lack of prosecutorial powers to do much to prevent any of it (Jones 2006).

Public outcry was immediate (Proudfoot and Habibis 2015). News of the Crown prosecutor's explicit account was replayed in all major broadsheets. "Sex abuse 'rife' in NT communities," declared one (Skelton 2006). "A culture of violence that must change," editorialized another.[2] The Intergovernmental Summit on Violence and Child Abuse in Indigenous Communities was urgently convened, involving ministers and senior officials from the Australian government and all states and territories. One month later, in June 2006, the Australian government offered the state and territory governments a package of funding worth $130 million over four years, a meager amount given the backlog, but represented as a generous fortune in media snapshots. Conditional on the removal of any references to customary law from each jurisdiction's crimes act, the funding was to build police stations and police housing; provide drug and alcohol rehabilitation services; establish "strike teams" to gather and share intelligence on Indigenous violence through the Australian federal police; conduct child health checks (looking for signs of sexual abuse) in remote communities; and establish a national truancy unit to monitor school attendance.

The NT government took the opportunity to additionally commission Rex Wild (a Queen's Counsel), and Pat Anderson, an Indigenous woman renowned for her advocacy in Indigenous health, to separately inquire into the extent of Aboriginal child sexual abuse. The NT would follow this commissioned inquiry in 2008 with an additional strike. It replaced sixty-two local community councils, many representing Aboriginal interests, with eight "super shires," recentralizing control (Michel 2015).

These amalgamations joined the chaos to come. Just now we are amid the buildup to the National Emergency Response.

A housing cure-all

> Aboriginal communities abundant with child abuse: Report
> Barker (2007)

Too many people sharing one house, the Wild and Anderson report warned, meant that children were exposed to adult sexual practices, were made witness to adult pornography in magazines and on video and television, or were vulnerable to the predations and assaults of intoxicated and drugged coresidents, lacking even the ability to lock a door or close a shower screen (2007, 195–198). These were representations of people locked in poverty, self-medicating and drug addled; of exhaustion, mindless aggression, tortures, and mutilations; of the financially broken and spiritually corrupted; and of children at the center of it all, exposed, neglected, and not even able to shut a door (Macoun 2011). The kinds of settings that Dudley David Davey might have emerged from, and contributed to, with his vicious depravity and wild ways.

Poor housing was also linked to low to no school attendance, infectious and chronic disease, and the inability to hold down jobs, given the impossibility of being a wage earner in a house full of unemployed kin, needy and indolent (Toohey 2011). Housing, together with systems of collective land tenure, was positioned at the heart of the dysfunctions wracking Aboriginal communities, causing everything from moral debauchery to welfare lassitude, unemployment to illiteracy. SIHIP was thus not only about housing supply (to be exact, 750 new houses, 230 rebuilds, and 2,500 renovations) but also meant to improve life expectancy, school attendance, training, employment, and health, while transforming sexual moralities, self-discipline, money hoarding, and family conduct. Houses would renovate psyches. Land tenure reform would open new economies.[3]

To encourage greater care for these heavy-lifting houses, additional reforms lurked in the fine print. SIHIP would only deliver new, refurbished, or replacement houses in sixteen particular sites that the government had newly categorized as "growth towns." The most any of the other fifty-seven communities would see was cosmetic refurbishments of existing stock. Later, following criticism that this pick-list neglected some of the most radically impoverished areas, the number of communities to receive major works increased to a total of eighteen communities and three town camps (Australian National Audit Office 2011, 164–165).

For their part, the select few growth towns would only receive money for those new or upgraded houses if traditional owners additionally assigned leasehold title over their town land to the government. Originally these were ninety-nine-year terms, later bartered down to forty years. Tellingly, only four communities willingly agreed to the ninety-nine-year leases. It was, according to Tony Wurramarrba, a traditional owner from Groote Eylandt, representing the first such group to agree to leasing, his "biggest regret." Township leasing had "taken away our self-determination," he lamented ten years later. "Looking back, I regret signing both those agreements [the leases and the partnership], but at the time I had no choice" (Akman 2016).[4]

The "no choice" argument was presented as follows: yielding leasehold title over Indigenous town land would create opportunities for private enterprise and private home ownership. (It would in fact do neither; but the convincing common sense being peddled was that existing leasing arrangements inhibited bank lending.) Any houses built under SIHIP would become the property of the government, to be let under newly sharpened rental tenancy regulations, with harsher eviction clauses, rather than follow the more intimate kin-based approach to housing management formerly taken by now-disbanded Indigenous community housing organizations.

It was as if everything that made life ferocious for Aboriginal citizens living beyond the metropolis could be reduced to the discipline of hard-line tenancies and the magic of private enterprise, which would somehow now flourish because the government held leases over Aboriginal land as the price of improved housing. It was not simply governance of the self that SIHIP sought but also a dehistoricized assertion of a contractual society built on indebtedness to the house and an idea of causality that pinned violence and psychic renovation to cement, support beams, and fiberboards, underpinned by the threat of tenure loss. But I am getting ahead of myself.

Six days following receipt of the Wild-Anderson report, the Australian government took the extraordinary additional step of announcing that the abuse of children in Indigenous communities in the NT constituted a national emergency (Altman and Hinkson 2007). The Intervention was approved in an overnight meeting of federal Parliament, receiving bipartisan support; SIHIP was one result. "We need to improve living conditions and reduce overcrowding. More houses need to be built and we need to control the land in the townships for a short period to ensure that we can do this quickly," declared Indigenous affairs minister Mal Brough (2007).

But if SIHIP and, before it, the ten-day passage of time it took to introduce 480 pages of legislation authorizing the original 2007 Intervention, were done at speed, my backroom access to document the program took many months to negotiate. I was positioned in July 2009, one year into SIHIP's operations, to track its unfolding. It was a time of intense enthusiasm, rash planning, humanitarian promises, and long, hectic hours. My access to it would be just as wild.

Inside a policy haunt

SIHIP's program headquarters, where I had carte blanche access to Jim's meetings, were in the Chan Building, opposite the NT's ornate Parliament House. Joining the SIHIP project management team involved a crash course on new acronyms, abbreviations, and elaborate planning structures. The program's organizational complexity mimicked the complexity of its social engineering ambitions. The engineering and design company Jim belonged to, Parsons Brinkerhoff (PB), was overall project manager. By April 2009, PB had recruited three alliance teams—Territory Alliance, Earth Connect Alliance, and New Future Alliance—to construct and refurbish housing in the growth towns.[5] PB organized the community consultations, controlled the design teams and the governance framework for all the work, and established the Strategic Alliance Leadership Team, a group Jim proudly convened and chaired. This was the SALT, and it mattered to Jim that I sit in on its agenda-jammed meetings. For him, it was the private-enterprise heart of SIHIP, the hub where the greater rationality of corporate players would finally deliver a professional housing product to Indigenous communities, different from the shambolic efforts of all governments hitherto.

Above the SALT sat the Joint Steering Committee (JSC) for the National Partnership Agreement on Remote Indigenous Housing—NT Implementation Plan. Each alliance team in turn subcontracted construction, repairs, and training services to other organizations, including some Indigenous-controlled companies within targeted communities; and each bureaucratic team had an army of other positions feeding off it, taking care of procurement or recruitment, for example. Before I was overwhelmed by the infinity of SIHIP's connections, I drew one kinship chart like this (figure 2).

Looking at the chart now, one can see that it conveys little information. It is the kind of fragment an anthropologist pins down, anticipating the case study to be wrangled out of isolated writing ventures to come. "You don't know what will become significant," I tell students. "Keep taking notes, every single day," I say, as if this will cure what will also come: the yawning immensity of discovering what we don't know and now can't find out—and how much becomes irrelevant, with time. This is, today, a posthumous ethnography, about a program that is widely deemed a failure or, at best, a squandering of valuable public housing money. Housing needs are as acute as ever, with no greater attention being paid to recurrent maintenance of public housing stock; and, worse still, there are fewer serviced lots to put any further housing on, because in the gap between fundable crises, there's been no money put into preparing any land, no surveying of subdivisions, no subterranean networks of sewerage and water laid down, no electricity grid upgrades. There's only the fastest-growing population with the greatest proportion of young people in Australia (Australian Bureau of Statistics 2016). I can write that the money set aside for SIHIP cannot meet the metric of 750 new houses, 230 rebuilds, and 2,500 renovations, and—evaluation piled upon evaluation, inquiry upon inquiry later—that the money will be siphoned, and the metric will not fulfill its raft of social objectives.

As journalist Nicolas Rothwell has reported,

[T]he flagship housing program [SIHIP] failed to build a single house in its first year of operation, had by its midpoint demolished more bedrooms than it had built, and had by its end mushroomed into a profit centre for several interstate conglomerates. Grotesque fees shelled out to consultants, quiet backhanders in the subcontracting daisy chain, unchecked overcharging, shoddy workmanship, ill-conceived designs—this was the Northern Territory's SIHIP in all its glory. The results are evident on the ground: Aboriginal families in many remote communities still live twenty to a home today, after a series of further, even more costly programs, and maintenance standards have become abysmal—a little detail that in itself does much to explain the persistence of poor health, domestic tensions and bad school results. (Rothwell 2017, 14)

In other words, the doomed alchemy can be prophesized as chimerical without sustained ethnographic recall. But because this is also an account that parallels

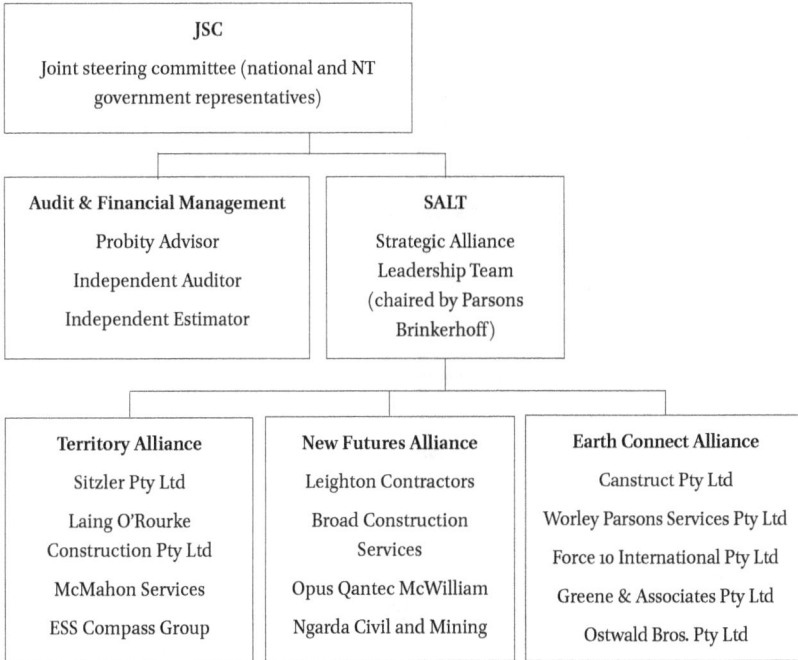

Figure 2. SIHIP kinship system.

what befell Grenfell Tower, a residential block in North Kensington, London, let's stay in this space of predictable outcomes for a while longer. Grenfell Tower housing estate went up in flames in July 2017, but was made incendiary *before* it combusted, in carpet-world back rooms where mundane budget decisions to lop fire extinguishers and stairwells out of buildings are made, by ordinary professionals without mayhem on their minds (McKee 2017). Anthropology of policy helps illuminate the tracks of not-so-bad, could-be-good, might-be-devastating, always-in-becoming pathways within social policy. It helps reveal how policy artifacts blend into ambient conditions that become unspoken future legacies, or what I call policy hauntologies, invisibly shaping differentially distributed obstacles and benefits in times ahead or, to cite the late Toni Morrison, invisibly shaping "the shared bounty of class" (Angelo and Morrison 1989, 120). In time, these inheritances lose their contexts, the ethnographic particulars become forgotten details, and only a select number of proper-noun policy artifacts are allowed to populate official chronological accounts. Simply, because

invisibilized legacies shape future possibilities, how they are enacted is important to capture.

I'd been promised "zero to hero," and the organizational labyrinth was an
expression of this spirit. SIHIP's extension of a "mainstream" public housing
management model to remote Indigenous communities also had a unique
name (somewhat contradicting its avowed normalizing intent). It was called
the Remote Public Housing Management Framework; and in time, this too
would assume an independent political life as a residential tenancy framework
that cascaded into increased fines and evictions. There were Housing Reference Groups in each community, established to bypass what the government
saw as the undue influence of powerful families and the petty corruption of
local overlords; and Government Business Managers, mostly middle-aged
white professionals of a generic helping kind (cf. Kowal 2015, Cowlishaw 2003),
who had been installed as part of the Intervention on behalf of the Australian
government.

Each targeted community was additionally provided a Local Industry Participation Plan describing the economic engagement processes to be applied to
it, and Local Service Agreements, which formed part of Regional Partnership
Agreements (RPAs). In turn, the RPAs are the offspring of wider intergovernmental agreements. Since the 2007 Intervention, these larger agreements have
metamorphosed into new pacts, such as the Closing the Gap in the Northern
Territory National Partnership Agreement between the Australian and Northern Territory Governments. Such federal–state/territory agreements each have
numerous subagreements, covering schools, early childhood development,
remote service delivery, economic participation, remote housing, health outcomes, and public internet access. (Where relevant, I sometimes name these
specific portfolio agreements, but have not attempted a compendium, simply
because, as an exercise in infinite label chasing among program bromides, it
promises no further clarity.[6])

Each of these agreements had specific correspondence histories as they
moved from serial drafts to official text on letterhead paper bearing multiple
logos, signifying the deepening entanglement of Indigenous futures and administrative imaginaries within dense systems of lexical authorization, as
government extended its administrative presence and decried Indigenous
dependency on government services in the same move. And each proclaimed
the moral imperative of preventing premature deaths and bettering lives. They

were talismanic, averting an abstract future in which the moral deprivation that precipitated the national emergency would finally be laid to rest. Sexual decrepitude, now exposed, would be eradicated, being a symptom of inadequate housing provision, tenancy management, and land tenure regulation. And the long-pursued goal of Aboriginal incorporation in the "real" economy would be realized.

Only, it wouldn't.

If, as the anthropologist of bureaucratic paperwork Matthew Hull (2012) has argued, the meanings attributed to discursive notations are governed by "graphic ideologies" (14), then the most obvious effect of the abundant representational genres multiplying within the Chan Building was symbolic stabilization, a graphic ordering of rampant project disorder. Without these attempts, SIHIP, and the wider suite of interventions it was nested in, would look like what it was: a chaotic collection of hastily conceived models and incompatible systems to cure catastrophic socioeconomic disadvantage. In this sense, the acronyms, the titles, the Gantt charts, the files, and the software, like the assumed panoptic gaze of settler colonial administrators, formed a "frail conceit" (Stoler 2008a, 23) masking greater anxieties and disorderliness. The chaos being kept at bay was not that of extraordinary death rates or child sexual abuse—that was the imprimatur for funding, not the reason for the administrative maze—but the splintering effects of partnering with private capital and profiteering while bureaucratically administering the inherent complexities of settler colonial biopolitics through housing and resettlement plans. This taming of wild bureaucratic ganglia also provides a glimpse into the artisanry involved in creating and sustaining policy artifacts, and the labor of pulling some good out of policy openings. But, despite all this exegesis, I cannot tell you, in retrospect, which bit was most redundant in holding SIHIP's imminent implosion at bay, and I suspect that the desire to locate such a culprit reflects the evaluative impulse we've imbibed as part of our generic policy conditioning. As a way of entering policy wilds, it is not a particularly insightful pursuit.

Administering chaos

Within the drab rectangular Chan Building, internally refurbished to allow for temporary offices and meeting areas, each room spoke of haste, busyness, and administrative density. Desks drowned in stacks of files, rolls of planning documents, and mismatched tea-stained crockery. This was a place not of curated wall art, or tasteful foyers with welcoming seating areas and freshly replaced nursery plants, but of long workdays filled with torrents of emails, meetings, urgent briefings, paperwork, data entries, and carb-rich lunches hungrily eaten from paper wrapping and plastic containers over keyboards. Personal adornments were few, and those few did not suggest precious memories. But the old Chan Building itself made up for the loss of mementoes, supplying lingerings of its own (figure 3).

On day two of following Jim, I found a handwritten Post-it note pasted within the personal address section of my diary, left open for me to find, I don't know by whom: *"If you are wondering—this building is haunted and things have happened to ladies in the toilet so we don't like to go ourselves!! Ha ha."*

The warning about the apparitional state of SIHIP's own amenities, in retrospect, was an insight, perhaps a second sight, into the appearances and disappearances that kept interrupting the marketing of SIHIP's institutional coherence. "Ghosts hate new things," Avery Gordon (2008) tells us, drawing on Zora Neale Hurston. "The reason why is because ghosts are characteristically attached to the events, things, and places that produced them in the first place; by nature they are haunting reminders of lingering trouble" (xix). The diary provocation to wonder about the uncanny, to avoid haunted areas in an otherwise drab industrial building, could be a summary theoretical statement of the upmost significance to the fantastic wiles of Indigenous social policy. And of its capacity to generate disappearances. Of the four men within the SALT whose hands I shook in July 2009—Jim and three alliance directors—only two would survive the year. More casualties would follow.

A departmental chief executive officer and several deputies would be replaced; a government minister would resign; the NT government would be brought to the edge of an electoral downfall; there would be six official inquiries and countless public consultations and hearings.[7] From it all, phoenix-like, a newly configured reporting tree arose, with far more nodes, as government bureaucrats replaced private-industry consultants to increase the look of probity within a shrouding of overabundant review and audit data. I was following dead men walking as they plotted the eradication of other policy specters: all the past, equally overoptimistic schemes to deliver houses that now sat as haunting souvenirs of poor material choice, bad design, cost-cutting, bypassed standards, no supervision, sporadic repair and maintenance systems, and no redress over landlord culpability (Lea and Pholeros 2010). I was following policy hauntologies in the making.

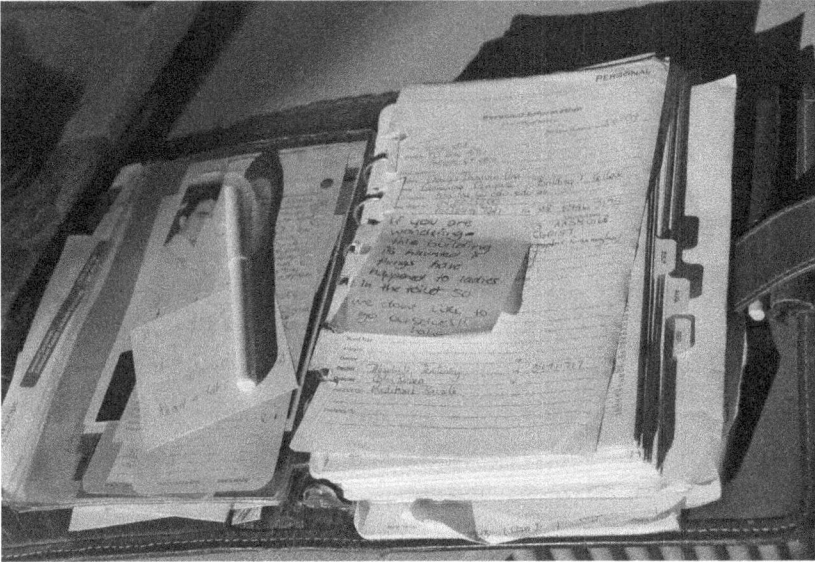

Figure 3. This building is haunted. Photograph by Tess Lea.

It would not take long for this anthropologist to also be eliminated, for as it happened, in the moment of initial fieldwork, with the rare invitation to name my meeting of choice, the SIHIP program was seized by a scandal of such political magnitude that in the end, the only thing that would survive was the metric: 750 houses, 230 replacements, 2,500 refurbishments. My eviction also took place as a phantom operation: how the new Labor federal minister who inherited the program, the Honorable Jenny Macklin, worded her rejection of my research, I never would find out. I was told instead to stop asking for a copy of her letter. I suspect the instruction was not written down. It had taken one-and-a-half years of entangled negotiation to gain approved access to the NT Department of Housing and Local Government in the first instance, and just over four weeks to have being there made an impossible matter of an unsigned research agreement. As public servants told me at the time, politicians were "anxious about the metrics," "no one wants another layer of review," and "everyone is worried about leaks and risks."

Just as ghostly, information on the previous most comprehensive Indigenous housing program, the National Aboriginal Health Strategy Environmental Health Program (NAHS-EHP), hovered in another dimension. It is not simply that ghosts hate new things but that new things hate ghosts. All the documents and plans promulgated under NAHS-EHP, plans that perhaps might have informed the current effort by way of that much-vaunted managerial category "project learnings," had been lodged with the vaults of the appropriately named archiving service, Iron Mountain. Filed in random order, they could now only be retrieved through official Freedom of Information requests, demanding long paperwork prequels with expectations of specificity. (At a minimum, one needed to know the title of what was being requested before it could be requested.) Of course, scholars of the function of archives have shown these treasured sites to be far from neutral systems for record keeping, but instead essential technologies of colonial rule (Stoler 2008a, Agamben 1999, Yale 2015). These are studies that point not only to the necessity of archival practices to empire but also, epistemologically, to the impossibility of archives; how one turns to them expecting revelation through windows or mirrors, only to confront their shadow plays and locked rooms, their partiality and politics. And that's when you can access them.

The labyrinth

Jim Davidson's job was a complex one, but its enormity had not eaten his spirit, at least not during my brief tumble through the SIHIP warren. The three chosen alliances had to operate over an extensive geographic area (one-sixth the Australian land mass), to install the largest Indigenous housing program in Australian history, one that was preloaded with multiple sanctions and reforms, including an intensification of dispossession efforts to centralize Aboriginal residents into larger "growth town" settlements—all within a five-year time frame. There would be a minimum of 20 percent Indigenous employment and training to be generated out of each contract for building works and allied services[8]; energy conservation measures would apply in the houses; there would be provisions for thermal comfort; and new tenancy and asset management regimes would follow when the keys were handed over. Sorting all this out was Jim's overarching job when I joined his team.

It's important to note that new SIHIP houses were also meant to have a minimum thirty-year life span, an ambition to be met by having construction comply with established building codes and best-practice guidelines for Indigenous housing. At first blush, such avowed adherence to codes and guidelines may seem rather ordinary; but in the context of remote-area Indigenous housing, this heralded a particularly radical insistence. Usually such regulatory requirements as, say, certification of safe electrical work or waterproofing of the wet areas of a house are left to qualified trades. Trust is rested in self-certification against set codes. But buildings on land seized by the national government as belonging to the Crown and later repatriated in fragments to successful Aboriginal claimants *do not* automatically have to comply with the National Construction Code. So, although this new requirement to build to codes that are not normally applied would also soon be dropped (along with fire escapes and flexible floor space) in a panic of blunt budget "corrections," they were part of SIHIP's frontloaded promises. Or to put this differently, invoking ghostly standards helped compose the mirage of services that were promised in exchange for tighter tenancy regulations and increased rent, higher levels of policing in exchange for increased fines and defaults, and greater family well-being in exchange for punitive management of welfare dispensations.

I began by vowing to follow the money, as if this would reveal a path to better realization of policy benefits; as if, by reporting on cuts and consequences, some kind of prophylaxis would stir into being, such as programs being done better next time. This is, after all, the policy discourse of evaluation and program improvement that also underlies the idea of (mythical) project learnings. But the money story is also a wild policy story, and following the money is no greater restorative than other methods (ficto-criticism would work just as well). SIHIP was majority funded by the Australian federal government, with a smaller contribution from the NT government, also using budget loadings gleaned from the federal government, which were given to the NT, in a roundabout way, for the fact of having Indigenous people in the first place. Let me briefly explain, because while I have claimed that overall, the reason policy cannot be gotten right is that there are no greater overall Australian population dependencies on getting it right, it matters greatly that Indigenous people can be easily counted and their disadvantage consistently measured.

The Australian system of governmental budgetary distributions operates on a rough socialization process run by a body called the Commonwealth Grants Commission (CGC). In theory, the CGC redistribution process gives each state and territory the same fiscal capacity to deliver a nationally standardized suite of services that, on paper, all citizens are entitled to. The process recognizes that the federal government can raise more money than the states and territories (this is known as vertical fiscal imbalance); that some states have greater revenue-raising capacities than others given market fluctuations and population variability; and that the costs of delivering services to a minimally agreed standard package also differs. When making its algebraic calibrations for redistributing national taxation revenues (through a process known as horizontal fiscal equalization, or HFE), the CGC accords different weightings to the estimated costs of service delivery. These weightings are known as disability factors.

Disabilities such as "'distance," "diseconomies of scale," and "Indigenous disadvantage" skew the HFE redistribution process in favor of mendicant jurisdictions like Tasmania and the NT. Notably, the above-average spending that servicing Indigenous populations might hypothetically require is not directly connected to any actual extra spending, as CGC determinations are "policy neutral." A jurisdiction can get money for dealing with Indigenous disadvantage but not direct the allocated funds accordingly (Smee 2018). How state and territory budgets are spent is up to the state and territory governments concerned, following protracted negotiations about headline policy agreements. The point is, having sick and disadvantaged Indigenous people offers a distinct fiscal advantage, as they attract generous per capita weightings. It is thus important to know how many Aboriginal people there are, which is made easier if people are in fixed addresses (proffering an additional purpose to "growth town" concepts, beyond questions of disciplining the subject, one might think). It is less important, either financially or electorally, to "fix" the pathologies that are indexed within disability weightings. Nonetheless, a key requirement is to appear to be doing all that can be reasonably expected.

Following the money, I learned that the *Memorandum of Understanding between the Australian Government and the Northern Territory Government on Indigenous Housing, Accommodation and Related Services* (the MoU) was signed three months after the Intervention. The MoU specified that a total of $793 million would be available to the NT government for the fiscal years 2007/08 to 2010/11, with two key provisos: first, that the Australian government would have no further responsibility for the delivery of any further Indigenous housing, nor for municipal, essential, and infrastructure services, from 2008. In future, that would all have to be done by the NT, the smallest economy with the largest remote-area populations. Second, the NT would also have to assume responsibility for servicing outstations (small settlements on traditional lands, established in the 1970s by the federal government at a policy time when being away from white population centers was figured as support for Aboriginal self-determination (Fisher 2015, 151)). And the NT would need to start looking after town camps.[9]

These were expensive legacies or, if you will, costly policy hauntologies. Outstations, or homelands, the sites where some Aboriginal people repatriated themselves following long land rights battles,[10] were specifically precluded from any SIHIP improvements, and, as noted, any new houses were reserved for designated "growth towns," title over which had to be ceded to the Australian government for a minimum of forty (originally ninety-nine, then ninety, then forty, in some places just five) years. In a new twist on an old battle, if landowning clan groups fell outside the new category of "designated town" for the purposes of the Intervention (which, confusingly for everyone, may or may not coincide with "growth towns"), they were suddenly to be treated as the owners of private rural property, so any future funding for infrastructure requirements (roads, sewerage, power) would fall entirely to them.

This is a distinct point of difference from the asset-rich but cash-poor estate owners in Europe: their assets might be in need of renovation and repair, but inherited infrastructure is already sunk in place. Roads exist, as do water and energy conduits. In fact, the whole concept of overnight private property with no state amenities and full internal development responsibilities contrasts with the symbiotic codevelopment of "private" property with government assistance long enjoyed by pastoral families and mining consortia in Australia too. In the main, Aboriginal people have won back infrastructure-free or infrastructure-liable title. With successful land claims, all infrastructure (or fixtures), including houses, fences, and sewerage ponds, becomes the property of the land trust. Ownership of town-based infrastructure was leased back to government entities under SIHIP. However, upon the expiry of the forty-year SIHIP leases, the responsibility for infrastructure provision for those assets (seriously depreciated after forty years of wear and tear) also reverts to the land trust. It is another policy inheritance, a provenance of broken things, for which the decision-making will likely also become spectral with time, allowing repeated government declarations that private property is the missing attribute within Indigenous development.

Exhausted? Wait—there was more. This list of requirements, reports, and interests, grueling to read, had multiple effects on implementation practices and sleights of hand. SIHIP had additionally promised attention to roads, sewerage, and power and water infrastructure, with the aim of ensuring that new, replaced, or refurbished houses would not suffer from inherited shortcomings in social utilities. At least up to $45 million (or make that $60 million; the amount kept changing) was initially announced for this purpose. Like the overall Intervention figures, this was akin to saying that SIHIP's infrastructure amenity program would not contribute much at all, given the backlog created after decades of sporadic attention and abandonment. Because the entire SIHIP budget could easily be spent on problems that lie below the surface without even touching houses, this additional infrastructural promise would also soon be dropped from the program and disappeared from future accounts, but gestural infrastructures mattered in the early days of public declarations about government's responsiveness to child abuse, before media attention waned (Weszkalnys 2017). Meanwhile, figuring it all out belonged to the hive mind in the haunted Chan Building, where all these competing requirements were taken very, very seriously.

In theory, the alliance contracting model chosen for SIHIP would remove conventional hierarchies between parties (Davidson et al. 2011; Jefferies, Schubert, and Awad 2011). In practice, it meant that consortium panels—comprising the head contractor; subcontractor; civil and building designer; material suppliers; and logistics, training, and support organizations—battled between and around multiple other administering nodes and related technologies, including intricately layered bureaucratic committee structures that multiplied in tandem with the distress of the program and its increasingly adversarial political destiny.

I quickly learned to favor Jim's more gripping management aphorisms. Alliance contracting was a "gain-share, pain-share model," he declared, showing me the flow charts expanded to full-color posters illustrating how it all linked together. "The obligations and risks are shared; it's all win-win."

Only it wasn't. For Jim's optimistic confidence traveled into briefings about the budget, in one set of open-book revelations taken too far, when he brashly told Alison Anderson, the minister for Indigenous policy in the NT government, that to truly meet the manifold design, durability, and social improvement qualities that SIHIP promised, the available budget was grossly inadequate. Under current estimates, he plainly advised, the program would not deliver the proclaimed 750 houses, 2,500 refurbishments, and 230 rebuilds but more likely only 300 new houses, less than half what had been roundly promised. It seemed that to build a robust house—one able to withstand the harsh wear and tear of coastal communities in monsoonal belts or the calcifying impact of hard water on the pipes and fittings of arid areas; that respected the need for gender separation in the toilet and bathroom arrangements when groups of kinsmen and kinswomen share the same space; that involved Aboriginal trainees and accounted for clan affinities; that insulated against the wilting heat of tropical savannahs and the piercing cold of desert winters; that dealt with wider infrastructural backlogs; and that introduced new tenancy management responsibilities—meant that fewer houses could be built for the available money.

The engineers and cost estimators also found that the $45 million (or $60 million) that government sponsors had budgeted for infrastructure and headworks (connection points on a property to connect to any existing water, wastewater, or drainage systems) was, likewise, well short of requirements. And where community leaders had wanted to reserve their existing serviced subdivisions for known future expansion needs and have SIHIP develop its own, the program would instead silently consume all currently available lots and create nothing new, effectively locking in, rather than alleviating, community overcrowding.

Another issue clouded the already murky picture. The initial program director immediately preceding Jim had known that the actual unit price of a new house was fast becoming politically untenable. Presumably in consultation with policy advisors, he had discretely made a decision to offload many of the attributed costs into the budget category titled "indirect refurbishment." (New houses had a capped notional price, but refurbishment was, at least at that point, much vaguer.) So while a house targeted for refurbishment may only be getting $45,000 of actual refurbishment activities, an additional 125 percent indirect costs might be budgeted against this activity, on the basis that the costs of labor, transport, and materials for both completely new and refurbished houses in a given community were being shared anyway, so it was legitimate to hold some of the total housing costs against the less politically troublesome category of refurbishments. This neither reduced the overall costs nor expanded the budget, but the hope was that it would keep the look of the average unit cost of a genuinely new SIHIP house within a politically acceptable range.[11] As sleight of budgetary hand, it more or less worked, until Jim's fatefully honest briefing.

The price of plain speaking

There was not much curbing Jim's enthusiasm for the completeness of the government's original housing commitments, I noticed belatedly. He genuinely thought the government would want to comprehensively fund the full costs of meeting the promising vision it had originally set. So he gave his unsparing ac-

count, when asked, to Minister Anderson, a Warlpiri woman born in remote
Haasts Bluff. Jim gave his briefing, and I think he expected appreciation in return. Having lived many of her days in the desperately poor central desert community of Yuendumu (Musharbash 2009), Anderson also brought experience as
a former representative of the (newly dismantled) Aboriginal and Torres Strait
Islander Commission, ATSIC, to her role. ATSIC had once overseen Indigenous
housing programs, and as a commissioner, Anderson had long decided that be-
spoke architectural consultations and prolonged backroom planning could be
taken too far. She wanted less talk, more delivery. For Anderson, the problem
clearly lay with the complicated SIHIP administration and expensive salaries,
and not with inadequate government allocations or capacious policy promises.
Discovering the trickery behind the bloated refurbishment costs simply confirmed her suspicions.

Anderson exploded; at first in private to Jim, then among her cabinet colleagues and, given the cabinet's apparent indifference, direct to a story-hungry
media. She accused the SIHIP SALT team of assorted scams to swallow the
money in fees and profits, with no actual houses to show for it. The counter-
claim that preparatory time had been spent planning the scope of works and
carefully consulting with communities, including over the vexed issue of securing leasehold tenure from communally owned land trusts (one of the conditions of receiving any new housing), came across as the hollow words of the
defensive and the incompetent.

Overnight, it was SIHIP, and not sexual depravity, that obsessed media reporting. "Head rolls over Indigenous housing wrangle" (Bolton 2009); "Indigenous housing bill 'to blow out to $1b'" (James 2009); "Slice of pie for building is
shrinking by the day" (Robinson 2009); "Macklin blamed for Indigenous housing wrangle" (Gibson 2009), ran the headlines. Although each government em-
ployee, contractor, and subcontractor, and each community organization and
town council was obliged to sign a confidentiality deed about SIHIP, everyone
had a story to tell. There were blog sites and tales told by taxi drivers who rolled
their eyes and said "Whaddya expect? Everyone wants to line their pocket." The
more the government tried to shut conduits, the more weird stuff seeped out.
Newspapers across the country hastily featured admonishing editorials (Robinson, Koch, and Owen 2009), and letters flowed offering one homily point after
another, everything from suggested mechanisms for quickly building prefabricated kit houses to supplying sturdy shipping containers or yurts; from mak-

ing Aboriginal people work harder to get/fund their own housing, to expressing outrage that any houses were being supplied at all.

To defray the scandal, federal minister Macklin and the NT chief minister, Paul Henderson, issued a joint press release, a solidarity of reassurance.[12] Together, they would get to the bottom of claims of funds being siphoned into consultancy fees and bureaucrat fiefdoms. Above all, they would ensure that the original metric of 750 houses, 2,500 refurbishments, and 230 rebuilds . . . Would. Be. Met.

Two trusted senior officials were seconded to undertake a four-week intensive "independent review," with the authority to enforce directives, bypass existing management tiers, and report directly to the chief minister and the federal minister respectively. One was a former lawyer, the other a former primary school teacher. Neither handpicked advisor had a background in construction, engineering, quantity surveying, cost estimation, or infrastructure development. Lack of knowledge signaled that they were untarnished by embedded expertise.

These personality breakdowns don't really matter, by the way. Or they do in the way of narrating the events as journalists do, as if the incoherency was a matter of individual personalities; as if, by removing a person here and adding a new one there, a system is changed. Colorful individuals made known through media dissections help the discourses and structures that allow penny-pinching and window dressing to slide out of view. Character profiling is like evaluation reports in this way: they identify culprits, as if future improvement is truly the main game. But such machinations reveal something about how scandals are defrayed to maintain policy trajectories—which is to say, how policies might be changed in order not to change at all. The same number of promised new and refurbished houses would be delivered; only now, instead of the hapless bureaucrats and contractors hiding costs under an uncapped refurbishment category, a worse kind of substitution came into play. Costs would now be hidden within narrowed design and construction standards, within smaller houses, dropped codes, no headworks, swallowed serviced lots, and uncounted public sector salaries. The houses would reembed Australian race politics into their material substance and return residents to their infrastructural backlog.

As the long days of those four review weeks unrolled, Minister Anderson was not appeased. Her displeasure especially mattered to the NT government, which held power by only one seat. Her decision—to remain or to resign from the Labor Party—depended on the briefings she expected to receive from the chief minister every three days, a reverse Scheherazade game of survivalist storytelling, and a siren call to an already frenzied local media, who followed her every reaction assiduously. Eventually, she resigned (Anderson 2009). On Friday, August 14, 2009, the decision was made to remove Jim Davidson from the program (Gibson 2009). The chief executive of the Department of Housing would soon follow.

Meanwhile, behind closed doors within the SIHIP program, before all the sacrificial departures, the paired über-bureaucrats charged with returning SIHIP to its target metrics convened their first emergency meeting in July 2009, a meeting to which Jim had urged my witnessing presence. This is how an ethnographer gets outed and evicted.

Their message was unmistakable: the SIHIP teams had to bring the unit price of each house down. There was, they explained, "an optics to the metric" to be protected. From here on in, the most expensive house in the most isolated and climatically extreme conditions could cost no more than $450,000, inclusive of indirect, freight, and labor costs; refurbishments would be capped at $100,000, all-inclusive. What was more, the original metrics would be met, and in the original time frame.

Q: How?

A: "All options are on the table," advised the line-by-line reviewers, meaning that all suggested cuts would be considered.

Q: What about the requirement for 20 percent Aboriginal employment on projects?

A: "It's on the table."

Q: Do we have to comply with the Indigenous housing guidelines?

A: "We should meet the key elements, not the 'nice to haves.' We need to reduce the footprint of the house. Are two bathrooms really needed? Verandas? A seven-star energy rating? It all needs to go on the table."

Q: (*From a frustrated Alliance member*) What about a roof? Is a house with a roof in or out?

Where art thou, killjoys?

The open invitation to put it on the table was a closing, a neutralizing device. Overstaying an objection to the pruning exercise meant becoming part of the problem. To be an institutional killjoy in this moment was to give up a lucrative

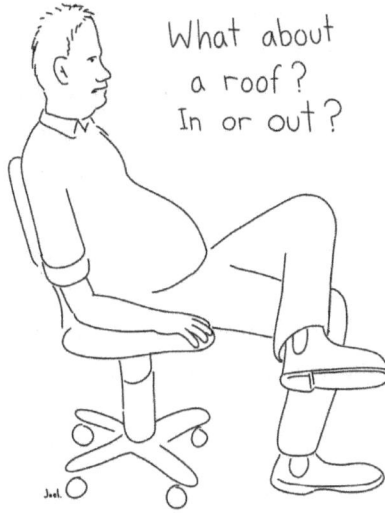

Figure 4. Putting it on the table. By Joel Tarling and Tess Lea.

contract and high-profile professional role and to risk not being at the table to put anything there. The discussion quickly turned to ways of building lower-cost houses at speed by dropping such seemingly discretionary design features as extended verandas—which, as an aside, we should note play a key role in reducing wear and tear from overcrowding by allowing overflow (see also Lea 2014b).New computer-generated floor plans accumulated rapidly: access ramps for the disabled, ambient temperature considerations (shading, siting, breeze-ways), energy efficiency, louvered or extra windows, even fire escapes—all became discretionary. An absence referred to periodically in the jab and parry of "putting it all on the table" was that of architects. Instead, their imagined protests were treated as the idealisms expected from those who do not know the hard decisions to be made when houses must be delivered at speed and on a restricted budget. Architects would focus on longevity, design, and cultural fit: as anticipatable killjoys, they weren't invited in.

There was a moment during this trial of strength, where the Commonwealth was reasserting control of the battle for political acceptability, in which all those seated at the table had to introduce who they were. At least thirty people were in the room: the engineers and building company leaders from the alliance consortiums; advising engineers and cost estimators; senior representatives flown in from the federal department in Canberra to reinforce the minister's new delegate and her speaking authority; the chief minister's matching delegate; the chief executive of the Department of Housing—and me: "Tess Lea, university," suddenly conspicuous as the only person not meant to be there. With my exception, it was a congress that otherwise could be taken to represent the program as a whole, right down to the absence of any Aboriginal householders in whose names decisions were being made. The scene was set: only those who accepted the problematization being enforced by the Commonwealth (that the unit cost could be driven down) and who passed through this obligatory passage point (the metric would be met), could remain in the program (cf. Callon 1986, 205–207). Those who presented nonnegotiable obstacles would find themselves removed. The ones who managed the twists and turns of the cunning new tricks (original metric, reduced cost, and an insistently asserted, albeit fictional, retention of all function and durability) would survive.

With only two days' notice, senior SIHIP leadership team members literally went back to the drawing board, producing a pared-down floor plan for a two- or three-bedroom house, which no longer needed to meet standards of good Indigenous housing design (now deemed fripperies). The different interests vested within the forced congress of alliance consortia also became more obvious. Alone, the Earth Connect Alliance team did not view this latest set of demands as a disastrous diminution of the social objectives of SIHIP. They instead rubbed their hands together, spying an opportunity to parade their company's ability to prefabricate housing systems off-site at a Brisbane factory and freight them in for local assembly at the desired bargain cost. Their promise was bold. They would take on the toughest project site of all—Groote Eylandt—and smash the unit costs and project delays.

Their model rested on foam-core "sandwich" panels and a metal connection system called Force 10, a system that had already been trialed on Groote, under a different name. Force 10 updated the old Logan Home foam-core panel housing that much of the community had lived in under other programs and hated bitterly. The Logan Home houses had completely corroded. Walls would swing in the breeze and sway when doors slammed, pivoting on what remained of their connection to the ceiling and the floor once salt-filled air rusted the frames, and water, insects, and rats entered the cavities. Cockroaches and termites ate the glue holding the polystyrene foam together within the breached panels. Then, when the bottom of the wall also corroded and came loose, the wall would empty like a beanbag, floating plastic foam balls onto floors and into cobwebs, leaving two thin layers of metal with no structural or thermal capacity as a flimsy carapace. The Anindilyakwans from Groote Eylandt knew all about foam houses, but they weren't in the room to put their prior knowledge on the table; and whatever might have been known institutionally was held under lock and key in Iron Mountain archives.

Acting as if policy is always immaculately birthed and unrelated to anything else, human or other, Earth Connect would truck and barge key housing components to Groote Eylandt in shipping containers, then assemble buildings on-site with a small team including a qualified builder, an apprentice, and as few as two unskilled laborers. Their buildings would not have disabled access, gender separation, or more than one entry point. But overall construction time, absent plumbing and electrical services, would take less than a month. Their speculative ideas had been rejected in the first fifteen months of the program. Now they could be placed onto the middle of the table with confident flourish.

In theoretical arguments about structure and agency and the agency of structures, it is when designs are still being parleyed that the "structuring force of a building" is deemed at its weakest (Gieryn 2002, 54). But I want to argue that the structuring force of a building begins here, in the muffled, inaudible sounds of houses being atrophied before they're built, as an anxious government sought to divert attention from itself. Failed social housing, or what I have elsewhere called nonhouses (Lea and Pholeros 2010), have their origin within these shrouded chains of decision-making. This is the spectral sound of a house falling apart in the nonspecifiable future. These are ghost houses in becoming.

In the months to follow, as the program descended into scandal, and audits became exercises in media appeasement, I also jettisoned the forensic task of accounting for lost accounts, even though these very cost cuts meant that shoddy future infrastructure was being composed before construction commenced. In my defense, Jon Altman, an economist with dedicated time, skills, funding, and research assistance for the task of evaluating evaluations of the Intervention to discern its impact, also had to jettison the effort (Altman and Russell 2012). Altman and Russell found multiple evaluations, but no central question being answered. Stacked together, evaluation reports about the Intervention towered over half a meter in height, raising the challenge of reading them, let alone categorizing their findings (7). Even excluding multiple possible reports from their purview, they devoured ninety-eight different evaluations, noting the plethora as part of an evaluation fetish that serviced a transparency aesthetic, fed by fit-for-purpose consultancy firms.

How do academics compete when the audit industry itself helps perform the reassurance rather than the actuality of audit, in a dark hinterland of regulatory capture enabled through entirely licit accounting techniques (Sikka 2001, Sikka and Lehman 2015)? Where reports become set-piece resources for pacifying critics, as showcases of scrutineering and recourse? When a report on town camp conditions runs for eighteen thousand pages, and project lessons are buried deep in Iron Mountains? Not for nothing did Balzac decry "the power of inertia called the Report!"[13] Instead of following the money or searching for program logics in the carpet world, I headed to Groote Eylandt, recipient location for the largest of the SIHIP packages; where other companions to entropic infrastructure joined Jim in the role of killjoys to Earth Connect's haste-fueled "cruel optimism" (Berlant 2006).

Interlude III

For all the headaches its anticipation had caused for those on the ground, Minister Wyatt's overnight visit to the APY Lands in early July 2017 was an anticlimax. When the minister and his entourage eventually arrived at the airfield in Alice Springs, waiting in the tiny charter aircraft office while luggage was weighed and bodies accounted for, the visitors seemed deeply absorbed in speculation: Who would be the next national secretary of defense, given the recent exit of the long-standing incumbent?

John Singer had stood to one side, the very picture of deep desert stillness, waiting for a question, long enough to infer that they had no immediate interest in gathering any premeeting details or Anangu context from him, before discretely taking his mobile for a short walk outside.

For the Nganampa attendees, it was a portent of sessions to come. In their inaugural meeting out on the Lands, attention may have been paid, but key symbols of attention-paying were missing. Perhaps the ministerial team had other matters on their minds, or perhaps the Nganampa team members were just oblivious to any dramas that were not their own. But Wyatt's entourage had appeared to fidget and pay greater heed to their devices, as Nganampa staff presented their achievements (reductions in sexually transmitted and childhood infections, maintenance of the highest immunization rates in the country); and tried to convey something about their new struggles. Nganampa has been in the business of remote health care under Anangu control since 1983, giving the council the rare institutional depth to operate a residential aged-care facility on the Lands, *Tjilpiku Pampaku Ngura*. Just as unusually, given the onerous paperwork involved with programs typically aimed at white metropolitan providers, they also tap into Commonwealth funding schemes to care for older or physically impaired people still living in their homes, maintaining time-consuming accounts of each and every conversation in order to acquit the funding, as blood sugars are checked, pharmaceutical regimens monitored, meals delivered.

After Gayle Woodford's murder, Nganampa needed an extra $170,000 in recurrent funding to pay for two caregivers—paired for safety, as was now required—to enable round-the-clock care at the *Tjilpiku* aged-care facility. The management team had decided to put this to the federal minister, believing that a story about the administrative burden of managing visiting care services (an acquittal burden inversely correlated with the small funding amounts involved) would not seem as noteworthy. In pre-deciding this among themselves, it seems to me that they were making a correlation. Just as administrative minutiae had diluted Nganampa's organizational abilities to provide care (given the way that onerous form-filling made the human interactions that are so core to care even more burdensome to enact), they also anticipated that bureaucratic care for, or knowledge about, the microsources of service impairment would also be paper thin. Amid their second-guessing of issues that would fly and those that wouldn't, the Nganampa team similarly figured that the minister's team would be uninterested in the bureaucratic paperwork making Nganampa's home visiting services for old people almost impossible to run, so they stuck to the story of how nursing costs had legally doubled since the murder.

Did their anticipatory tactics work? As ever, it is hard to know. Wyatt appeared noncommittal, the muscles in his face working a neutral visage. Where politicians usually offer soft stalls through vagaries like "I'll take your request back to the department" or "Perhaps you could set out these details in a letter, and we will see if anything can be done," here there were no obvious performative utterances of concern. The visitors may have been taking everything in mentally, but they didn't ask questions, and they didn't take notes, at least not where anyone could see them. They packed up quickly after the briefing, announcing their eagerness to complete their first day on the Lands with a tour of the community art center. The following morning, departure day, the group was close to two hours late for its scheduled tour of *Tjilpiku Pampaku Ngura*, delayed, they explained upon belated arrival, by the need to view another art gallery.

"It's different now," John Singer says, reflecting on the lackluster interactions. "In the old days, you could really argue with Commonwealth bureaucrats. But this mob don't really have enough knowledge to even have an argument. I reckon they'd just get upset if you tried.

"Perhaps they may have been expecting to get that briefing in the specified agenda time, when we all got to Umuwa. Maybe, yeah. But it left me feeling like—well, that I was not the chief executive in their eyes."

But this isn't completely new, I prompted, reading aloud field notes from a nearly identical visit, four years earlier, from a different ministerial entourage. On that occasion, Nganampa Health Council was hosting the new South Australian minister for health, who was likewise making his debut visit to the Lands. This visit had similarly disrupted all other business, and the minister had equally emitted radical unfamiliarity with the portfolio. He appeared unaware that the South Australian ambulance system did not service the Lands, for instance, or that emergency aerial retrievals usually took patients north across the border into the NT, and not south to the distant city of Adelaide, seat of the South Australian government. Anangu country interrupts the meaning of governance borders—borders that take little account of where people might move to enact their ceremonies and to look after country, visit others, shop, gamble, attend sporting events, appear in court, pay fines, recover lost driver's licenses, escape humbug, negotiate banking systems, or access health services.

Or, closer to his ministerial portfolio, that border crossings also become protracted payment disputes that entangle finance bureaus in fee-recovery battles, for all Australian states and territories are required to meet the cost of their residents' inpatient services regardless of where treatment is received (Tew, You, and Pircher 2008, 16). This transmutes into pressure on doctors, nurses, and patient travel personnel to horse-trade for hours and days at a time to coax and cajole patient placements, dealing with the irritability of their counterparts in other institutions, for even though Alice Springs is much closer than Adelaide and makes sense for cash-strapped and ill patients from the APY Lands to access, money will then be owed between institutions, generating other kinds of unwelcome paperwork. Thus there are small but real resistances to accepting cross-border patients, behind-the-scenes navigation of which saps wit and energy—wit to coax cooperation, energy to get past the institutional foot-dragging. In all, an infuriating system of wasting dollars to save cents.

Can policy fix this? Or is this already policy, in its spectral, fragmented, "street-level" form? How can people be expected to make more of an effort when making an effort is against the grain of tacit institutional expectation, when such expectation is not explicitly acknowledged as being part of policy? Are health care workers meant to make the system work by spending all their spare time making the system work? Ghost policy haunts everyday practice exhibited in what people know to do without being able to articulate the policy rules they are obeying. Unwritten rules of rationing, but not rules of efficiency, equity, or effect. Rules that are not written, so no one can say these are the rules.

The South Australian health minister, although a former finance minister, hadn't appeared to know about any of this cross-border charging stuff. Perhaps carpet-world people so far from policy field sites can be forgiven such missing ethnographic detail. Theirs needs to be the expertise of electoral geniality, cabinet rooms, and press briefings; of hectically staffed offices and down-to-the-minute chauffeured itineraries. Though not yet an old man, my notes recall, he was clearly a carpet-worlder, his skin pallor already reflecting overtime in artificially lit habitats, his arms having lost their muscle definition, his stomach its clench. But he was at least listening and asking questions, hands grasped behind his head, elbows winged, hips slumped forward on the seat. His assistant had seemed more distracted, clearing eye grit with a fingernail before returning his gaze to the ceiling; but eventually I captured him "taking a note, or at least, pulling his mobile out to thumb something in."

John and I laugh at these jottings, which sit alongside so many recordings of similar meetings in Indigenous settings, which are just as often accounts of conditions of inaudibility and of cruddy, low-level impediments, such as broken photocopiers and insensible forms; and John amends his verdict of the Wyatt visit. It was not the worst at all, he agrees, but simply an iteration of a growing contemporary trend, centered on high turnover of external visitors who arrive without deep content expertise. The politicians then get associated with the seemingly arbitrary policy vacillations between hypervigilant detail required in one program (every transaction with an aged person and the detail of each conversation recorded), and complete inattention to other issues; or to paraphrase Lucas Bessire and David Bond (2014, 441), a simultaneous narrowing of areas of legitimate concern and widening of the scope of acceptable disregard. It doesn't reduce to political identities so easily after all.

We talked then around the inability of bureaucratic imaginaries to digest the profundity of continued A*n*angu existence despite all the reasons not to prevail ("*I know* we are sophisticated people out bush, and through our law—but other people outside, they only see what they see in the newspaper," John says); and the Faustian toll exacted when Aboriginal people embrace any part of the health sector, including those helpful home deliveries of food, medicines, and firewood that Nganampa Health pulls off through its dazzling paperwork acrobatics, which might help prolong the time that ageing bodies avoid residential settings, but keep old people off country even so.[1] Local organizations are the same, we conclude. They can't cast adrift from mercurial policy formulators either, but engagement likewise has a price.

Chapter 3

Moorings, mining, and minutes

The story of housing debacles on Groote Eylandt, the empirical case study at the heart of this chapter, is also a story of ships, maps, legalized thefts, and a settler colonial logos; of military policy and the wider extraction dependencies that militarization feeds, sustains, and protects; and more simply too, of small-scale petty corruption within fields of neoliberal outsourcing. And it shows the other companions occupying the poor living conditions that justify interventions and their withdrawal in the name of Indigenous health and well-being: the rats, salts, winds, fungi, and insects whose driving role in material entropy can haunt residents and sometimes help drive policy whistle-blowing.

This is to adopt an understanding of policy and bureaucratic effects as phenomena that can be concentrated in formalized organizational settings and official encounters *and* as spectral, temporally unmoored, wild phenomena operating across time and place. The chapter blends policy artifacts, ambient policy surroundings, hauntology, and ecology, all in one, to showcase just what it is that Aboriginal organizations are mediating when they broker and translate "policy." It begins with a ship entering the Gulf of Carpentaria in January 1803, as Captain Matthew Flinders and his crew sail in on their leaky vessel, searching for a mythical inland river to establish the wealth and fortune of all who sailed with him and the imperial financiers behind their endeavor.

I will emphasize that the desire for extraction, and corresponding ontological blindness, pulses through history into the present and remains entwined in infrastructural enactments on Groote Eylandt. Imperialism reaches through the past in the assumed fact of Aboriginal illiteracy; an assumption that, in the present day, sees interveners remaining oblivious to the fact that they are indeed being noted, and that this noting is often an essential form of reverse accounting, a vigilance that is increasingly necessary to pulling any good from policy arisings. Meticulous accounts of promises as made and regulations as coded can hold visiting officials and would-be masters of regimes of accountability to literal account. In these strange new times of high-speed administrative entanglements—at once hastened, deepened, spread, and hollowed by digitization, 24/7 communications, repeated structural metamorphoses within the public sector, and increased outsourcing of such mundane but vital organizational functions as asset management and telecommunications (Froud et al. 2017)—field officers and political representatives alike turn over too fast for coaxing either trusting or combative intercultural relationships. In many cases, it is *Indigenous* organizational record keeping that provides crucial administrative continuity in the business of hauling some good out of the compromised policy mires that we are all differentially located within. In this way, keeping records can be an underacknowledged form of guerrilla accounting (cf. Hetherington 2011).

Even so, such Indigenous interventions, using an arsenal of records, plans, files, and accounts, are not necessarily expressions of being antistate or even of becoming like the state (cf. Scott 1998, 2009). Rather, they are historically embedded responses necessitated by "nonsensical violence, rampant environmental devastation, humanitarian NGOs, neoliberal economic policies, soul-collecting missionaries, and tradition-fetishizing ethnographers" (Bessire and Bond 2014, 444). I am not seeking to locate redemption, rupture, or reconciliation in such administrative struggles. Fighting through and within the interstices of historically thickened bureaucratic entanglement is simultaneously a resistant, compliant, coercive, and creative operation. It is unavoidable and painful, for paying attention to fine print is also the terrain of what Anishinaabe cultural theorist Gerald Vizenor has termed *survivance* (Vizenor 2008a, b). Vizenor was challenging concepts of Indigenous victimhood or simplistic survival narratives, to convey something of the effortful nature of sustaining Indigenous ways of being, and of truth-telling, despite the suffocating force of settler cultural efforts. Indigenous organizational settings can be activity zones where, with exacting, stressful, and, for those who stay the course, high-burnout work, policy benefits can be extracted (Lea, Howey, and O'Brien 2018). The toll of needing to countermand policy to make any of it work tends to be unseen by those creating the need for countermanding. That this unseeing has long been part of the permit of intrusion and intervention explains why we begin with English men first meeting the Anindilyakwan[1] people of the Groote archipelago in the Gulf of Carpentaria, as our prequel to the establishment of plans and strategies for betterment in the present day.

A captain's log

WEDNESDAY 12 JANUARY 1803 (on Chasm Island): In the steep sides of the chasms were deep holes or caverns, undermining the cliffs; upon the walls of which I found rude drawings, made with charcoal and something like red paint upon the white ground of the rock. These drawings represented porpoises, turtle, kangaroos, and a human hand; and Mr. Westall, who went afterwards to see them, found the representation of a kanga-roo, with a file of thirty-two persons following after it. The third person of the band was twice the height of the others, and held in his hand something resembling the *whaddie*, or wooden sword of the natives of Port Jackson [Sydney]; and was probably intended to represent a chief. They could not, as with us, indicate superiority by clothing or orna-ment, since they wear none of any kind; and therefore, with the addition of a weapon, similar to the ancients, they seem to have made superiority of person the principal em-blem of superior power, of which, indeed, power is usually a consequence in the very early stages of society. (Flinders 2015, 166)

Flinders's diary is remarkable both for its incidental notes and for what is considered incidental. When he first sailed into the Gulf of Carpentaria, with two-hundred-year-old Dutch maps to hand, Flinders initially bypassed an ex-ploration of Groote to take in as much of the surrounding mainland as the shal-low waters would allow. In among turtle nests, the shore parties also found huts, bamboo stands, nutmeg trees, human skulls, and "several skeletons . . . standing upright in the hollow stumps of trees; . . . the skulls and bones being smeared or painted, partly red and partly white, [which] made a very strange appearance" (Flinders 1814, 161). Seven days later, now at Blue Mud Bay, there's an armed exchange. The master's mate is speared, and in the following melee, Morgan, a crewman, loses his straw hat to the "Natives," who audaciously steal it. Morgan, hatless, becomes delirious with sunstroke and dies "in a state of Frenzy" later that night (174)—prompting an unauthorized revenge party to sneak back to shore, to shoot a native in the back.

The next day, Flinders himself heads ashore to retrieve the murdered corpse, because, as he notes in his journal, the painter [William Westall] was desirous of making a drawing, and the surgeon wanted the cadaver "for anatomical purposes" (174). Seaman Smith's separate diary notes make the crime scene more explicit:

[O]ur Boat went on shore & found one Savage dead of his Wounds, he being shot through the Back. Being hoisted in the Surgeon Cut off his Head & took out his Heart & put them

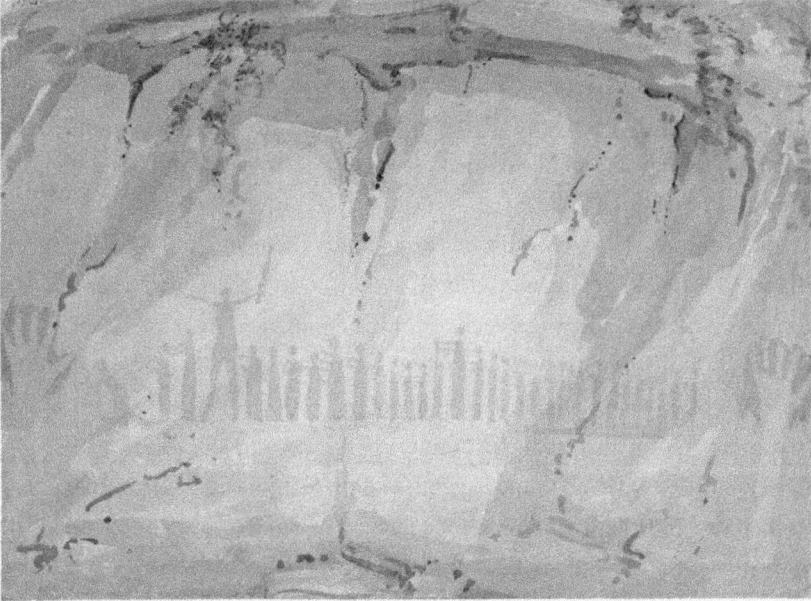

Figure 5. William Westall (1803) *Chasm Island, native cave painting*, National Library of Australia, nla.obj-2108209.

in Spirits: most of his bones seem'd to have been broke, & his beard Very long. This Day we Interr'd Morgan according to the Usual serimony perform'd at sea, afterwards the Native was hove overboard & seen to be devour'd by Shirks. (Cited in Brown 2003, 39)

When he finally got to see William Westall's sketches (see figure 5), Flinders wrote down what he thought he had seen. A kangaroo and a file of people following. An elevated leader and a crude sign of society in development. For Westall's part, as the photographer and ethnologist equivalent of shipping times, his interests in recording the recordings of others was impelled by boredom. His youthful interest in life as expedition chronicler had long since been dulled by the seeming repetition of the Australian bush, as they'd sailed on and on through the mosquito-heavy, crocodile-infested waters of coastal northern Australia. Frustrated with unexciting landscapes and "dreary Indians," Westall instead recorded Indigenous notations at Chasm Island, north of Groote, inadvertently becoming the first non-Indigenous artist to make paintings of Australian rock paintings (Findlay 1988). On the cave walls shimmered the hunting prowess of those who had traded trepang, turtle shell, pearls, pearl shells, and manganese for the steel sent down via Macassan fleets—fleets urged by

Dutch imperialists sitting in wait for the lucrative "black gold" of dried Arnhem bêche-de-mer (trepang or sea cucumber) to feed their multinational profiteering racket (Macknight 1976, Sutherland 2000, Russell 2004). Metal meant axes and grander dugout canoes and harpoons and thus the ability to support larger populations on that literally named great island, Groote Eylandt (van Egmond 2012, 7–8, Chaloupka 1999, 19).

But this prior story of trade, metal, population density, and skillful hunting (figure 6) is not what Westall captured with his water brush, nor what Flinders recorded about the depicted rock art in his chronicles. The Groote section of Flinders's diary is replete with comments on the likelihood of manganese given the deep-blue colors of the sea channels in their ongoing search for profits (the promise of which financed Flinders's epic circumnavigation), and on the need to find arable land, minable gems, and that elusive inland river that surely opened into the continental interior somewhere along this tepid coastline. The diary also gives his alphabetic reading of Westall's artistic recording of Indigenous graphics on the cave wall (Flinders 1814, vol. 2, 132). In describing how primitive hierarchy had to be displayed in the absence of superior bling, the ship artist and captain both misapprehend the vertical prow of an extended dugout canoe, seeing instead a kangaroo. Where there is a hunter wielding a harpoon, they install a leader brandishing a primitive wooden sword, while the hunting party helping to power the open-water search for large dugong (on the rock wall, clearly speared, with ropes tethered to the harpoon) become simpleminded followers (Chaloupka 1999, 19).

The inability to *see* Indigenous accounting haunts present-day Indigenous policy. In the place of strategic nous, administrators still assume managerial naïveté on the part of their Indigenous counterparts. It is akin to the settler insistence on alphabetic literacy as a key index of cognition and cultural advancement more generally. These are not innocent emphases. Yoked to the imperialisms of alphabetic literacy come intricate links to state building and imperial conquest, as existing Indigenous methods of record keeping are simultaneously denigrated. then smothered (Mignolo 1992; Biddle 2000, 2016). As Walter Mignolo has argued, referring to South American imperialism, it was the "natives" who, learning the language of their colonists "to translate their world and answer the questions posed . . . were the only masters of the two worlds" (in Castro-Klaren 1998, 142). The question of how much of what is perceived as them is really just us brings together Flinders's expeditionary notes of 1803 and

Figure 6. George Chaloupka's reconstruction of the original scene, from *Journey in Time: The World's Longest Continuing Art Tradition* (Chaloupka 1999, 19), reprinted with permission from Reed New Holland Books and Eve Chaloupka.

attempts in 2010 to build houses on Groote Eylandt under the Strategic Indigenous Housing and Infrastructure Program. (That, and the blithe unawareness among external parties of any reciprocal notations.)

At this point it is instructive to know that the fertile homelands of the Anindilyakwa, an island of pandanus palms, shell-encrusted shorelines, and small streams cascading over multihued rocks, has another identity as the site of an open-cut strip manganese operation, producing more than 15 percent of the world's highest-grade ore. Groote Eylandt sits opposite the aptly named Blue Mud Bay on the Arnhem Land coast, the deep-blue colors noted by Flinders reflecting the particularly rich bedrock deposits of manganese platforming beneath the tropical sea. The mine is run by the Groote Eylandt Mining Company (GEMCO), a jointly owned venture between BHP offshoot South 32 Ltd (at 60 percent) and Anglo American Plc (at 40 percent). South 32's biggest manganese operations are in the Kalahari basin in South Africa, but its website boasts that Groote represents one of the largest and lowest-cost manganese ore production sites in the world.[2]

This is not simply a function of GEMCO's recent investments to modernize and mechanize Groote's crushing, screening, washing, dense media separation, and freighting logistics. As the earlier Dutch traders already knew, the ore itself is quite pure, requiring little further refinement. Usually, the ore is processed on-site at the mine to produce a concentrate that is then transported by road train to GEMCO's Milner Bay port facility on the island, to be shipped to global markets. In some instances, "due to the nature and quality of the manganese ore type being mined, it is not [even] necessary to wash the ore and this material is able to bypass the concentrator and be trucked directly to Milner Bay port facility" (Hansen Bailey 2015, 13).

Manganese has been ripped and shipped at scale from Groote since mining commenced in 1964. The first load was freighted out in 1966, when the archipelago was still controlled by the Anglican Church Missionary Society (CMS) and the NT Administration's Welfare Branch. The CMS had taken out permits both to prospect and to seek mining titles on the island in response to growing interest from geologists, thus securing its own key role in subsequent negotiations with then owner BHP and ensuring that the meager royalty payments it had negotiated would be channeled to a church-run trust account.[3] Anindilyak-wan consent was neither required nor given. We will revisit these extractions in chapter 5.

Also relevant to our discussion, there are three main settlements, marking former missions and mining activity: Umbakumba, on the northeast coast of the island, infamous for its armored gangs and school lockdowns; Angurugu, an inland community located next to freshwater streams, reached by leaving the sealed highway and bypassing the island's only sealed airstrip; and Alyangula on the northeastern shoreline, a white service center complete with golf course, developed to house mining industry personnel, where tourists can also be luxuriously accommodated, and from where various administrations center their operations.

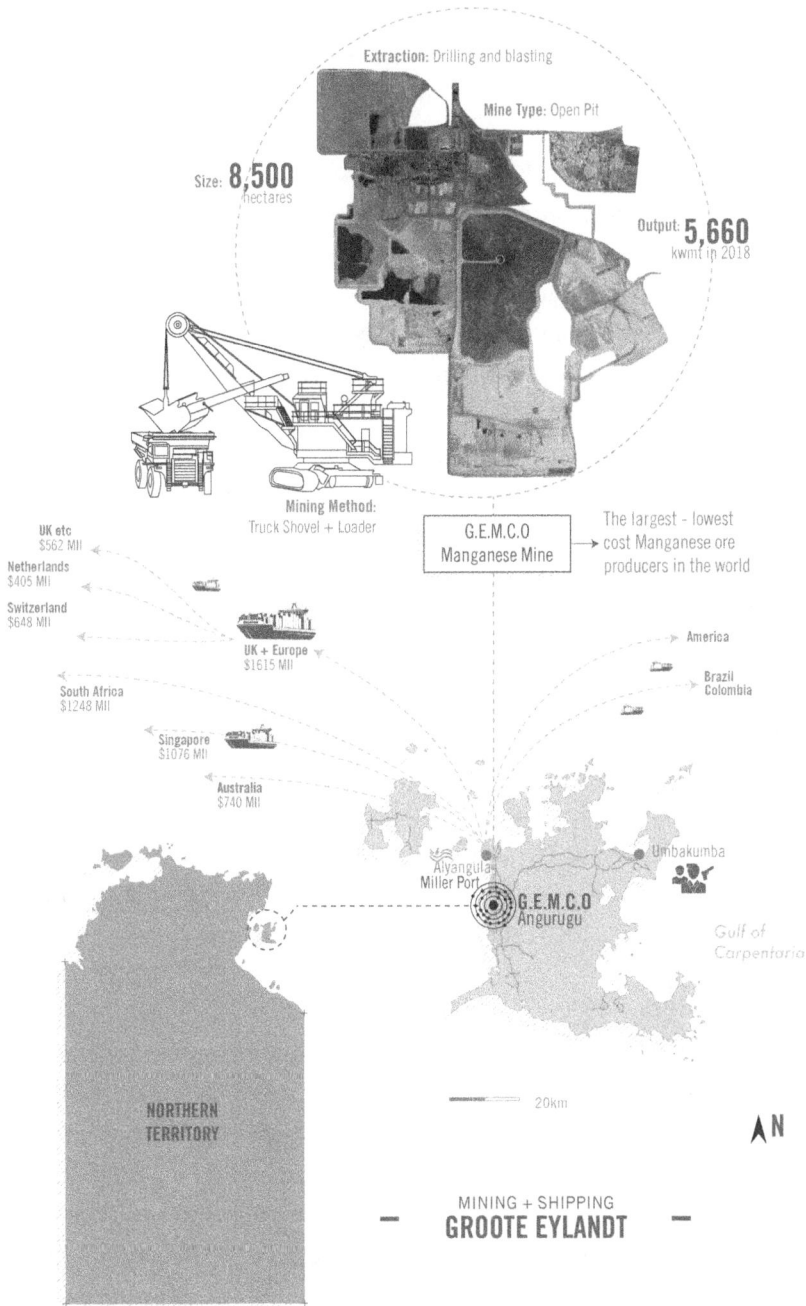

Figure 7. Groote Eylandt manganese operations. Map by M. Barbagallo.

We can picture these sites as the government did, when it drew up its Baseline Community Profiles at the beginning of the 2007 Intervention period (SGS Economics and Planning 2009). Alyangula, with its non-Indigenous population of approximately one thousand people, clubs, coffee shop, swimming pool, church, shopping facilities, bank, post office, school, travel agency, courthouse, and police station, received a good rating across the indicators of income levels, school attendance, morbidity, and mortality.

By contrast, Angurugu's services expressed impoverishment and the material evidence of ambient policy. Alongside the usual cluster of a school and small health center, in 2008 it had a renal dialysis unit; men's and women's shelters; an aged-care and respite center; a substance misuse facility; a desultory store housing the community's single public telephone; two run-down takeaway food shops (akin to backyard "greasy spoon" joints); a Centrelink office for managing the dispensation or cancellation of welfare payments; a sport and recreation building; a weedy football oval and a basketball court; inadequate street lighting across the community; insufficient water capacity to meet peak daily demand; and chronically poor housing with some of the country's highest levels of overcrowding. Umbakumba was worse again, reachable mainly by an unsealed road with high fatalities. There was no permanent police presence in any of the towns, with all police being stationed at Alyangula several hours' drive away from Umbakumba's infamous strife; no full-time resident teachers or nurses at either Angurugu or Umbakumba; and no fluoridated water.

Everything the 2007 Northern Territory National Emergency Response offered (aka the Intervention), the island desperately needed.

Brawling tribes

Across the north back in 2015, when former prime minister Tony Abbott and assorted state premiers were threatening community closures, mean daily maximum temperatures had begun their relentless march toward record highs. In the sweltering heat, on Friday, November 6, a fight broke out between the Warnindilyakwa Mamarika and Warnungwamakwula Amagula clans in Angurugu. Two young men, ages nineteen and twenty-nine, died from spear wounds, and another was hospitalized, seriously injured.[4] In interpreting the events, the media and police typically described it as a petty dispute between two jealous women that spilled into revenge attacks involving men, including a truckload of armed relatives who drove in from Umbakumba to add their anger to the seething fire. A woman was knocked to the ground; a feud grew out of control.

According to Ben Hall, a young anthropologist hired to chart the extensive *everywhen*[5] (Stanner 1968) connections between the archipelago and the mainland, the Mamarika and Amagula clans are aligned closely by their shared ceremony and songs, and the broiling tensions had another origin (Hall, email communication, November 9, 2015). The people of Groote had been involved in long and strained negotiations over GEMCO's plan to extend new leases into the southwest corner of the island, instead of closing the mine at the end of their assorted tenement leases. With governments, NGOs, and corporations alike each facing the imminent loss of vast sums of mining revenue, locals were under intense pressure to agree to more manganese extraction on the island or, alternately, have the songlines[6] connecting and separating them from the mainland ripped up through proposed seabed mining, where they would have neither say nor recompense.

Land-based mining ensured some recognition of rights; seabed mining none at all. Since 2008, Aboriginal title to the seabed and waters above it were deemed to be exclusive, at least to the low-tide mark, meaning that others need to have the permission of the land trust to access waters for fishing (or anything) in the intertidal zone.[7] But rights where salt water permanently covers land out beyond the intertidal zone, within Australia's territorial seas, are nonexclusive. Mineral leases for seabed mining crucially do not require the right to negotiate with native title holders at all, who thus have very little in the way of procedural leverage. (By comparison, native title holders would be able to negotiate a mining agreement if a mineral lease was granted on the mainland where native title rights were held.)

The sea channel flowing between Groote Eylandt and the mainland, where Flinders and his surgeon dismembered the first of many murdered bodies to come, is thus part of a new frontier for mining, using new military technologies; and the best that policymakers in the NT have thus far managed in the face of this emergent frontier is a temporary restraining order on exploration, in the form of a moratorium (announced first in 2012, extended in 2015, and extended again in 2018 until 2021). The lurching moratorium in turn is also metaphorically accurate, symbolizing the ongoing precarity of life within settler colonial extraction zones, the permanent unpredictability of what will be threatened next. Ann Stoler (2013) has separately described imperial formations in terms of constant "states of deferral" wherein future autonomy is the promissory note for accepting compromises in the present (8). Within conditions of chronic de-stabilization, you might still hope for control, and sometimes you might just lose hope.

The tension of such relentless uncertainty is borne in bodies. Someone slams a car into a tree; someone else throws down a challenge to a fistfight; others binge-drink alcohol or smoke gunga; a few loudly press local organizations to take some kind of charge of the policy churn surrounding them; a smaller few persevere in driving organizational attempts to take that charge; others are simply on the take. And so, some people were resisting the prospect of an expanded mining operation; others could see no alternative but to yield to GEMCO's in-tensified pressure, given the alternative, lesser-known emerging evil of seabed mining; others wanted mining royalties to continue in the absence of any other reliable funding for desperately needed civic investment;[8] still others saw royal-ties as poison money and lamented everything already lost. "Once it's started [seabed or land mining], it's here for good, it doesn't go away, the nightmare doesn't end" (resident interview, March 17, 2011).

Six months after the breakout of supposed "sexual jealousy" that left two people dead and others permanently maimed, on June 28, 2016, the Anindi-lyakwa Land Council granted South 32 GEMCO additional access to forty-four hundred hectares (nearly eleven thousand acres) of land in the center of the island, and exploration rights over a huge twenty-six thousand hectares (sixty-four thousand acres) in the island's southern half, having tried in the years prior to initiate sufficient postmining economic alternatives. Those postmining alter-natives included submitting to the government's reform agenda of the previous decade, which, with the Intervention of 2007, pegged government support for essential services such as housing, infrastructure, and schooling to a require-ment that existing royalty revenues be channeled to the "omnibenevolent" goal of "jobs and growth" through capitalized resources and private labor integration (Neale 2017, 26).

Back then, Indigenous communities were also told to sign over the lease-hold of the towns on their lands to the Commonwealth for ninety-nine-year periods (see also chapter 2). The Anindilyakwa Land Council, having negotiated this down to a shorter eighty-year lease period (comprising a forty-year lease pe-riod, with a forty-year option to renew, exercisable unilaterally by the newly cre-ated government position of executive director of township leasing), became the first to sign up for township leasing and an associated Regional Partnership Agreement (RPA). At the same time, the NT government chose to dismantle fifty-four mostly Indigenous community government organizations in favor of eight "super shires" (Michel 2015). The self-government arrangements at Angurugu, begun in 1979, and Umbakumba, begun in 1982, were absorbed into the East Arnhem Shire Council in 2008. In 2018, the Anindilyakwa Land Council negotiated fiercely to return it all to local control, including management of housing and township leasing, opening a new chapter on an old battle. But when SIHIP houses were meant to be constructed, it was the Australian government that insisted on being the leaseholder.

The choice

Within all this externally led policy tumult—an ambient surround of project stutters and perennial rearranging—township leasing was promoted as a mechanism to simplify Aboriginal land tenure arrangements to enable the business investment and private home ownership that would miraculously solve the chronic infrastructure and service deficits that decades of lucrative private sector mining had not. Townships would be controlled by a newly formed government agency called the Office of Township Leasing, which would then lease blocks of land back to occupiers. The idea of leasing being a solution to the problem of absent private development is itself a fictional policy invention. As Leon Terrill's (2016) work details, section 19 of the Aboriginal Land Rights Act has always enabled the granting of individual long-term leases for home ownership, and even hairdressing salons, but that is a separate story, too complicated to more than sketch here.[9] The widely accepted common sense then prevailing about leasing is otherwise best captured in the words of News Corp journalist Paul Toohey:

[T]he federal government had seen dysfunctional, alcohol-wracked communities on Aboriginal land, and the stultifying lack of economic activity due to the fact that the land could not be sold or traded.

It also took the view it did not want to keep building houses and services just to see them wrecked, with no one held responsible.

They wanted a circuit breaker, some form of tenure so people could privately buy homes on Aboriginal land and take responsibility for them; and so businesses could get backing from banks, which refused to loan money because they could not call in a bad debt on communally-owned land.

The idea was the 99-year township lease, in which the land effectively became free-hold. The traditional owners would lease whole towns to the Office of Town Leasing for a period long enough for several generations to buy, sell or hand down their homes. (Toohey 2017, 20)

The forms of enterprise that the Anindilyakwa Land Council hoped would re-place mining royalty revenues were imagined as a composition of more kids at school, more young people in training, more homes under private owner-ship, more commercially operated local businesses, medical clinic upgrades, improved roads to facilitate cross-island access throughout the monsoonal rains, standardized street names, and support for the preservation and promo-tion of local cultural knowledge through a series of cultural centers.[10] These would be funded through mixed Groote Eylandt and Bickerton Island Enter-prises (GEBIE, the Anindilyakwa Land Council's royalty investment company), government, philanthropic, and mining contributions. In other words, unlike many Indigenous groups without their own land council and royalty stream, the Anindilyakwa can direct resourcing pathways and substantively influence policy because of their ability to put money on the table. They are also expected to subsidize public services, an issue we revisit in chapter 5.

Taken in their isolated parts, Groote's post-Intervention strategic plans made undeniable sense. For instance, an upgraded health service and residen-tial high-needs facility are desperately needed in an area that features Machado Joseph Disease (MJD), an inherited neurodegenerative disorder for which there is no known cure—a disorder that leaves people wheelchair bound and fully dependent within ten to fifteen years postdiagnosis.[11] The same can be said of the need for housing to alleviate chronic overcrowding, for schools that retain students, and sealed roads that deliver something other than the highest road-kill and disability rates in the country (Lea 2016). While academics can nos-talgically critique the colonization each cookie-cutter component seemingly represents—what with schools representing thick socialization in a western curriculum, and houses the sedentarization of former hunter-gatherers[12]—these are necessary contemporary infrastructures for which people will yield much, even the bitterness of more mining, to have available.

The pressure to have Aboriginal people consent to renewed mining is also distributed, part of a wider ecology, conjoining Aboriginal survivance with greater population dependencies on extraction (Lea 2016). Take, for instance, the demand for uranium. As this book later elaborates, Cold War politics brought intensive Commonwealth, Russian, and American interest in stockpiling the resources for making nuclear weapons. However, this was also a time when civil rights and anticolonial agitation made old tactics of violently seizing desired resources far less tenable. This potential complication saw governments, established miners, and swarms of geological prospectors calling for that euphemistically termed vehicle for extractivism: policy continuity (Harris 2011). A mutual benefit system was imagined. The Aboriginal Land Rights Act (Northern Territory) 1976, the first piece of Australian legislation to enable Indigenous repossession, provided precisely such a vehicle. Title carried within it an exacting clarification of the legal processes for mining exploration, extraction, and recompense; and for the Mirarr of Kakadu, the first claimants under the act, a specific schedule precluded their right to veto uranium mining (see chapter 5).

In other words, although land rights can and should be interpreted as the culmination of long campaigns for political recognition and prior sovereignty, the legislation can be read a different way: as establishing clear mechanisms for securing exploration and mining rights, by specifying the exact conditions under which a veto of exploration and mining might be exercised. In most settler colonies, creating "business uncertainty" remains key to pronouncements about the public risk at stake with recognition of Indigenous title (Pasternak and Dafnos 2018, 740). Not in Australia.

In addition to establishing clear pathways for mining access, land rights also changed social and economic relationships among Indigenous people. For freehold rights to be granted, settler law required named individuals. To this end, Australian land rights also literally invented a new category of empowered decision-maker and beneficiary, which the land councils had to inventory, known as the "traditional Aboriginal owner" (TO). The concept of the TO in turn enshrined fixed descent lineages and an idea of bounded spaces into the legislation. The interests of openly affiliating, flexible, and diasporic groups were now contained in the hands of a serendipitously advantaged few.

In a policy master stroke, the four original land councils that came into being with the NT legislation also owed their own continued existence to mining revenue—arguably to guarantee their independence from government interference.[13] The key challenge for a land council or a TO, or, more accurately, the key challenge for those TOs for whom country is still resonant and demanding, is to minimize environmental damage when mining or other incursions are made inevitable, and maximize the promised benefits, in situations where the right to negotiate this compromise is one of the only bargaining tools left—and there is no time to ensure that the promised benefits arrive.[14] Like much Indigenous social policy in Australia, land rights have a "'damned if you do, damned if you don't'" hologrammatic quality, offering opportunities and inveiglements at the same time. Put simply, companies get their profits, consumers like me get their goods and services, and Indigenous people get an invidious choice about livelihoods and least-worst paths, while redistributed dis/advantage is categorically indexed to allow budgetary loadings for governments, and goods and benefits too.

Groote Eylandt's predicament in needing to establish an indigenized capitalist economy beyond reliance on mining—through the planning efforts of a land council whose main source of discretionary investment income has its origins in mining royalties—perfectly represents the binds. Anindilyakwans share this pressure with other groups, such as the Mirarr Gundjheimi in Kakadu National Park, who have likewise endured the consequences of having desired resources, of being dragged through early years of fantastical development schemes (crocodile-shaped hotels and assorted other investments) to now be at the stage of assuming control of soon-to-be abandoned mining town amenities (see chapter 5). Unlike the clan estates of the Mirarr, who were fighting the mooted introduction of nuclear power in Australia and the prospect of expanded uranium mining, the Groote archipelago was in the direct line of sight for Intervention programs. Because building and renovating houses to alleviate overcrowding, disease, and disorder was a key part of fostering future capacity for future autonomy, it was also a central part of why the Anindilyakwa Land Council was among the first to agree to the harsh terms of Intervention-led policies and, in particular, to the requirement that members partly cede their collective jurisdiction over land, including the houses on it, to the delegated authority of the state, in terms of construction, tenancy management, and, later, repair and maintenance regimes. (This turned out to be a dud bargain, for reasons earlier chapters make clear, and the Anindilyakwa Land Council has since insisted that government should stay out of key areas of service delivery on the archipelago, unless invited in.[15])

Dissolving houses

I visited Groote Eylandt periodically throughout 2009, 2010, and 2011 to spend time with the small band of mostly non-Indigenous, mostly male engineers, project managers, and tradesmen who were then trying to ensure that the new and upgraded housing promised as part of the SIHIP got off the ground. Literally off the ground.

Early upon my first arrival, Andy Irvine, an engineer commissioned by the Anindilyakwa Land Council to coordinate the housing program from the community's side, had taken me on a tour of the sites where new housing was meant to go, to reveal what nearly $48 million and the resurrected SIHIP program, clawing out of its early scandals, had brought residents thus far.

Andy was simultaneously establishing a new building and roadworks arm for the Anindilyakwa Land Council, called GEBIE Civil and Construction Pty Ltd, with the ambition of training locals to assume future maintenance and construction contracts across a suite of infrastructural works, from roads to drains to houses (see also chapter 5). We had walked around four sorry-looking house footings and stood by a stack of glued laminated structural timber, freighted all the way from New Zealand, now lying half wrapped in thick orange builder's plastic on ground worn down from many steel-capped boots. Bits of cladded foam wall boards could be found jettisoned on sand dunes, repurposed as sleds that local children surfed on, while other expensive materials had been parked who knows where. There had been no secure storage for the construction equipment, no close auditing of supplies. For all that the newly empowered Earth Connect Alliance approached the project as a done deal that simply had to be accepted, given the unruly reputation of Groote Eylandt residents and the pathology portraits justifying the Intervention, locals had their own notations. They had experiential records of the rash new prefabricated designs, which weren't so new after all, but had been tried before. And so they rejected the Force 10 prefabricated foam housing the moment they learned what was on offer, haunted by still-fresh Logan Home memories (see chapter 2).

As a compromise, Earth Connect had then come up with the idea of laminated veneer lumber (LVL) houses, constructed on-site. I was now touring some of the results.

The four semibuilt LVL houses had been abandoned, and Earth Connect sacked, leaving the Anindilyakwa Land Council in an intense dispute with the NT and Australian governments about how the costs would be recovered and who would resume the works, with what bits of kit. Andy's team had to res-urrect Earth Connect's failures with the now-scattered gear—failures they had systematically, wearisomely called attention to for two long years before Earth Connect was finally removed.

How did it get to this point with Earth Connect, the confident alliance that had promised the media-ravaged government swift delivery of Groote's suite of housing works at the speed and cost required?

Every time I think about SIHIP's hectic beginnings, I remember the political panic about up-front costs and the need to return the program to an acceptable optics (chapter 2). Amid the stress of meeting impossible deadlines and demands to bring the price of any new house down, Earth Connect's swagger had stood out. The alliance had promised kit houses, delivered fast and cheap. Put to the test on Groote Eylandt, Earth Connect swiftly discovered that its prefabricated designs had no place in a cyclonic region. Earth Connect's designers also met residents who were fully aware of the radical unsuitability of these hasty backroom plans. Their plans rejected, Earth Connect contractors switched to what is colloquially known as a "stick build" approach, constructing on-site, learning as they went.

The abandoned footings tell part of what happened next. They tell a story of processes of ruin, of man-made (they are male-made) disposability, of perme-able materiality, and of policy hauntologies in process. Ordinarily, LVL beams are much stronger than milled or "natural" timber, and less likely to warp, twist, bow, or shrink. Being straighter and more uniform, they also require less manual labor in a build. They can even withstand extreme atmospheric conditions, shrinking and expanding in dynamic response to changing moisture gradients—just the thing for an exposed island lashed by an annual monsoon with massive infrastruc-tural deficits, one might think. Only, before being used, LVL beams cannot be left exposed to the elements; they must be kept flat and well ventilated, dry and out of the sun, elevated off the ground on level bearers, and, especially, kept away from termites, critters that particularly hanker after the adhesives used to glue these beams of engineered wood together (see also Lea 2015b). The beams left lying half wrapped on the ground beckoned ants like a discarded burger would a camp dog. As with the foam inside the metal cladding for Earth Connect's proposed-then-abandoned prefabricated homes, LVL glue was ant nectar.

According to anthropologist Tim Ingold, the distinguished Portuguese ar-chitect Álvaro Siza says he has never been able to build a real finished house, for such a thing cannot exist:

Rather, for its inhabitants it calls for unremitting effort to shore it up in the face of the comings and goings of its human inhabitants and non-human inhabitants. . . . Rainwater drips through the roof where the wind has blown off a tile, feeding a fungal growth that threatens to decompose the timbers, the gutters are full of rotten leaves, and if that were not enough, moans Siza, "legions of ants invade the thresholds of doors, there are always the dead bodies of birds and mice and cats." (Ingold 2010, 5, citing Siza and Angelillo 1997, 48)

"Whatever free time you may have is not enough to deal with the madness of nature," Siza adds (1997, 48). Following Siza's lead, we can see Earth Connect's inexperience as a certain unworldliness, expressed in not knowing how to shore up materials against known pressures from human and nonhuman forces. In other words, before they were built, Earth Connect's liminal not-yet-houses were already fighting the elements. Like policy and people, housing is always on the move. It deconstructs from the moment of construction: rusting, corroding, sinking, sliding, expanding, shrinking, cracking, dissolving, incubating, weathering, and being chewed, rotted, or nibbled at (Graham and Thrift 2007). With Earth Connect, the bridge between postconstruction and decay was introduced even earlier in the process. The decay began before any buildings appeared. When corner cutting is built into its design, housing deconstructs even as it is being proposed in meetings and drafted into plans. As contemporary ethnographers of things infrastructural have made clear, infrastructure can be defined by its inherent instability, as being in a constant state of threatened breakdown, always veering toward its impermanence (Jackson 2015, Leigh Star 1999). Tracing the vagaries of infrastructure, one confronts its entropic default. The airplane has always held the possibility of its crash in its very assembly. This is also part of the decolonial notion of haunting, caught in material immanence. A slow water leak blotching a ceiling is, for decolonial scholars Eve Tuck and C. Ree, "the ghost's *memento mori*, that we are always in a process of ruin, a state of ruining." They write, "Our ruins lie within the quick turnover of buildings, disappearing landmarks, and disposable homes, layered upon each other and over again" (2013, 653).

This is the dynamic more-than-human space that standards and principles for Indigenous housing design attempt to fill, as a partial block to the manifold and constant threats to the integrity of human-made materials in vitally alive built environments. A recommendation for a dimension and ideal compositional material for a drainage pipe, for instance, incorporates expected use loads and the known depredations of soft water, hard water, vermin, or earth movement. But given the financial pressure and media scrutiny the wider SIHIP was under—pressures that had originally catapulted the bargain-basement promises of Earth Connect to the archipelago—the requirement to build to national Indigenous housing guidelines (a voluntary best practice at best) had already been waived.

Guerilla accounting

What interests me here is not only the inevitably inadequate and partial nature of standards or the inherently decompositional nature of building materials (Lea 2015b) but the tactics required to draw attention to Earth Connect's disastrously inexperienced efforts. For it was not the squadrons of visiting politicians, bureaucrats, media, engineers, planners, or even financial auditors trekking in and out of Groote's luxury accommodation facilities at Alyangula, nor the plethora of official program reviews of SIHIP, that eventually blew the whistle on Earth Connect's failings, but personnel within the Anindilyakwa Land Council. Using meticulous records comprising planning documents, minutes, correspondence, spreadsheets, budgets, and records of phone and Skype conversations, Indigenous organizational "guerilla accountants" (cf. Hetherington 2011) could remind fast-changing visiting officials precisely what had been agreed at previous meetings, or what the guidelines required, or what the official funding was being spent on, or what past program ghosts needed warding, in far greater detail than bureaucrats were able to do of their own programs. Locals became the continuity editors in the surreal movie that SIHIP implementation had become. Their campaign was a perfect inversion of the specter of single-minded bureaucratic oversight, where public officials are (meant to be) forensically keeping program information, and Aboriginal groups are (meant to be) the naive subjects of governmental technologies (*pace* Batty 2005). As Earth Connect houses struggled to assemble, different representatives of assorted government agencies would attend project meetings, each time bringing scant memory of their own prior commitments and promises, while Groote's local servers groaned with mirroring paperwork, forming an arsenal of counteraccount.

I have since come to see such phenomena as a very ordinary kind of administrative violence (Graeber 2012; Lea, Howey, and O'Brien 2018). Such noneventful, unremarkable, sloppy kinds of dealings, like the casual rudeness of visiting

dignitaries or the transactional costs of hollowed-out expertise within bureaucratic ranks, are indisputably part of what enables poorly conceptualized and
poorly executed programs to be reliably reproduced in Indigenous settings; yet
analytically, they do not compete with the clear, media-worthy scandal of, say,
an alliance squandering millions of dollars with nothing to show for it (Hall
2010). Highlighting the nonnarratability of the second-rate, of corner cutting, of
superficiality in business as usual, of high speed where hesitation is warranted,
in turn requires an analytic counterinsistence, to draw our anthropological attention to what it takes to question the underdone, the half-baked, the blithely
accepted. To insist that a problem exists, Sara Ahmed (2012) reminds us, is to
make oneself into a problem. Insistence takes effort, causes stress, is not well
rewarded. This is the impossible terrain of the institutional killjoy.

When the scandal of SIHIP had finally come out of the headlines—inquiries
conducted, Jim Davidson removed, a minister replaced, bureaucrats exchanged,
the ethnographer evicted, and a new metric hammered into public acceptance
(750 new houses, 230 rebuilds, and 2,500 refurbishments)—so much work had
gone into managing the renovated look of the Intervention's signature policy,
the last thing anyone wanted was fresh evidence of ongoing failures and mis-
spends. Accompanying this self-protecting state reluctance is the settler colonial habit of seeing any Indigenous insistence on honor to the written word,
on follow-through for promises, as somehow immature or inexperienced, as
unfaithful to the compromises expected of institutional partnerships, and most
certainly as introduced by external troublemakers (cf. Neale 2017). The default
assumption is that, as recipients of government social policy funding, Indigenous people should be grateful. Any in situ critique is thus easily trivialized.

Consider then the effort of refusing to be shaken off and flicked aside, when
mutual complicity in compromise is the expected price of being "in partnership." Consider the disapproval such efforts of refusal also face within, as well as
without, organizations. Sara Ahmed has recently turned her attention to intrain-
stitutional suppression of complaints as a collective will not to hear, and a thor-
ough socialization in institutional fatalism.[16] People admonish themselves with
"What's the use of complaining?" toggling between that discouraging thought and
another—a foreboding, self-censoring knowledge about what happens to those
who complain. This is the force field I am invoking here. Within communities,
Indigenous and non-Indigenous alike, there are thick hinterlands of entangled interests, of different subjectivities involved in fighting for different versions of what

a good life is meant to entail and how best to acquire or deliver it, different financial and even drug dependencies, alliances, and allegiances. Different complicities. It took a persistent and deeply unpopular campaign of counteraccounting to call the SIHIP machinery to account; and it was no easy fight, for lying inside each half-done, neglected process, within the dismissals and the trivializations, are also mundane biographies of idle self-protection. When being complicit with corner cutting in the grand name of cost containment is taken for granted as part of a matrix of transposable dispositions, competencies, institutional know-how, and instinctive preservation of professional reputations, to overstay objection beyond a ritual protestation is to become too demanding. It is to ruin collegiate relations. Refusing to share coffee and cake in "strategic" meetings in simulations of authentic collaboration is to become a killjoy. Killjoys are targets.

By complaining about Earth Connect, Andy and his team made themselves the objects of complaint. As they mounted a detailed critique of Earth Connect's increasing disarray, providing undeniable documentary evidence and reminders, using records as technologies to interrupt the default return to "no problems to see," they became problems to be removed. They were accused of nepotism, of recruiting mates, and of paying these imports lucrative wages to do (what should be) local Indigenous jobs. They were equipping the GEBIE company too quickly with expensive plant using money that could and should be for local community development. The local jobs they were generating were indicted as superficial, of being trainee roles while professional positions were still held by outsiders. These are the easiest accusations to make stick in Indigenous organizations, and claims that the trainee roles were pathways to qualified roles sounded like so much defensive self-interest.

Reading this account, Andy wrote me back:

I know it is probably not the thrust of your writing but the overwhelming part for me of the whole episode was the pointless urgency. . . . The biggest killer was the ridiculous urgency of the SIHIP rebuild and renovation project. $16 million of work that had to be done in 18 months . . . for what end? This meant lots of accommodation and infrastructure for FIFO staff to meet this deadline and a huge rush and cost.

This project could have sustained a smaller business for many years, seen locals get through [apprenticeships to qualified] trades, established the business, built better houses, kept the money locally, and been far more effective, but no one would listen. What is always missing is the complete accounting [of costs] across and forward. (Email correspondence, December 17, 2018)

He is left with multiple what-ifs. What if SIHIP had been staged at a more manageable pace? What if those local recruits had stability and support over years and not weeks and months to acquire the missing qualifications? What if business plans reflected comprehensive development achievements and not just a simplistic immediate cost accounting? What if the budget analyses had been estimated as a cost per person housed, not as a cost per square meter or cost per bedroom? What if the protection of being able to live adjacently for kinship and camaraderie, for protection from thuggery, for food security and child care could be answered with homesteads boasting flexibly larger houses, with generously sized bedrooms with storage, robust common spaces, and high-functioning wet areas (laundries, bathrooms, kitchens) that allow affines to share and retreat, to convene and withdraw? What if the metric had not been propelled by scandal-driven media concern but by community history and environmental need? (Some better news: a decade later, with the Anindilyakwa Land Council now more firmly in charge of housing design, construction, and maintenance, the still unfolding infrastructure story is heading in these directions.)

Eventually, one of the original three alliances, Territory Alliance, replaced Earth Connect on Groote, after the government paid the departing consortia a contract dissolving penalty (of $40 million) to have to start again. Territory Alliance proceeded to build a different style of prefabricated dwelling, known as Ritek houses, under which wall frames are erected, then vertical and horizontal bars are inserted for later wiring and piping before concrete is poured into the cavities. Like Earth Connect before it, Territory Alliance also had to build a certain number by a certain time on a certain budget— one that was now even more strictly capped. To further shave costs, veranda spaces were removed; houses lost rooms; there was little shaping of the yard sites; and there was no or minimal landscaping for controlling surface-water runoff from houses in heavy rainfall, for controlling dust in the dry season, or for orienting shade. Combined, these nips and tucks neutered householder capacities to create makeshift arrangements to manage visitor overflow; to manage, that is, the overcrowding that ostensibly SIHIP was resolving to interrupt child sexual abuse. Remember all that? The children who needed to get to showers unseen by anyone else? The reason why land tenure had to change, and so on? In the era of increasing temperatures, the thermal performance of Ritek properties is also unknown (Horne et al. 2013).[17] But the houses themselves are human-proof, and between the tenancies of more easily disposable and interchangeable occupants, they can be blasted inside out with high-pressure water hoses.

Out of all this we can say: a program to get houses built can build no houses, can build houses that are not houses, or can build houses that dissemble, and still be a program for building houses. The processes for building nonhouses may even be evaluated positively. Even after the unrelenting local effort to broadcast the dissembling finally does its work, the subsequent idea that removing problem contractors removes the problem of poor housing is how the problem of poor housing is continually reproduced. It is the kind of response that individualizes endemic processes and entrenched structures. Bad housing is, in the Latourian sense, an accomplishment, the product of commitments and expectations that ease into habituated practice with the key aesthetic enabler of unruly householders down the line, destined to bear the liability of dysfunctional outcomes; and of policy processes that are beyond exhausting to interrupt. Indigenous people have long learned to pick their fights or ignore the whole scene, while non-Indigenous killjoys quickly expire. My own what-if: Can artifactual policy fix what it is such a part of?

Interlude IV

November 2017, a searingly hot day in Adelaide, the capital of South Australia. I met John Singer in the foyer of a hotel on North Terrace, a street that sets a casino, gentlemen's clubs, and greasy spoons in competition with Adelaide's other civic symbols: its famed churches, creative industries, and multiple universities. Instead of the craggy hills and endless horizons of the APY Lands, we sat amid the hotel's faux Roman furnishings, the walls craftily distressed with fake cracks and seams to match the marble tabletops held aloft by heroically draped Romanesque pedestals. Caught in the clattering noise of breakfast eaters silting the machine-cooled air, we both refused to reengage the blazing furnace outside to search out a quieter venue.

John's phone vibrated repeatedly with incoming message notifications. He was in town for a series of meetings, as his new role as chair of the National Aboriginal Community Controlled Health Organisation (NACCHO) kicked into gear. Operating with the motto "Aboriginal Health in Aboriginal Hands," NACCHO represents an alliance of 143 Aboriginal Community Controlled Health Services across Australia. Aboriginal-controlled health services employ more Aboriginal people than any other sector and boast the greatest proportion of female chief executives, John explains. As he launched into a description of his current leadership challenge (how to showcase the sector's forward-facing relevance when the government is ideologically opposed to ceding to Indigenous control of anything), John had become as distracted by a buzzing device as all the ministerial touring parties had been whenever they visited the APY Lands.

"Did you like what I wrote about Minister Wyatt's visit?" I asked, referring to my draft of his meeting with apparently disinterested visitors, mildly anxious about depicting his private reactions now that he's leading a national representative body.

"Yeah, that looked like a pretty good account of what happened there. I think they asked me like, two questions. 'Are you living in Adelaide or out on the Lands now, John?' There might have been a few other questions maybe, I can't remember!"

He paused to sip his cappuccino through a violent clanging of crockery nearby.

"Usually, people we've had in the past, they could pick up that we were making an impact on the ground; they could see what we were doing's effective and was actually giving us the chance to reduce that health burden or risk, and they could see we were putting in the best measures that we could do in terms of different areas. Some [of our approaches] worked, some struggling to work, but the plans, steps we taking, were well researched and well prepared, looking at what has been done before, not just in Australia but sometimes internationally, trying to get best practice and all that.

"And they could see that and be satisfied, be confident that the money was well spent and all those sorts of things. . . . That's sort of not there anymore."

There was, by now, a growing list of issues for Indigenous health services needing urgent attention. The Australian federal government had announced a review of its Indigenous health funding models, to further constrain expenditure by funding organizations for discrete "episodes of care." Theoretically, it has always funded clinics in this way, but now it would adjust the patient information software ("Communicare") used in clinics to bundle together any number of items of attention delivered on a single calendar day—be it for sickness, injury, screening, counseling, or preventive care—and have all these counted as a single episode, no matter how many things were done.

The implication was clear: rather than supporting holistic attention, the model incentivized filleting a patient's issues into discrete, fundable episodes to be spread across different days, heedless of the inconvenience for patients or the additional resources needed to then coordinate appropriate referral and follow-up care. The work associated with managing medical emergencies—of stabilizing a patient sufficiently until the Royal Flying Doctor Service can land on an airstrip, wind and light allowing, or driving 450 to 500 kilometers to the nearest hospital—would likewise be treated as a single episode of care, based on an urban model where a patient from a health service can expect an ambulance to arrive within the hour. With these tweaks to Communicare, the money granted to cover primary and preventive health care costs could be whittled under the guise of introducing greater transparency. All told, Nganampa stood to lose over $2 million from its base funding, enough to shut at least one of the seven clinics it operates across its 110,000-square-kilometer service range. In other words, Nganampa would need to mount yet another paper fight in the undeclared policy wars of settler colonial Australia, simply to do what it is ostensibly meant to.

Nganampa had continued operating the *Tjilpi Pampaku Ngura* Aged Care Facility at Pukatja on the APY Lands, despite not having recurrent funding for extra positions to meet the new nurse-safety policy following Gayle Woodward's murder in 2016. Only now, following extensive renovations of the aged-care buildings, the organization was confronting separate regulatory issues. The aged-care facility comprised four small buildings or pods, positioned close together, each with shared toilet and bathroom facilities. Each pod had two rooms, with two beds in each. Before the upgrades, the facility had been operating according to a Class 3 classification under the National Construction Code of Australia; post the renovations, they had been reclassified as Class 9c. Such dull titles, for such highly consequential effects. Class 3 buildings are residential buildings that provide for both long-term and transient accommodation for a number of unrelated people, such as boarding or guest houses, hostels or backpacker lodges, the dormitories that might be workers' quarters for shearers or fruit pickers, or the "care-type" facilities that might accommodate children, the elderly, or people with a disability.[1] Class 9c buildings are aged-care buildings proper, such as high-care, high-density nursing homes in metropolitan areas. They provide "for elderly people who, due to varying degrees of incapacity associated with the ageing process, are provided with personal care services and 24-hour staff assistance to evacuate the building in an emergency." The South Australian certifiers said, in point of fact, that the *Tjilpi Pampaku Ngura* aged-care facility should always have been Class 9c, a categorization that was never mentioned by the Commonwealth government in any of three previous reviews.

Although the facility was down on the recurrent funding required to reliably maintain the said twenty-four-hour staff assistance, its renovated bricks and mortar now met the requirements of a fully fledged residential aged-care facility, a shift in classification that came with tighter fire safety requirements. Among other things, each of the bedroom units must provide for automatic fire sprinkler systems. It seems perfectly reasonable, but for the fact that the whole community of Pukatja, nestled high in the arid Musgrave Ranges separating the Great Victoria Desert to the south and the Gibson Desert to the north, receives its water from six main bores pumped into three storage tanks. Population growth had seen water pressure dropping over time, and the tanks are unable to provide adequate flow and pressure for fire hydrants, fire hose reels, or fire sprinkler systems.

Nganampa would now need to install an independent water supply to feed the sprinkler systems, at significant additional cost, and because there is no category of funding to apply to for such infrastructure, the remote-area health service was plundering its own cash reserves, meant to cover wage liabilities and emergency contingencies, to ensure accreditation, by looking to build itself a large water tank.

"So let me get this right," I spluttered, stabbing out my left thumb, then index finger, middle finger, ring finger, little finger, each angrily raised digit expressing the latest organizational assaults. "You are forced to cannibalize the funds you must maintain for emergencies, to cover the safety of *tjilpi* (elderly A*n*angu); there is a premium on putting locks and bolts on doors for nurse safety, but not on providing dollars for new nurse salaries, even though this is now legally mandated; you are looking at potentially losing a clinic?"

"*Uwa* [Yes]. That other one [SA minister] you talked about in that paper [Interlude III], he's gone already. And now we the old show in town, and they really don't trust old Aboriginal-run organizations. Not really.

"It seems to be a bit of a thing with government, to look at these big companies like PricewaterhouseCoopers who might be have a little Aboriginal section in there, advising them around things, consulting . . . maybe this is a new way forward, they [government] think. Maybe put Aborigine in a company and fund them instead of community mob. They don't trust Aboriginal organizations, and if they don't have to fund them, they won't."

John returned to this theme two years later, in August 2019. "I was thinking the other day and thought that even though ATSIC [Aboriginal and Torres Strait Islander Commission][2] had its problems, at least they had a presence on the ground, and funding was focused on Aboriginal community priorities. Like CDEP [Community Development Employment Projects, a work-for-benefits scheme]. People could work sixteen hours a week, then [have] the rest of time available to practice cultural maintenance, and homelands movement was supported and funded, as homelands generally were strategically placed near cultural areas of significance. As well as allowing flexibility for Aṉangu when ceremonies or other significant cultural activities were taking place.

"Aṉangu felt like we had control, then when ATSIC was suddenly dismantled, the priorities were changed as ATSIC monies went back into mainstream departments; our priorities were at the bottom of mainstream priorities, or just abandoned.

"That's when we saw the closing and abandonment of homelands policy and funding for homelands. Everything was centralized, so that meant . . . less focus on programs that were about cultural maintenance and Aṉangu being in country."

Meantime—March 5, 2018 to be exact—the Australian Broadcasting Commission (ABC) aired a newly harrowing episode on Gayle Woodford's brutal murder for its documentary series Australian Story.[3] Representatives of Nganampa Health Council had struggled to remind the investigating journalist that not all Aṉangu are violent murderers, amid their deep distress over Gayle's loss. It was a dilemma whether to talk at all, given the omnipresent dangers of misrepresentation. Could they point to the government's refusal to fund staff positions, or would this further position them as troublesome activists cleaving to outmoded models of community-controlled organization? Nganampa's general manager was haunted by a trauma memory of Gayle's vibrant presence. After the documentary, he resigned.[4]

SafeWork South Australia had initiated an inquiry into Gayle Woodford's death, driven by worker's compensation insurance concerns. The health service proffered records over its decades of operation detailing how every staff anxiety about safety was noted and acted on, as the insurers probed their liability. For his part, John chafed at the need to talk about *this* murder over all the others, given the overpolicing of his friends and relations, and their simultaneous underprotection. He understands all too well the requirement that he stay silent about the racial profile of senseless deaths that do and don't matter. A murderer let loose on the APY Lands is a correctional services issue, he still thinks. But he also thinks that governments rely on constituting Indigenous people as underdeveloped and wild, the better to use Aboriginal issues to audition their varying policy experiments. Strategic silence is a necessary condition for the always imperfect but sorely needed funding that such experiments offer. Even agreeing to let me write these interludes is a risk.

To channel money (officially granted money, that is), Indigenous people need to belong to incorporated organizations, inviting a tsunami of subsequent requirements (Sullivan 2008, Smith 2008). To inch toward its mandated tasks, an incorporated body must seek annual state and federal government funding and any other grants it can attract, topped up by Medicare and pharmaceutical benefit reimbursements, with all the tangled lines of (always ideologically loaded) negotiations, reporting, accounting, stop-start deliveries, and evaluations that such dependencies invoke (Neu 2000, Sullivan 2009, Michel and Taylor 2012). Many Indigenous services are so drained from extracting small concessions from the swill and swirl of policy happenings that claiming anything bolder or more comprehensive becomes too difficult to contemplate, especially without independent or recurrent funding. Relentless distraction begets issue captivity. As John and I insulated ourselves from the baking heat outside on that hot Adelaide day back in 2017, I heard no prominence given to such issues as climate change in Nganampa's policy preoccupations, no mention of this ancient continent becoming more inhospitable to mammalian occupants, of the future costs of power generation, long-distance freight, or the repair and maintenance of anything; nor of what will hold remote areas together, what with hunting and gathering skills already atrophied by forced sedentism, the jailing of knowledge holders, and nothing much left to hunt (Douglas 2015).

Policy dramas in health do not include the risk factors of lost decoding skills—how to look at signs and know from the looking, this is a buck kangaroo; this one's a female still carting a joey, we'll leave her alone—even though being a successful hunter remains the most likely indicator of being successful at gaining employment, securing a vehicle, providing for a family, and managing the impact of chronic diseases, and thus a key part of the stronger futures that all published policies say is wanted for Indigenous people (Garnett et al. 2009, Dombrowski 2007, 2010; Altman 2005). It is hard to activate other possible worlds when the footholds of the worlds you are surviving in are constantly shifting.

Instead, at the local level of policy translation, an astounding amount of work goes into securing program gains that are so slender, so provisional, they cannot make a dent even in the more myopic needs they are immediately intended for. Those involved are suspended in the distracting work of mind-reading high-turnover ministerial and bureaucratic personalities; of writing endless submissions to redirect centralist assumptions; of forcing actual benefits out of underfunded, competing, or conflicting systems; and then, over and over again, of managing public sentiments. Of course, the distraction list could also expand to include the compliance, audit, and reporting activities associated with the fractal system of funding allocations under new public management logics, forces that strangle initiative in their own right. Or the multiple official reviews and inquiries that cannot be ignored, but never yield easier outcomes.

Despite their extraordinary survival tactics over the years, the population of the APY Lands is as sick as any in remote Indigenous Australia. Approximately 26 percent of Anangu over the age of fifteen are diabetics. Over 50 percent of all diagnosed cases of rheumatic heart disease in South Australia are on the APY Lands. In recent years, although Nganampa has done much to reduce the number of patient evacuations by the Royal Flying Doctor Service, this still occurs more than two hundred times per annum. More than 54 percent of the population over the age of fifteen are current smokers, and approximately 65 percent of patients over the age of twenty-five have a body mass index—a measure of bodily fat levels—that suggests they are either seriously overweight or clinically obese. Approximately 5 percent of adults are on injectable antipsychotic medications; and 6 percent have hepatitis B, a virus that infects the liver and, without early detection, dramatically increases the risk of liver cancer.[5] Child and maternal health is only partially addressed. Babies are plumper, children are immunized, and pregnancies better cared for, but families are embroiled in conditions that shorten their lives even so.

Why does John stay? Because this model of community-controlled decision-making is still the best one, he says, "even if they are trying to wipe us out."

The noise of the hotel foyer had become deafening. An airport courtesy bus had arrived, with the sounds of confused tourists arranging luggage disposal and room bookings, all clangs and raised voices, crunching into the ambient interjections of a hissing espresso maker and brunch-to-lunch changeover. We gave up on further talk, agreeing to meet again when I had more writing to share about Nganampa's refusal of the relentless elimination tactics of the state and about my attempts to capture how all this is also part of what policy *is*, in its unadorned, ambient, and hauntological guise. In its wild and natural state.

Chapter 4

Almost a miracle

It is almost a miracle wherever you find a really solid Aboriginal-defined vision
forging its way through a maze that only seems to work to destroy possibility.

Wright (2016, 56)

It is "almost a miracle," writes the novelist Alexis Wright, a member of the
Waanyi people of the Gulf of Carpentaria, describing life under continuing occupation in Australia, a nation that has cleared for itself unimpeded rights to
subsurface minerals, and cast Indigenous people collateral roles as an absorb-
able, commoditized, or surplus people in the process. Audra Simpson (2016)
makes a similar point. For the *Kahnawà:ke* of North America, the choice offered
to Indigenous groups under continuing occupation is "a half-life of civilization
in exchange for land" (328). That land, and what can be extracted from it, feeds
and sustains every urbanite in every city across the world (Graham 2010). I am
talking about Australia's policy ecology in this book, but the extractive condition
is global. Extractive systems subtend settler existence in all colonized spaces.
The food dragged from soil, water, petrochemical, and flesh-fed industrial agri-
culture; the militarily carved freight systems across land and sea that distribute
goods to different markets; the defense-funded research that preserves per-
ishables to extend shelf lives over larger distances—even the prosthetics and
extension methods for perishable human bodies—are dependent on an extractive foundation (Belanger and Arroyo 2016). We are thus all implicated in the
tolls exacted on Indigenous and other subaltern groups, through mass tributaries of administrative, carceral, and ecological violence and remediation, in the
very metabolism of our shared freight-dependent, militarily enabled existence.

In emphasizing the chaotic policy entailments this all engenders, I have un-
derplayed Indigenous creativity and resilience or, to return to Gerard Vizenor's
concept, Indigenous survivance. Turning to the work of the Karrabing Film
Collective, a group I have allied with for some years,[1] this chapter attends to

grassroots creative efforts to reinterpret different policy assemblages, without overclaiming the potency of such creativity to order incoherent state effects. In less than a decade, Karrabing films and commentary have appeared in the most prestigious art houses of the global north, and the humblest too—their work has traveled to Palestine, Manila, Korea, and remote Australia. In the beginning, when making movies was still new to everyone, a professional film crew was involved.[2] Most films have since been shot by Karrabing members themselves with stabilized smartphones, a technology that matches less militarized film shoots and more psychedelic treatments of time, spectral coexistence, and policy fates. Now liberated, their films reflect what the Potawatomi scholar Kyle Whyte describes not with a figure of hauntology but of "spiraling time," experienced and lived "through narratives of cyclicality, reversal, dream-like scenarios, simultaneity, counter-factuality, irregular rhythms, ironic un-cyclicality, slipstream, parodies of linear pragmatism, eternality" (2018b, 229).

Karrabing filmography thus draws attention to the infinity and simultaneity of incommensurate policies under continuing occupation, to apertures that close and open in the traffic between policy pronouncements and their daily enactments, as "Aboriginal-defined visions" are pursued. Karrabing endurance and probing in turn invite reflection on what it is that its members are maneuvering in and through. What kind of policy-scape sits within and behind Karrabing films?

As I have insisted, policy encounters are not restricted to moments when this or that coded policy artifact—this legislation, that regulation—is directly in play but are part of a wider policy ecology, in constant states of intra-action with other matter, organic and inorganic, from across time and space (Barad 2012). This "other matter" is also inescapably policy inflected. Policy and lives, matter and time are not occasionally intersecting but otherwise separate dimensions: they are comerged. The air and ground traffic I can hear from my makeshift office (usually, a kitchen table), traffic that inextricably shapes cultural habits in profound and intimate ways (Lutz 2014), is an ambient reminder of policy-enabled technologies in my everyday surroundings, complete with bitumen subdivisions and air-carved military and civilian territories in the sky above.

These surroundings are at once legacies, here-and-now elements, and are already shaping our lifeworlds into tomorrow. They form a settler colonial project that is annexed to the uncertainties of climate change and material shortages to come. Policy ecologies are thus neither singular nor time bound. They are monumentally extant in some moments and more atmospheric in others. Like houses, policies can thus be thought of as assemblages of people, stuff, nonhuman matter, and colonial legacies, which are both "violently thrown together and banally and incrementally sifted into each other" (Schlunke 2016, 219). Further, if policy is part of what one is inhabiting in the everyday, then the obstacles that are pushed through and manipulated in changing one's conditions are always at least partly policy encounters. That these manipulations do not necessarily take place in carpet worlds or through the prosecution of black-letter edicts does not make them lesser examples of policy intra-action. Thus, to repeat a point made throughout this book, forms of policy teleology, whether hagiographic or critical, have little to offer in analyzing Indigenous worlds under continuing occupation. Nor does the convenient separation of policy as a citadel concept severed from haphazardly implemented programs as "that which happens beyond policy." It is *all* policy, manifesting in different densities and configurations.[3]

The point of considering policy more ecologically is not to multiply the subclauses of a master category called "implementation effects." Rather, it is to multiply the entry points for analysis and action. Policy interventions can be activated by many actors across manifold dimensions, not just in sites of formal governance or official state power. As an important disciplinary bonus, an ecological framing also rescues the anthropology of policy subfield from its grand distraction with correcting the normative logics of political science, by instead inviting ethnographic attention to more widely distributed policy phenomena.

To further build these points, in this chapter I first describe the conditions subtending Karrabing filmmaking, focusing as much on wider contexts of production surrounding film plots, to pull into view the multiple policy operations that are always a constitutive part of everyday phenomena. Karrabing tactics open a way to describe the mesospace of policy possibility, a concept I adapt from Isabelle Stengers (2009, 2012, 2017). To give proper due to this concept of settler policy's everywhereness and longue durée—its ephemerality and presence in the before, here, and to come—this chapter also deepens the concept of policy hauntology. My concern is to emphasize how policies accumulate and linger, operating less as a singular mission and more as a porous force, akin to water in its ability to saturate the surroundings with a mix of old and new matter, even when policy is not apparently in place (cf. Neimanis 2017). That policy is never operating de novo is almost certainly part of policy's capacity to ex-haust, but it is also an invitation toward hope.

Faking it: On how the Karrabing came to be

Jayden (not his real name) had punched his uncle so hard in a drunken melee one night, the older man had to receive hospital care. Uncle Lamar had not wanted to press charges, but under section 125 of the Domestic and Family Vio-lence Act 2007 (NT), health professionals are required to report assaults visited by one family member upon another. It had been a stupid, no-good fight, Jayden told me later. They had hit and slammed each other, cursing and pushing; but Jayden, younger and faster on his feet, hadn't stopped until blood gushed like a faucet from that old man's broken face. He'd gone too hard, he admitted now with an attractively sheepish grin, creating one charge too many on a police re-cord mounting from petty acts of shoplifting, driving offenses, and one of police assault, for that's what cussing at officers can be called. Charged and released on bail, he was awaiting trial. Among his specified conduct requirements, Jayden had to report daily to police, remain at another relative's address (well away from Uncle Lamar), and obey a strict curfew. My job was to collect him from his newly fixed address, take him to the station for his daily police report, then whisk him to the ferry terminal some twenty-five kilometers away, so we could both quickly cross Darwin harbor, meet up with Uncle Lamar, and, together with other friends and family, participate in a collectively conceived film shoot, then dash to make the return ferry before curfew—a subterfuge we would re-peat the next day, and the next.

I had pulled up in the near-empty parking lot behind the Palmerston po-lice station, in the lone bit of shade I could find, as the tropical sun steamed the bitumen—a fieldwork location I often find myself occupying. How ironic, I noted in my journal, that we are bluffing these bored police with our diligent reporting so that they can complete their red tape, to enable a different kind of make-believe, that of a film, when in adjacent scenarios, making art is the way Indigenous youth are meant to be reanimated.[4]

How did we get to be here, a collective of friends and relatives who toy with fiction to better tell the truth? There are any number of origin stories to the Kar-rabing's work as a film collective, including a story about Elvis Presley. To keep this short, let's say it started through long discussions about how best to repatri-ate philosopher and anthropologist Elizabeth Povinelli's expansive archive—

old photos and recordings, notes and footage, the memorabilia of lifelong friendships and exchange—in ways that might return stories to the country that generated them, while crafting new knowledge and income. Rather than store this mass of material in static archives, the Karrabing envisaged something far more dynamic, ideally on country, learning in the way you should, sweating your identity as a calling card to the animated world around you.

At first this was imagined in terms of a "virtual living library" where that same archival information would be merged with new, old, and organic factual and storied information about the land and sea. Access points to our imagined new media would be literally embedded within the landscape and animated via augmented-reality technologies using data registries annexed to global positioning system (GPS) satellite data and the geographical information system (GIS) software that makes sense of GPS information. In this original project vision, we visualized all the different types of visitors to what I will call, for shorthand purposes, Karrabing country, referring to some members' partially recovered estates either side of Anson Bay, the mouth of the Daly River.

The shorthand is necessary, given the vexed nature of what is Karrabing country, complicated precisely because time-spiraling policies are always haunting any present-day constellation. To briefly elaborate: members of the Karrabing Film Collective bring eight different sacred ancestral links or *every-when* (Dreamings), and members are linked in custodial relations to multiple others. Individuals are further separated by (heavily ethnologized) notions of clan, estate, and language group, the key policy indexes for determining who is and who is not a traditional owner. Some members have been given this recognized designation as TOs; others have not. Some might have to answer the demand: Whose land do you think you're on? Others do not. Moreover, the Karrabing Film Collective does not include all members of the various clans, estates, and languages that individual members are also part of. This means that even as members insist they are connected and obligated to each other through shared friendship, history, and ancestral narratives, and formed their corporation to manage this alliance, they do not represent any single landowning group or globally representative body (see Biddle and Lea 2018, 10). Expressed differently, the Karrabing Film Collective is entirely recognizable as mainstream small-to-medium enterprises are often constituted: a part family, part ally, and part friendship network, based on shared purpose, shared histories, and shared affinity.

But in the early days, this mainstream alliance configuration was the basis for their nonrecognizability. For official funding, members were meant to be geotagged to a singular "clan" or "community" belonging to a discrete settlement. They were thus not legible to policy even as they pursued perfectly aligned policy goals. Instead, as Daniel Fisher has accurately summarized, "they exist in large part in their coming together for the film, a fact which makes them nearly invisible to many Australian agencies and funding bodies" (2018, 296).

The challenge Karrabing members set themselves: Could such policy impasses in turn be bypassed? Might cultural tourists, fishers/hunters, land managers, and estate custodians, the different folk visiting Karrabing country, purchase Indigenous cultural and ecological knowledge? Such questions informed a vision for a sustainable, cross-generational, semicommercial enterprise, based on transforming material from members' lifeworlds and other sources (historical archives, scholarship, reports) into media that outsiders would be so intrigued by, they'd pay an access fee.

At this stage, films were just one potential way that such material might be animated. Photomontages and factual environmental material about the best places to hunt or fish were also anticipated. We imagined visitors using their smartphones to photograph two-dimensional barcodes strategically placed on land that Karrabing members had rights to, prompting a webpage download. Then and there, in situ, participants might discover key items of local environmental knowledge or, for the adventure tourist, receive information about good places to fish and hunt. Perhaps they would enjoy a video stream about an aspect of Indigenous life, a Dreaming, or a neorealist fictional story about the ghosts of other lives lived there, about life under occupation from the time of early white settlement or what happened during a shared historical moment, such as the Japanese bombings in World War Two, when lands up and down the coast either side of Darwin were bombed over a period of eighteen months, to flush out American and Australian militia (Lea 2014a, 24–28).

Alternately, a sacred sites registration body like the Aboriginal Areas and Protection Authority[5] could select a data set for an area according to its secret sacred nature—essential documentation should future mining prospectors arrive and sacred sites need subsequent protection. Land management professionals such as ranger groups[6] would orient to other forms of metadata. Given their interest in invasive species (weeds, animals), fire management (managed burns and wildfires alike), the appearance of ghost nets on beaches and in waters, and environmental monitoring (soil, water, biodiversity), rangers might work with Karrabing members and *pay them*[7] to iteratively add information over time.

To help make this GPS/GIS, or augmented reality, project (metareferenced as "the project" in various Karrabing films) generate income and not just data, premium information would have a small purchase price, akin to purchasing media through iTunes or supporting a podcast's special extras through a subscription payment. The scheme needed to generate livelihoods that would join older and younger generations and tap into their many talents as hunters, builders, mechanics, storytellers, improvisers, rangers, analysts, comics, critics, and geographers. It also needed to be fun, to lure younger generations into caring about country (or anything at all): the alternatives—jail, one-off training, aimlessness, drinking, drugs, and stop-start uninspiring jobs—needed intercepting.

By being their own cultural entrepreneurs, revealing and holding back information on their own terms, the Karrabing also wanted what policy says it wants for them too: to create meaningful work; keep families intact and whole; quit dysfunctional community life; have reasons to believe in further education and training; become self-supporting; and attend to the consubstantiating conditions of their fundamental health and well-being by taking care of time-spiraling bodies and country. Their vision presumed a pluralism within policy communities, and genuine receptivity to forms of self-organizing Indigenous economic and cultural activities within the funding flows that such policy communities shepherd into place. In other words, the vision represents both continuing possibility and overoptimism about the truth of proclaimed policy ambitions for Indigenous people.

Escapes and entailments

Whatever the shape of the eventual Karrabing enterprise, it needed to enfold people's sweat and stories back into geographical sites, for ancestral lands were missing their memories and have been punishing contemporary populations in retaliation.[8] Karrabing forebears had been run off their country repeatedly during the killing years of cattle ranching and the slavery of subsequent mission times (Rose et al. 2011). If punitive raids and pestilent diseases didn't kill people, the settler state plied slower lethalities through the entrapments of its drugs (sugar, alcohol, tobacco), control and theft of water, blockades to hunting, and spatial detention. Karrabing forebears were compounded at one such internment camp, Delissaville (now Belyuen). Thus displaced, as vibrant people do, they set about re-creating place anew, transforming their dislocation into ontological belonging and new diplomacies, reading the "intensely interested" new world around them and setting "their analytic focus on the nature of the responsive relationship between themselves and the lands across which they traveled and in which they were interned" (Povinelli 2016b, 77). By "intensely interested," writes Povinelli,

they meant that every region of the world was pressuring existing forms of existence and creating new ones—one specific form was the European settlers who wanted space and goods that could be transformed into market values and who claimed that Indigenous people were merely breathing fossils in the way of progress. (Ibid.)

But such a dynamic relation between sentient, sensing, judging country and its inhabitants met with the force of settler misrecognition within the new black-letter policy constraint and opening known as the Aboriginal Land Rights (Northern Territory) Act 1976. The land rights policy process did not encode legal interest in the cultural means by which Indigenous people transformed myriad dislocations back into location. It did not recognize long-standing forms of socioecological responsiveness, which enabled people to effectively take new policy entailments into their own hands. Instead, an anthropological accounting of an abstracted and fixed idea of traditional knowledge was the barometer (Povinelli 2002, Vincent 2017). Across the NT, this fossilizing approach divided members of newly formed communities into winners and losers. Subsections of interconnected families and people were singled out as traditional owners and given the benefits and responsibilities of this new designation.[9] Feuds, rivalries, alliances, and new formations—such as the Karrabing Film Collective—are among the many entailments.

Before the land rights act radically changed worlds again, there were other major displacements. Back during World War Two, families were evacuated from the Delissaville compound to a new internment area known as Donkey Camp, hundreds of kilometers away on the Katherine River. Beginning on the morning of February 19, 1942, and continuing intermittently for the next eighteen months, the Japanese dropped more bombs and sank more ships between Delissaville and the port of Darwin than in Pearl Harbor, which was hit a mere three months before by the same commander, using the same squadrons (Lea 2014a, 17–23). The bombings prompted wartime emergency measures, using powers that would again come into view in 2007, when the Australian government likewise declared a state of emergency concerning Indigenous people. From early March 1942, all NT land north of Alice Springs was placed under military control. Nonconscripted white civilians were evacuated to southern ports, while Aboriginal slavery was continued anew as interned people were put again to labor: running cattle, tending market gardens, building fortifications, being abused sexually, leveling the way for roads, mattocking ditches, and more besides (Powell 1988, 204; Cowlishaw 1999).

On the night of September 19, 1943, Karrabing forebears escaped Donkey Camp and made the arduous journey back to their home country hundreds of kilometers away. They were caught and returned, and then escaped a second time, hiding from soldiers, other whites, enemy air raids, and the bloated dead bodies they saw floating in rivers and creeks (Lea 2014a, 27). This is explored in the film *Night Time Go* (2017). With a characteristic mix of drama and humor, history and satire, the film begins by hewing closely to the actual historical details of this heroic escape, but slowly turns to an alternate history in which a wide-scale Indigenous insurrection drives settlers out of the Top End of Australia altogether.

As it happened in legalized reality, far from being driven out, settlers multiplied in the postwar period, and Indigenous battles to repossess lost country likewise intensified in new forms: the weapons were no longer guns and poisons against spears and stealth, but legal claims and depositions. Following long civil agitation for land repossession, the Aboriginal Land Rights Act was the first attempt by an Australian government to legally recognize an Aboriginal system of land ownership and put into law the concept of inalienable freehold title. It was meant to be national legislation; it was confined to the Northern Territory. It was meant to restore lost title; it created new classes of propertied and dispossessed. It was meant to open country; it became a time-limited scramble for repossession. In the end, claimants had two decades (from inception in 1976 to 1997) to learn and perform what was required of them to go to court to reclaim some of their lands, lands that if won, would still be "over-regulated piecemeal concessions" (Moreton-Robinson 2015, xi).

A policy hauntology sits within these title battles, within rents and gashes that still slice through peoples' lives, down into the bones of families, one set against another (cf. Vincent 2017). Reflecting these painful title battles, at one point there were riots at Belyuen, and Karrabing families hid in their ceiling cavities before fleeing, fearing for their lives:

[O]n March 15, 2007, members . . . were threatened with chainsaws and pipes, watched as their cars and houses were torched, and their dogs beaten to death. Four families lost rare, well-paying jobs in education, housing, and water works. (Povinelli 2011a, n.p.)

At the time, police dismissed this terror as "tribal" and did not investigate. Perhaps, when Indigenous people are just a risk to themselves, it doesn't matter; but when their presence impacts on the privileged, they get police(d). Even so, the government's initial response to this displacement had been vaguely hopeful. The families were promised new housing, proper schooling, and better jobs at Bulgul, close to the mouth of the Daly River, a site that, though small and with meager to no civic infrastructure, was at least closer to their ancestral countries. As a founding Karrabing member Linda Yarrowin recalled this time to me,

In 2007, that's when we been fleeing from Belyuen. [We were] homeless people because we never had that house, you know, so we all had to live full house in Minmerrama [a public housing estate in Darwin] and then we all decided in wet season we just going to move to Bulgul [Daly River] and sleeping under the trees [in tents].

While families were living in small tents and waiting for the promised new housing, jobs, and schools, government policy just as swiftly changed, unleashing what felt like a new wave of violence. Aboriginal people could no longer receive funding for infrastructure on their customary country, but as part of the 2007 Intervention, were now told to shift to arbitrarily determined "growth towns," a newly invented category introduced to explain the government's latest bout of funding withdrawals here, arbitrary investments there (Markham and Doran 2015). Alternately, they could move to the welfare suburbs of the capital city, Darwin.

Producing neorealist fictional film projects to tell their stories and restore their sweat back into their traditional lands replaced the original project. Film pursuits enable members to reassemble in ways that do not suffocate who they are, that do not presuppose bountiful infrastructure or the moral bettering of that fictive category called "a community" (Lea and Povinelli 2018).

Making do with make-believe

Perhaps the augmented reality project as originally conceived was before its time. When the Karrabing first made representations of their enterprise vision, potential sponsors did not understand the possibilities of streaming material onto phones; instead they asked questions about whether Aborigines knew enough about computers to make such a thing work, or worried about the absence of Wi-Fi in remote areas, ignoring the global band of satellites geo-synchronizing around the nearby equator. At any rate, to raise money, the Karrabing needed to incorporate themselves as an officially registered body with the Office of the Registrar of Indigenous Corporations and register with the Australian Taxation Office as a "Deductible Gift Recipient Organisation." Before any films were made, we thus encountered the raced and classed differentiations embedded in agnostic procedural realms.

Making the corporation subject to the law of charities—essential for donors to be able to claim donations as a tax expense—was predicated on applicants having key infrastructures already secured. Technologies as neutral as a landline telephone proved essential when one is waiting for six hours on hold to secure a uniquely generated code to complete just one of the manifold application forms. The raced and classed nature of this may not be immediately clear. At least it wasn't clear to me, and I study bureaucratic formations as my academic lifework, so let me step it out.

A land line is a threatened species for many, but is particularly rare in the average Indigenous household. Prepaid cell phones are preferred precisely because of their actual neutrality: they do not presume the fixed address and stable income needed for service plans.[10] They can lie idle when there's no credit. But, back in the day, when someone with a cell phone was placed on a phone queue, charges were prohibitively expensive.[11] The phone queue itself also assumes affluence—people with the time and relevant literacy to forebear the inane loop of electronic messages and barely interpretable application processes. As Melissa Gregg (2018), a cultural analyst of temporal and productivity techniques for the self, reminds us, the ability to delegate waiting is a sign of classed, raced, and gendered privilege. There is an acute asymmetry between who waits and who can delegate or outsource their waiting. This is a patience-testing system that is simultaneously a sifting system. And this is to say nothing of who benefits most from being able to protect profits from taxation by claiming charitable losses.

Identifying the stratification effects of policy operations in such minutiae recalls two points. First, as Akhil Gupta notes, the commonly held notion of the state as a monolithic object, as an institution—what he calls its ontic status—is deceptive; or rather, the seemingly singular state is a magical illusion created out of thousands of humdrum, routinized practices, such as the pursuit of a tax form registration number (Gupta 2012, 55). Policy is acting when it directs the route that actions can take. And, second point, noting the minutiae of policy operations reminds us that phenomena that are not seen as policy issues—such as the 1-800 helpline number for setting up a nonprofit corporation with deductible recipient gift status—are more than tacit tests of resources and capacities. These minor processes that have no clear policy status reinforce privilege in the mode of feigning access to opportunities. After all, what is creating a tax break for giving financial support about, if not ensuring that the gift is no true debt for the giver?

Structured into these infuriatingly trivial mechanisms are deniable and denied distributional tributaries of privilege and their thoroughly dispersed cultivation. There are no threatened bodies or catastrophic events, but as David Graeber (2012, 109) has pointed out, there is an undertone of violence to the senselessness of bureaucratic procedures, which remains obscured in the abstractions of social scientific accounts.

At any rate, deep breath: making fictional films—originally envisioned as part of the catalogue of mixed-media items that paying consumers could download onto their smartphones as they toured Karrabing country—has since superseded the living library project as such—but not the ambition of engaging with continuing settler occupation in resistant terms. There was no official evaluation to redirect Karrabing efforts away from augmented reality and to fictional films, just a constant collective readjusting, activating new possibilities using relationships and networks within policy-practice-place intra-actions.

Karrabing films invariably comment on policy openings and closings without this being the explicit agenda. For the most part, everyone plays some version of themselves (including sometimes me, as the fumbling, helping, or intruding white person), drawing from real-life scenarios to show the resilience of people pushing through new and sedimented obstacles and hauntings with wicked humor and insistent endurance. Take *Windjarrameru, the Stealing C*nt$* (2015), the Karrabing's second major work, where who goes to jail for what kind of offence is the universal saga sitting behind a more immediate story of a group of young Aboriginal men who stumble across two cartons of beer in the bush and settle in for an impromptu party, unaware of the dangerous eddies they are now immersed in.

The film begins: Cameron, a young Indigenous ranger, sits, leaning against a tree in some scrub, flicking through his mobile phone in between looking up and squinting into the surroundings. We don't know what he is looking for, only that he is scanning and keeping a low profile. The click and impatient strumming of his thumb over the phone's screen, and his boredom, are the key orientations, until the scene shifts to an incoming group of age-mates, gleefully carting cases of beer. *Join us*, they sing out, *look, we found this beer!* Initially, Cameron shrugs them away. His task, whatever it is, is important, if slow moving. Eventually Cameron succumbs to the lure of fun with mates, explaining his prior distraction cryptically. We later learn they are all near a sacred site, which is simultaneously a contamination area filled with dumped military chemicals, and an illegal mine operation. Cameron was on the lookout for miners violating the site, but it is he who ends up being arrested.

As the youths enter an alcoholic haze—one sunbaked beer devoured, another can crushed, empties tossed over a cliff face to a beach below—plot tendrils gather and collide. The discarded cans cascade upon two senior men, Trevor and Darrell, who are on the sands below, mysteriously painting a danger sign on the rock face, warning people to stay out of the area. Trevor curses a drinker he recognizes as his nephew, but the young men ignore Trevor's protests. Instead, as the youths speculate about their bonus beer carton (was it left by campers or by miners?), their guesswork operates as a casual critique of the number of trespassers Indigenous people can expect on their country at any given moment in time.

The drinking continues. There are young male slurs about sex had or denied, and advice about what to expect in Berrimah jail, the largest detention center in the NT. This too is casually done. There is nothing out of the way in the young men swapping survival tales about prison. In the NT, *Windjarrameru*'s backdrop, Indigenous people make up 85 percent of the total prison population, but less than a third of the overall population (Northern Territory Government 2017). The people you might meet in jail come from all over the place, there for "acts intended to cause injury" (47 percent), sexual assault and related offences (11 percent), and "offences against justice procedures, government security and operations" (8 percent) (5–6). Everyone knows someone on probation, in detention, on parole, in community service. No one is unaffected, a fact underlined by the life-art-life relay that Jayden was also reenacting, taking part in a filmed drunken spree and improvisational jail talk while absconding from his remand conditions, aided and abetted by the helping white girl, Tess, in turn playing a hapless legal aid officer in the shoot.

Documenting biographical verities, reconceived as representative fictions, the drinkers show us there is no such thing as free beer. The angry uncle calls in the police to arrest the irritating boys, but initially the police only nab Cameron, who hadn't realized he was drinking with "thieves," while his comrades escape into the undergrowth, entering a barricaded area known for its poisonous contaminations. *The police won't follow us in here*, they reassure themselves, as they find a new cramped place to hide for the night; and they are right.

Two middle managers from the Windjarra Mining Corporation soon turn up, driving ominously slowly, their utility truck sporting the logo We Dig You. They don't want the police to inquire too closely into what Trevor and Darrell were doing painting warnings on the cliff face.

"You rang the police—what for?" the Windjarra managers demand of Trevor.

"Those mongrel shit faces were chucking a beer can at me," he answers, incubating his outrage.

Thus we learn that Trevor and Darrell are working on the sly, helping Windjarra Mining Corporation conduct illegal blasting. The uncles need to earn cash to repay the state the "$1,300 and 32 cents" and "$500" each respectively owes in fines; the real amounts these actors have actually accrued from public drinking, driving without a license, or driving an unregistered vehicle (Madden 2015; Povinelli 2016a).

As an aside, because I lack the space to elaborate properly,[12] liberal governments worldwide have boasted of cutting direct taxes. Under this pretence, prisons, aged care, child care, land title records, electricity, welfare, employment services, and multiple other public amenities have been privatized, outsourced, and converted into "user-pays" and other forms of rentier capitalism. Remnant service bureaus do less with less, as successive governments feign their low-taxing bona fides. Money is recouped indirectly, through semiprivatized fees and tolls, fines and penalties—seldom income adjusted or benchmarked against personal capacity to pay (Cooper 2018). The poorest and most service-dependent members of the community pay an exorbitant price in the regressive revenue-raising regimes they are suspended within. Even the forfeiture of court bonds can generate income in this mercenary complex (Seigel 2014, 2018).

The Windjarra mining managers, sinister behind their mirrored aviator glasses, watch the police, who, in turn, are watching for the escapees to leave the contaminated grounds. The mining representatives must ensure that the police do not accidentally discover what they've been doing in the area. They need to make sure Cameron's witnessing is not believable. As darkness descends, the young fugitives hiding in the contaminated swamp worry that they might die themselves, as surrounding *nyudj* (ancestral spirits) remind them that this sacred area is haunted from its maltreatment over time and is yearning for better care (Povinelli 2016b, chap. 3). Is it grog poison causing the boys' hallucinations, or radiation sickness, the intending country, or ghosts from all the bodies ground into this place in earlier invasions? In this way, the one space into which the police won't follow Indigenous people remains distinctively Indigenous, alive with sentience and memory, but also a site of ingested and emitting toxicity, troubling the distinctions between past and present, inside and out, life and not-life, and, I would add, policy and not-policy.

Time contracts and moves through this material. Present action is constantly circulated through and assessed by black and white state representations and public fantasies about "traditional" versus modern practices, even as ancestral creatures and their sacred areas (Dreamings, durlg, therrawen), are being decomposed for their mineral content and recomposed as composites of crushed beer cans, plastics, wire, and chemical effluents. (Povinelli 2016a, n.p.)

Come early morning, the fugitives yield, preferring police custody over the demands of their terrifying bolt-hole, a toxic hiding place that is nonetheless also a form of lacerated yet resilient Indigenous sovereignty, and a policy haunting too. Stoler (2008b) would call this the resistance to be found within the long durée of imperial ruination; Eve Tuck and C. Ree, the revenge that is a form of double wronging (2013, 654); and Avery Gordon, a reminder that "entire societies [are] haunted by terrible deeds," which are systematically denied by "every public organ of governance" (2008, 64).

With the boys locked up, a neophyte legal aid officer attempts to meet with their mothers and aunties to decipher the issues. To the officer's (my) ears, the boys' relatives are making incoherent claims. They're saying something about a conspiracy where beer is deliberately planted to thwart local Aboriginal evidence gathering about illegal mining in a sacred site; and something else about a husband failing his duties to a son he should have cared for—or is it his nephew?

These come as fragments toppling one over the other, half-audible, half-shouted, and the inexperienced lawyer can't work out the connections. If we know anything about this scene, we also know she will not be in the job long enough to ever join the dots; nor will she be directed to any detailed jurisprudence showing the material role of extraction activities within the commonplace of youth-crime prosecutions already clogging her backlog of files and cases in the underfunded Indigenous justice NGO she no doubt works for. As I have previously insisted, the microactions of such policy brokers and translators are highly consequential, whether they are wielding words or wrenches. For the usually shortened times they are in their roles, they will have to strain against rules, bending and questioning them, invoking other policies—such as privacy laws, building codes, occupational health or environmental protection regulations, sacred-site protections—to deter or propel favorable actions for the Indigenous people they are allying with. If they become killjoys by straining too hard to protest the austere rationing norms they are meant to comply with, they will likely turn over as quickly as the bureaucrats with whom they are wrangling in the tangled policy wilds. But will the neophyte lawyers have time to also grapple with the wider political economy of what they and their Aboriginal clients are embroiled within—to know that legacies of militarized extractivism lie behind grog gifts and toxic sovereignty? Unlikely.

On the ground, institutional allies like the confused lawyer are necessary, but insufficient. The policies that require young people to be mandatorily detained for evading police, resisting arrest, and stealing exist alongside policies that perfectly enable the desecration of sacred sites through mining activities, with symbolic reparations made, if they are made, in the insulting form of two Toyota Land Cruisers (PricewaterhouseCoopers 2016, 35). Another life-art couplet. Southwest of our film shoot, there was an Indigenous sacred site known as Two Women Sitting Down, a site that links with songlines all the way across to Kakadu in the northeast. For the Warramungu custodians, the story of this sacred site is of two female Dreaming figures, whose skin names were Namakili and Napanangka. One was a bandicoot and the other a type of marsupial rat (Butterly and Pepper 2017, 1326–1327). The bandicoot had only two children; the rat had many. Lonely bandicoot did the obvious and made to kidnap herself some children. The vicious fight that followed was so violent and prolonged, their bloody outpouring colored the manganese outcrops deep red. But most of their tracks had been destroyed in the 1950s by mining extraction of surface material, leaving the Two Sisters Sitting Down as the last intact record of their travails, containing rocky outcrops where the two had staged a separate brawl over bush tucker fruits. (They were typical siblings, really, fighting all the time.)

OM (Manganese) Ltd was fully aware of the significance of the Two Sisters and had negotiated careful access around the site at its Bootu Creek Manganese mine. But then, after a quick meeting with a single Indigenous representative and a junior legal officer from the Northern Land Council (far from a properly negotiated approval process), in full awareness of the desecration risks, OM Mining set off an explosion near the base of the site twenty-six meters below ground level, tumbling seventeen thousand cubic meters (the equivalent of four hundred loads of a two-trailer road train) of ore, soil, and vegetation into the pit, destroying the Two Sisters forevermore.

Institutional killjoys within the Aboriginal Areas Protection Authority (AAPA) took OM (Manganese) to court and won. The company was fined $150,000 as a "stern warning" to others.[13] More shocking than the trivial caution is the fact that this was the *first* and to this point the *only* successful prosecution AAPA has been able to mount since its inception in 1979; a prosecution that was swiftly followed with threats of AAPA's defunding and, in 2016, a review of its mandate (PricewaterhouseCoopers 2016). OM Holdings Ltd, by contrast, has become one of the top performers in the Australian stock exchange.[14]

Mesopolitics and policy hauntology

Isabelle Stengers, a Belgian chemist turned philosopher, provides some tools to conceptualize what this entangled policy activation space is. Frustrated with the perennial micro-macro toggle within critical analysis, Stengers refers instead to the potential in between, within what she calls mesopolitics. Because Stenger is a chemist, her illustrations concern the physical properties of materials and practices. As soon as one starts looking closely at materials and practices within a milieu, she suggests—understanding what makes them bend or fatigue, have limits or be elastic, be sticky or fluid—by definition, one needs to move beyond macro and micro terms. To use her words, the meso "concerns not matter, but material. Why does glue stick? Why do metals tend to stress and break? This is a science of the interstices and the cracks" (Stengers 2009, n.p.).

Analytically, the concept of stickiness conveys the idea that humans are not free, autonomous agents operating separately from situationally specific socio-material contexts—or, as Stengers prefers, milieus—but nor are circumstances permanently "stuck." Movement might be burdened, but movement is still possible. Stengers continues:

[E]ach time, the meso affirms its co-presence with a milieu. This sticks—that's a relation to a milieu. This breaks, this bends, this is elastic—that implies an action undergone. Every material is a relation with a milieu. (Stengers 2009, n.p.)

Paraphrasing, as we attend to the specificity of different policy-shaped situations and the capacities or potential "good" each situation holds, we are obliged to grope our way through the middle, through the sticky, slightly malleable milieu in between. This is what Stengers refers to as "the meso."[15] Individual transactional, micropolitical, or street-level bureaucracy encounters—such as when a young man must genuflect to police to complete paperwork about his conduct requirements in between an assault and its judgment—are happening all the time, all over the world, in infinite variations and contexts. Part of their tenor of inevitability, what makes us shrug our shoulders with fatalistic resignation, is the well-socialized sense that this *is* what poverty (racism, sexism, inequality, homophobia, anthropocentrism, overcrowding, ecological degradation, animal cruelty . . .) everywhere feels like, is like, will always be like. But *the meso*: this is about creation and possibility, about what can yet be made of each different milieu, when people act together; think together; pay attention; strive toward different outcomes through experiment, play, probative analysis, grit, and determination.

As Karrabing examples demonstrate, with the right kind of playful techniques and tactics, collective desire and striving can transform into an activating force, never quite transcending the stranglehold of late liberalism, but enough to bend or stretch situational possibilities in new and capacitating directions. Indigenous sovereignty is neither unconstrained nor ever eradicated. Choice remains fettered, and yet, with coalitions, choices can also be activated. Alternate world-makings are always simultaneously hindered and enabled by sociomaterial conditions and forces. This constitutive tension of immanence and constraint "offers an opening to the possibility in the present by embracing the fundamental incompleteness of power and persons alike" (Bessire and Bond 2014, 448).

Stengers's concepts help account for what is being transacted in the enacting of alternatives, and what might make pressing for alternatives hard, beyond a vague implication that people will hit walls in otherwise inevitable systems of injustice and inequality and rapacious settler extractivism. The meso concept is productive for thinking through the detailed efforts that every attempt to realize the potential within each policy-imbued milieu involves, speaking directly to my probe "Can there be good policy?" However, read in isolation, Stengers's conceptual framing seems to position milieus within singular moments in time. To cite Bruno Latour, not one known for pulling political histories into his analyses, "to say that every local interaction is 'shaped' by many elements already in place, doesn't tell us anything about the origin of those elements" (2005, 194). Neither stickiness nor slickness, ease or tension, are neutral properties of timeless matter. The efforts required to wrest benefits against the grain of policy norms suggest an overdetermined *prior* grain or, better, other oiled and other sharded relationalities. Digging into Stengers's work further, perhaps her separate call to think beyond capitalist imperatives (2012) opens to these missing (hauntological) dimensions.

With Phillipe Pignarre, Stengers has explored what keeps us spellbound by capitalism; how it comes to appear inevitable and unstoppable; how it attaches to us, binding us to its programs (Pignarre and Stengers 2011). Other possibilities are turned aside, made difficult, curtailed, as we are lured in and entrapped by capitalism's enchantments. Thinking of being spellbound, we might consider settler colonial justifications of ongoing dispossession as itself a kind of possession, as a way being possessed, of being put under a spell and alienated from other ways of thinking and being.[16] It takes new spells to weaken the force of these powerful ontological bindings, and they cannot be cast by individuals operating on their own. Alliances matter.

What might be called spellbinding can also be called haunting, depending on one's standpoint. Invoking the spectral can bend social policy ethnography toward the hauntings that policy also bequeaths as trace effects, residues, and sediments, within any present-time "milieu." Recall that real ghosts haunted the women's toilets of the Chan Building, from where the Strategic Indigenous Housing and Infrastructure Program was coordinated (chapter 2). Women were afraid to enter the ablution area, sensing something apparitional in there, gaping yet hidden. Who knows what happened in the corridors of that old building, or on its soil prior, that a ghost might still be wandering there? For women who police their physical movements based on absent-present threats every single day, it is not too hard to think of possible scenarios.

Policy hauntings thus might literally refer to spectrally inhabited bureaucratic spaces that are animated by invisible yet felt forces. And there are metaphorical phantoms. Let's not forget that the minister who banned my presence from that haunted Chan Building issued her edict as a verbal warrant, becoming an apparition in another guise. Unauthored bureaucratic edicts have their own spectral powers.

Hauntings can also refer to the ways policies past and present are physically incorporated, having (insidiously or noisily) seeped into lives, affecting probable destinies and shaping overall circumstances, if not immutably then certainly as a powerful stimulus. Individuals are hindered or facilitated by the ghosts of policy pasts manifesting, for instance, as privileged or underfunded schooling, as life-sustaining potable water or water so contaminated that deaths are inevitable. Policies past and current adhere to bodies and things, making privilege feel earned and inequality feel natural, the product of personal destiny and pure choice.

Perhaps a more familiar way of understanding policy hauntings, at least since Foucault, is to consider the dominant paradigms that are encoded within black-letter policy documents or, as I have referred to them, within policy artifacts.[17] Policy vocabularies reflect (are shackled by) their own deeply invested socioeconomic logics. They require all things (animate and inanimate) to serve the settlers' currently dominating form of existence, as a necessary condition of citizenship within the nation-state. Policy emphases and abandonments aggregate around an inherited and taken-for-granted cultural core. It is not simply paperwork about or served to Indigenous people that encodes what happens to whom, how, for what kind of money. Policy involves paperwork—the artifactual—but it is also an inheritance (which I have termed hauntological) that shapes conditions of possibility in the present and future. As a cultural formation, settler policy is an ancient mode of draining lifeworlds entirely legally, without visible violence or notable theft, via contracts, grants, regulations, negotiations, standards, accountabilities, and enumeration, and the avoidance, thwarting, attenuation, noncounting, or perennial bastardization of all these mechanisms, which together constitute a settler colonial policy hauntology that Indigenous people continually weather (Lea, Howey, and O'Brien 2018, Neu 2000).

Here we might think about files, and what is kept in and what is missing from them (Vismann 2008). Forms, and what they do and don't count (Hull 2012). Archives, and what they attract and repel (Yale 2015). Regulations, and what they protect or safeguard: a river occasionally (Neale 2017) or, more commonly, "deregulated" banking with financial regulations directed into banking's profitable favor (Sikka and Lehman 2015). And I would include in this mini-gathering myriad other forms of policy blindness, where phenomena are not investigated in order that they cannot occupy a named policy existence—the levels of lead, cadmium, and other contaminants in groundwater where mining and people coexist being one such institutionally endorsed sightlessness (Kristensen and Taylor 2016).[18]

Policy hauntology encompasses these kinds of governance assumptions and adds something more. Tottering infrastructure and hollowed and gutted regulatory supervision are policy inheritances too, reflecting relational histories of human and other agencies. These relational histories include the gestational and corrosive contributions of water, soil, contaminants, human and nonhuman critters and their unstable, shifting sustenance systems—representing an intra-active metabolism with different ingredients reappearing and disappearing over time. Policy hauntings exist even where they don't seem to. One day you might push against foam-filled wall cladding and have it spill cockroach leavings, for the wall's insides have been eaten hollow by termites welcomed in by their friend, electrolyte water. Water pushes into weaknesses in buildings shaken by storms then left porous by the baking of hot days and the slaking of more rain; a permeability that can be made more, or less, fragile by the quality of policy-fed interventions and resurrections. By the quality, that is, of meso-level (in)attention at multiple points in a policy's mutations as it intra-acts with the environments that summon and authorize policy interventions.

And then there are the hauntings of past violations that some Indigenous people might carry inside themselves as secret wounds stemming from micro- and macropolicy: from the abuses of a disdainful school clerk to the heart-wrenching moment when a family is evicted, merging with inherited memories of murders and massacres haunting contaminated swamps, still too close in time for emotional neutering; and always, a sense of a judging sentient environment that might be pleased, or likely disappointed, with a person's level of attunement and care within the meso of a particular clan member's kin and country.[19] In Karrabing hands, settler policy operates like viral matter, with discarded ideas and jettisoned programs from long ago still able to intercept contemporary lives, mingling with new openings and foreclosings. Karrabing members' probative work and counterfactuals show that the contemporary is not "now" in the singular but a composite formation of multiple times. The contaminated swamp our fugitives hide in overnight is the real site of a real asbestos dumping ground, shoveled there from leftover military installations, from and through which new connections with ecologically altered and somewhat hostile ancestral forces are also forged.

As untrained actors and amateur production crew, the Karrabing have been using techniques members would say are "story but true": taking things from life that could have happened to challenge configurations of "the truth." People are shown to be many things at once: hunters; families; married couples; loving parents; lovers in and out of love; cohorts squabbling across the generations; welfare beneficiaries and public housing tenants; jobholders; students; hospital patients; bush people and city people; drinkers; smokers; fighters—and people who, obliged to their country, get things done, when push comes to shove. The improvisational realism of film scripts mirrors the makeshift workarounds of everyday life, where obstacles include jail time, hospital episodes, negotiating lost bank-card details, the spatial tethering of a court order or a suspended driver's license, and incarceration or eviction from accumulating fines. Members are resilient without this being a romantic way of being, as policy hauntings render both city and bush life equally precarious.

Mesoleverage

Karrabing mesopolicy effects are both small and heroic. Jayden didn't end up in jail, and Karrabing's work is reaching new world audiences. And although being taken up by international curators does not resolve landlessness, poverty, illnesses, incarcerations—that is, although it doesn't end policy entrapment—film productions energize an ongoing analytics of this entrapment. Karrabing counterfactuals serve as a discovery process about what exists and why, even if only through second-order reenactments of the madness and injustice of much settler colonial policy, "faking it with the truth" (Biddle and Lea 2018).

Still, for all its life-imitating-art-imitating-life notes of hyperrealism, Karrabing filmography is not principally about one-to-one documentary representation. Rather, the films are a mechanism to explore alternative explanations for things that were, are, and yet might be. Scripting films, members get to imagine

Figure 8. Elizabeth A. Povinelli, Karrabing Annual General Meeting. By Joel Tarling and Tess Lea.

what might have happened if Indigenous people in the north had truly used the chaos of World War Two to rid their lands of settlers (the fear that had seen them impounded in the first place)? Other segments show that the environmental violations that are so dreaded by climate change analysts are already here, as in wetlands filled with slabs of abandoned asbestos cladding, likewise war legacies.[20] In Karrabing film treatment, these contamination zones are also sites of irradiation that sicken bodies but provide a toxic protection too. The films offer policy critique without addressing any singular policy, by depicting policy-saturated environs with their everyday resistances and affordances. Karrabing films and lives do not connect neatly to chronological policy history but to spiraling time, policy hauntologies in the ambient surroundings, and the possibilities of the meso.

As we sat sketching out new storyboard possibilities and corporation business on bits of canvas and cardboard, with plastic milk crates and empty fry-

Figure 9. A training center. By Joel Tarling and Tess Lea.

ing-oil drums as furniture, a fleet of Toyota Land Cruisers circled a single-story air-conditioned building nearby. I was curious. What was going on over there?

This was the training center, its keys denied to us. That day it was hosting a gathering of functionaries to plot the education, training, and employment needs of "the community" as we sat in the dirt and heat and activated the same issues. Our apartness was real, yet fictive too, for we are enjoined, not only in an ostensibly shared focus but through the transnational tributaries creating that wagon circle of Toyotas and the well-salaried bodies within.

Karrabing work explores the flows that connect colonial extractive industries with shifts in schemes for community development through such devices as the provision of public housing and tenancy reforms, welfare control, education, or training and employment programs. Without being explicitly policy focused, for that is my concern, not theirs, Karrabing work nonetheless shines a torch on social policy unfurlings in urban, regional, and remote settings, moving from microethnographic to macrolevel accounts of the connections between Indigenous circumstances and the welfare of others in Australia and supranationally. Their successful reassertion of a probative analysis of why things are as they are and what they are becoming operates in the meso. Karrabing work unpicks taken-for-granted faiths in the key institutional forms of betterment— such as the provision of housing, or enterprise facilitation—through the analysis that takes place beforehand, when improvising, and once a film assumes new forms of life as a product for unknown viewers. As Povinelli has put it,

Perhaps the central purpose of Karrabing's films is to discover what we never knew we knew by hearing what we say in moments of improvisation. We suddenly see what we have been saying, what we have been sensing. But knowing something is not equivalent to solving something if by solving we seek an intelligible action. (Povinelli 2015b, n.p.)

Povinelli's conclusion about the importance of hesitation—not promising to problem-solve in any normative sense—points to my lingering proposition, to the "no" of good social policy: namely, that the militarily enabled conditions of global extractive trade subtending human existence, especially but not only in countries like Australia, remain to be reckoned with.

Interlude V

After Gayle Woodford's murder, everything changed. Nganampa Health Council immediately adopted a community escort system, which stops community members going directly to a nurse's residence after hours without officially designated company. It might not have made a difference for Gayle. Her reasons for going beyond the security cage encasing her home, without her clinic bag or keys, still in her pajamas, are unknowable, and the only remaining witness is unreliable. In *R v. Dudley Davey* (No. SCCRM-17–50), heard June 8, 2017 in the South Australian Supreme Court, Dudley's untrustworthiness is made clear.

"It is not easy to say exactly how these events unfolded," Justice Ann Vanstone concluded, directing her remarks at Davey:

What caused Ms Woodford to leave the security of the house is a matter of inference rather than direct proof. It seems clear from the material I have about the care she took for her safety and from what Ms Woodford was wearing that you must have tricked her into opening the security cage. Perhaps you made a false claim about the need for medical assistance related to your grandmother. But I am satisfied beyond reasonable doubt that you must have immediately overpowered her. She would not have left willingly with you, dressed as she was, without her nurse's bag, or even her house keys.

Even so, the new escort system was an action Nganampa could introduce, and, who can tell, it may help in future. Under pressure from journalists and nurse-safety advocates, the South Australian government additionally introduced the Health Practitioner Regulation National Law (South Australia) (Remote Area Attendance) Amendment Act 2017, or as it is known more popularly, Gayle's Law.

Under this act, which first came into effect on December 12, 2017, health practitioners responding to out-of-hours or unscheduled callouts for emergency treatment in remote areas must be accompanied by a second responder.

The act's original scope was telling. Initially, Gayle's Law applied exclusively to regions with Indigenous-controlled health organizations, where staff funding is provided by the national, not the South Australian, government (figure 10). This clearly made Aboriginal people the absolute threat, and not drug-addled or psychopathologically violent people in general, or notoriously violent mining towns in particular. As of November 2019—after two years of intensive lobbying, letter writing, and agitation from Gayle's Law proponents—the act now defines *remote* more comprehensively.[1] The revised act does not align "remoteness" with the Australian Statistical Geography Standard,[2] but introduces a different boundary, capturing the regions where Indigenous people dominate. Violence is still given a racialized character through a flexible rearrangement of policy definitions.

The act is even more difficult to decipher when it comes to other contingencies. What happens when a patient needs to be evacuated by the Royal Flying Doctor Service and the airstrip needs to be cleared for landing, because of recent rains or the possibility of camels, donkeys, or kangaroos on the dirt runway? If the nurse stays with the patient and the "second responder" leaves to clear the airfield, they are technically in breach of the act. What if patients can't be collected at all (given that not all places offer night-safe airfields)? Who stays with the patient, who drives to collect the evacuation personnel 50 kilometers, 100 kilometers, 200 kilometers, away? Say a grandparent brings a suffocating infant, nearing death, a hard sweet lodged in its throat, but the second responder is resting at home, on call but not immediately there. Should the nurse treat the baby instantly or say no, you must wait, as I need to have a second staff member beside me before I can provide emergency care? Does the baby die for the rule to be followed, or is the rule expected to be broken? If a rule is broken and a nurse is attacked, where is liability assigned in the run for cover to follow?

And what of uncertified Aboriginal health workers: Are they included under the provisions of the act, or not? In my reading (I am not a lawyer), if Aboriginal health workers are not fully accredited, they do not meet the criteria of "health professional" under the act. Naturopaths and masseurs are included, but the group most likely to experience violence—Indigenous people themselves—are most likely to be excluded. Separately we can note that getting Aṉangu candidates through the full health worker accreditation process has become formidably difficult. In former times, Nganampa Health Council operated as a registered training organization (RTO) and was thus able to supervise health worker train-

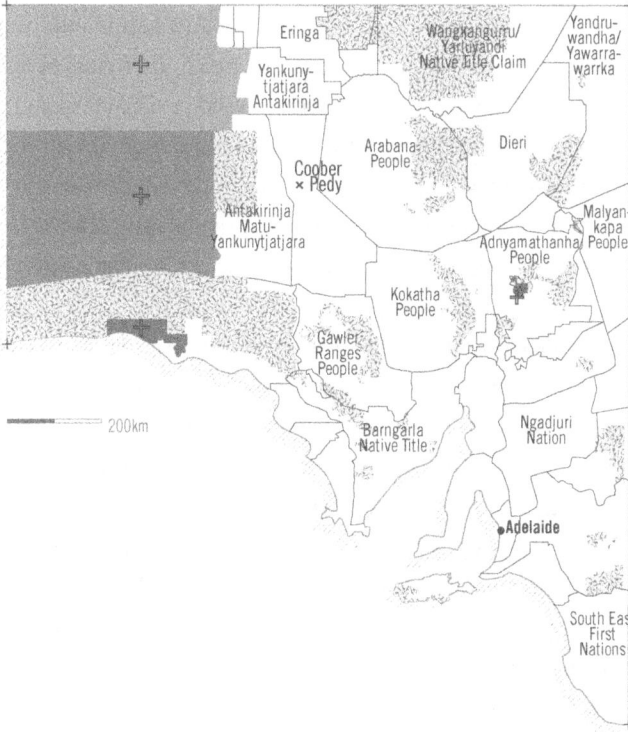

Figure 10. The original danger zone. Map by M. Barbagallo.

ing in situ. Thirty years of such training support has not left the council with a brigade of fully qualified health workers. At certain stages in the process, alphabetic literacy and numeracy skills increasingly transcend practical skills, and Aṉangu candidates are left behind. Then, a few years ago, Nganampa found the costs of meeting the national government's tightened accreditation requirements for RTOs too high (a regulatory tightening that reflects another policy entailment, from a miserable industry squeezing money out of migrants for fake diplomas). So now Aṉangu candidates must leave the APY Lands and study alone in Adelaide, which means they don't. At any rate, most Aboriginal health workers on the Lands are excluded from the safety provisions of Gayle's Law.

Back when John Singer was still chair of the National Aboriginal Community Controlled Health Organisation (NACCHO) (he resigned in November 2018), he had hammered the organization's point that the health sector is the country's single largest employer of Aboriginal and Torres Strait people outside of government.

"Twenty years ago, thirty years ago, when we first started, Aboriginal people [were] coming in as Aboriginal health workers. Now we got a few Aboriginal doctors. We got nurses. Aboriginal nurses. We got Aboriginal CEOs. Who else can show that or demonstrate that they've been able to develop that over the last twenty, thirty years, in a national setting? No one!

"So that's the stuff that I am pushing coz no one knows about that unique setup we've got. We are the only ones with a national footprint. We have pathways from welfare to employment. A lot of us, a lot of our staff, come from unemployment into that health service.

"Instead of making out that the Business Council of Australia, or whoever, that them having an Aboriginal employment plan means something, when—that's just bullshit. Small business can't do it either. They just only about families, you know. They only have the capacity to recruit two, three people. So, who or what else are you looking at? What, Twiggy [Andrew Forrest] putting his hand up to employ five hundred people to go to work, get smashed, visit hookers on the way home [from mining jobs]?"[3]

John is not alone in thinking that this is what much-vaunted mining jobs amount to, viewed ecologically. Occupying a postnatural environment of isolated men's camps, mining towns, time-lapsed airport transits, and no-frills licensed premises, mine workers inhabit a pharmacologically altered, temporally jagged human landscape that might not be the panacea for Indigenous impoverishment it is claimed to be. Criminologist Kerry Carrington has tracked such hypermasculine spaces over decades (Carrington, McIntosh, and Scott 2010; Carrington and Scott 2008). In one Western Australian mining community, her team found a violent crime rate at 2.3 times the national average (Carrington, Hogg, McIntosh, and Scott 2012). "The workers then get bused to these pubs that are surrounded by wire mesh, they drink hard and get plastered, get into fights, sleep it off and go again," Carrington told journalists (Fenech 2010) (and John Singer separately said to me, using different words).

Aboriginal community-controlled health services, he still reckons, are a national answer to the constant call for Indigenous pathways out of welfare. This is the model national policymakers should think with, hesitate about de-funding, and deliberately promote and sponsor. But back at Nganampa Health Council, the reality of having entry-level positions recognized as portals to se-cure and sustainable employment in hard and isolated areas confronts a more immediate organizational need: that of attracting and retaining resources for any services at all.

Whichever way one looks at it, more resources are required in the fallout from 'Gayle's Law'. Any service provider that fails to meet the requirements set out in the new nurse-safety regulations cannot be contracted to provide health services. But even though Gayle's Law exists, funding for it doesn't. The policy impacts flowing from the brutal slaying of remote-area nurse Gayle Woodford in March 2016 are at once everywhere and nowhere: already a hauntology, lin-gering, shaping, and not fully materializing. John Singer hardly needs to tell me that there's little happening politically to give hope of recurrent funding for staff positions any time soon. I can see it in Nganampa's preoccupation with retaining a new general manager (the Health Service had gone through three recruitment rounds since the murder) and with holding on to its old people in local residential aged-care accommodations.

After eighteen months of working through a lawyer, the South Australian Fire Service, Housing Department certifiers, and various government officials, *Tjilpiku Pampaku Ngura*, Nganampa's aged-care facility, now boasts an extra water tank and new fire-alert panels. It fully meets accreditation requirements. But having solved the issue of fireproofing to keep the doors open, the facility is now running at a loss from providing round-the-clock staffing. The federal min-ister for aged care, Ken Wyatt, had forwarded Nganampa's written request for staff funding to the Remote and Aboriginal and Torres Strait Islander Aged Care

Service Development Assistance Panel (SDAP). SDAP comprises "suitably qualified organisations engaged by the Department to provide specialist advice and assistance to eligible aged care providers." (The multinational consultancy firm KPMG is a member.[4]) Two "panel" consultants visited the APY Lands, requested additional data, and added to email backlogs, before helpfully confirming that *Tjilpiku*'s expenses have indeed risen more than the income received.

Thus Nganampa's jewel-in-the-crown service, a remote-area residential aged-care facility—one that already does what advocates are calling for in wanting services like renal dialysis made available closer to home—is now to be outsourced, likely to a provider headquartered in either Perth or Adelaide. The longevity that should have given Nganampa confidence in its community-controlled model has instead seen this powerful organization show increasing signs of fatigue and fatalism, as it battles to survive.

Actually, it is not true to say that the minister's eventual visit to the Lands back in May 2017 yielded nothing, I've been wryly corrected. It appears that Minister Wyatt was particularly captured by a side story of vaccines and medicines sometimes decaying in refrigerators due to occasional power outages. In June 2018, a surprise arrived in Nganampa's service agreement. In the paperwork, an additional $314,000 appeared as an orphan line item without specification. Could this be recurrent funding for nursing staff, heeded at last?

Fruitless phone calls to Commonwealth finance officers in Adelaide escalated to the most senior bureaucrat in charge of Indigenous health in Canberra. The money was for . . . drum roll . . . diesel generators for each clinic. Ah. But still, might it be diverted to the more urgent purpose of staff salaries? No, department officers advised. It was a one-off to protect those pharmaceuticals.

This is where Gayle's Law sits, somewhere between ghosts and generators, in the netherworld of wild policy, with its relentless turbulence of intervention and neglect, funding largesse and tightfistedness, and a foundational refusal to resource Indigenous issues any more than must be done, given the lack of any true national imperative to do so. It shows the strength of continuing Indigenous refusal, that such profound policy inadequacy and quiet voiding of the conditions for living well remain insufficient grounds for defeat.

Chapter 5

Militarized social policy

It took me a while to see the relation between militarism, extractivism, and Indigenous social policy. Just as "the geopolitical context in which anthropology grew to maturity" has been largely ignored as the discipline's routine reflection premise (Gusterson 2007, 157), so too anthropologists of Indigenous Australia do not ordinarily make militarism and its tributaries in transnational trade and long-distance logistics their object of study. State policy categories for describing the most determining influences—assimilation policy, self-determination policy, and so forth—tend to be favored instead (Lea 2012a). The Northern Territory National Emergency Response of 2007, infamously marshaled into being by a former army major, Mal Brough, warranted much critical commentary on the hyperpaternalistic colonial heraldry associated with deploying army personnel to enforce domestic policy (Watson 2009, Stringer 2007). But where a uniformed military involvement is not on conspicuous display, the conditioning background presence of a military political economy within Indigenous social policy is less often analyzed.[1]

Nor did ideas about contemporary militarization sit inside my journals and transcripts, awaiting release through close analysis and pattern hunts. I had somehow managed to undertake fieldwork in multiple sites over many years—with different organizations, individuals, and family groups, tracking the impact of Indigenous health, education, housing, infrastructure, and other social policies across cities, suburbs, and settlements—all the while ignoring what these policies were geostrategically embedded in. All the while ignoring what *I* was geostrategically embedded in, what enabled *my* presence. By which I do not simply mean the conditions of white academic privilege and of being non-Indigenous in a settler colonial nation, but rather the extensive infrastructures subtending my existence or, more accurately still, the militarily enabled territories and technologies of extraction I/you/we depend on (Belanger 2018,

4; Akhbari 2017). As I write this, my fingers plod over a sophisticated piece of technology that comes to me via convoluted journeys: quartz chips and carbon (coal) are extracted from pits, and freighted along trade routes long established by military treaty, to be smelted in an electrical furnace to 2,000° C to form molten silicon and carbon dioxide; this material is in turn purified of sludge (its toxicities to reenter another part of the environmental chain) to become industrial-grade silicon ingots that travel to another refining company and are combined with hydrochloric acid to form trichlorosilane, a volatile liquid that is repeatedly distilled and purified, then converted to polysilicon blocks that travel to a wafer fabrication facility to become the silicon chips that are the base for microchips to come. The plastic journey, the rubber journey, the cable journey, the labor issues are part of the genealogy for this academic tech, all of which can be simultaneously rendered as a militarized entanglement: the computing know-how, the presence of the internet, the logistical techniques, the secured trade routes, the extraction "rights." This chapter necessarily scoots over quite a bit of historical and sheer geographic space as twentieth-century uranium, manganese, and military research and security concerns are taken in, to argue that militarized trade enjoins my conditions of affluence to the extractivism that drives Indigenous social policy, writ large. In summary, the chapter sketches our geostrategic conditions of possibility, relating these conditions to Indigenous policy dysfunction and my own existential investments in the foundations of Indigenous inequality. It asserts a connection between the technologies of existence that I depend on and the extractive complex that state-sanctioned aggression is designed to reinforce.

My slow dawning

Although the beginnings of self-cognition are notoriously hard to pinpoint, I am going to say that my recalibration toward recognizing that the most consequential Indigenous social policies have military kin started on Groote Eylandt. Having been evicted via spectral instruction from Minister Macklin out of the public-private sector headquarters of the Strategic Indigenous Housing and Infrastructure Program in the haunted Chan Building (chapter 2), I had relocated to a new vantage point on Groote. Australia's third-largest island was host to the most expensive round of SIHIP housing, out of all the intended communities, and the policy translators battling on the ground with government officials and contractors flying in and out with increasingly erratic survey and construction

plans were happy to have me ethnographically document their exhausting brokerage efforts.

Viewed retrospectively, one set of fieldnote entries documents a slow
dawning point. They capture a fragment of a story about roads, quarries, and
Indigenous enterprise (see also Lea 2016). Andy Irvine and Jeff Green, two contractors working with the Anindilyakwa Land Council (ALC), and key allies for
my ethnographic efforts, were in the thick of a negotiation with six government
officers, all men, variously qualified in engineering, town planning, and project
management, aged somewhere between their late twenties and mid-thirties,
judging by their well-nourished, well-protected bodies. They had flown to the
island the day before on a chartered light aircraft, stayed overnight in tropical
bungalows at the luxurious Dugong Beach Resort, and were now discussing a
potential gravel contract.

Andy had recently helped establish a subsidiary enterprise to the ALC's
investment arm, Groote Eylandt and Bickerton Island Enterprises (GEBIE),
known as GEBIE Civil and Construction (GCC). A new road joining the communities of Umbakumba and Angurugu was in the offing, with Anindilyakwa funding forming the majority contribution, supplemented by government financing.
There is a complicated backstory to why Indigenous Australian citizens often
must pay for civic amenities, which can be summarized as a compounding
extraction model: extractive mining extracts compensation payments, partial
return of which is necessary to further extract partial provision of government
services. (A separate book is needed on these substitution effects.) At any rate,
GCC planned to run and sell gravel from quarries to be established around the
island, to sell back to any entities engaged in cement making, road construction, or general infrastructural repair and maintenance, with the forthcoming
Umbakumba–Angurugu road in sight as their launch project.

The contract negotiations had stalemated. Days flowed into weeks, weeks
into months. The government officers now wanted to see a full business plan
from GCC before embarking on the procurement spadework needed at their
end to arrange a direct tender. For GCC, this sounded like yet more prevarica-
tion, after years of government urging on the need to create sustainable remote-
area enterprises based on private sector models. To establish an Indigenous-run
quarry and related road construction and maintenance business, the new
company would need to purchase expensive plant from Japan and elsewhere,
freight it to the island, and do the work to have a combination of credentialed

and in-training workers ready to hand, before the monsoon season made timely commencement impossible. Their efforts would be fruitless if immediate future work related to the new road was not guaranteed.[2] Trucks, hauling vehicles, excavators, graders, and rollers, once assembled, would lie idle, costing rather than making money. Without a direct tender, and soon, the only other organization poised to supply plant, gravel, and skilled personnel at scale for the promised road was GEMCO, the Groote Eylandt mining company, providers of the cheapest and most productive manganese operation in the world.

It was the sort of conundrum that fills my journals. The state constantly urges Indigenous groups to emulate the liberal capitalist economy to survive on something other than mining royalties, government grants, or welfare payments; but the criteria for doing so seem tailored for permanently imperfect realization of any local vision or need. The obstacles are always defensible. The bureaucrats' demand for a business plan is completely reasonable, inarguably rationalizing delay while meeting the aesthetics of transparency. But in curating the imperfectability of Indigenous policy completion—be it through foot dragging, microimpediments, fantasy investments in rebadged programs, overambition, unrealistic deadlines, rationing disguised as eligibility criteria, proposing business possibilities in premonopolized sectors, or [insert diagnosis]—the rhetorical push for market simulations to promote Indigenous wellbeing mimics the essence of consumer capitalism itself. Just as the next object of consumer desire promises, but can never deliver, complete psychosocial fulfillment (Taussig 2012), the perfect unrealizability of Indigenous policy compels deeper bureaucratic inveiglement, in the endless search for that time, always around the corner, when the promised scheme truly delivers (Lea 2008).

In this way, the futility of policy realization can be thought of as cellular mitochondria that are permanently powering governmental reproduction (see also Ferguson 1990). The state will always be needed while soever Indigenous fault or deficit is thought to exist. As I have argued, here and elsewhere, the point of social policy writ large is survival of the apparatus of policymaking, rather than the success or otherwise of individual policies as such; and in relation to Indigenous issues, this is tied to the ongoing rights to do things on and to Indigenous lands and waterways. It thus makes sense that the arena of Indigenous (and perhaps any) social policymaking is far from the coherent and orderly myth of political science caricature. Governance is not a transient formation. Acknowledging this we can also say, by definition of any intra-active matter, that governance is a mobile, entropic assemblage, not a fixed one, which implies innate instability through the very motions set in play—even if the point is to be maintained in place as a seemingly permanent and inevitable presence.

My scribbled field notes caught the cut-and-thrust of Andy's meeting with the six officials. "We need to see your full business plan to have confidence, specifying capability, sustainability, key objectives, the Indigenous employment targets, in as much detail as possible," they said, to Andy's repeated requests for corresponding assurances that a contract would then be forthcoming, in this seasonally dependent place where a year is not really a year.

"What's in the ground will provide the specs," Jeff muttered furiously as we later drove to one of the proposed quarry sites, traveling in separate cars. "They [the government officers] think they're the ones wielding the stick. But it is the dirt that's in charge."

The ridgeline we head to is a place where Jeff, a man with no patience for bureaucracy but with deep gravel expertise, believes that the dirt holds the most promise. It offers what he calls "floaters": rocks sitting on or near the surface, turned into laterite through extensive weathering, ready to be crushed and compacted into road material. A small rectangular pit roughly the size of a twenty-five-meter pool has already been scraped clear of trees and shrubs; and we watch while the grader driver, Wally, directs the spiral probe of his digger to the spots Jeff indicates next, testing the soil like Goldilocks with her porridge. Hole 1 holds too much clay; hole 3 hits a hard base and may or may not be useful later; but hole 2 captures a perfect mix of manganese and laterite, ideal for immediate use (see figure 11).

It is hot and humid out on the ridge, and although the conditions do not faze Jeff or Wally, the government officers have kept their vehicle air-conditioning rumbling. The aesthetic and technical sensibilities Jeff and Wally show in their work—a loving, expert attention—did not seem shared by the visitors. Some sat with their legs swiveled out of the car, a symbolic gesture to exiting; others hovered in the envelope of the engine's cooling efforts. But their senior man made his way over to where I stood in my patchy shade beneath a straggly eucalyptus, sketching the digger and where the holes are being trialed, to ask what my notes are about and whom I am working for.

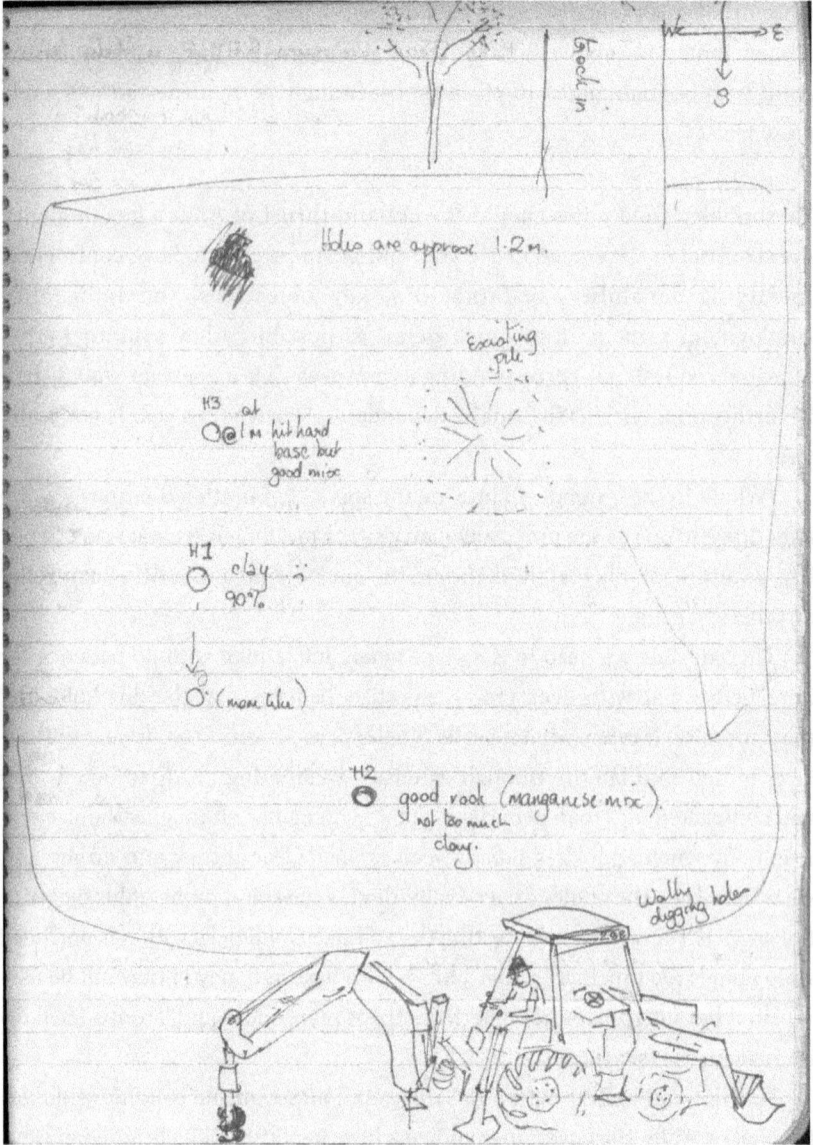

Figure 11. Mapping the quarry. Tess Lea fieldnotes.

"I am an academic writing about the leadership efforts of organizations like the Anindilyakwa Land Council, so others may learn from it," I say, improvising my no-good answer: "I am writing about people like you, and how people like you are endured, in places like this."

The leadership answer works somewhat, but not quite enough. He wants my contact details—and a copy of my notes. Just as I was mentally composing a different polite refusal, Jeff bounded over, arms outstretched, hands cradled, as if carrying melting ice or a fragile baby bird. It's dirt that he offers, straight into my one free hand. "Feel it," he excitedly commands, keen to share its perfect gravel qualities, before urging the official to likewise participate in this sensory exploration, letting me slip away to entertain Wally with my scrappy sketch of him in his digger.

The government officers do not quickly forget me or my notes. That night, when we saw each other again at one of the island's few licensed eating venues, a more junior delegate, "David," tried a new tactic. Because David was tasked with taking minutes of the earlier meeting, and hadn't, Andy had apparently promised my fieldnotes, David now claimed, handing me his business card for follow-up, his slight tremble catching the lie.

For Andy had not offered up my journal but had promised a concise meeting summary. My notes were safe. Even so, I privately vowed greater discretion in future fieldwork, to avoid courting another eviction. In place of cotton skirts and sundresses with sandals, suitable for the tropics, I sported what Australians call "hard yakka" clothing: tough cotton trousers with multiple pockets, a plain leather belt, a yellow-and-navy long-sleeve shirt with high-visibility strips, a cap, and well-worn R.M. Williams subbing for steel-capped boots. Even my notebook went undercover, transforming from a candy-colored spiral pad to a black vinyl clipboard, engineering pen sensibly connected with cotton twine.

On my next Air North flight back out to Groote, I disappeared. My imitation outfit operated as camouflage, the "high viz" becoming low viz on an airplane majority-loaded with men in similar gear, prompting a question: What exactly was I in?

What was I in?

1966. In the year of my birth, the first load of manganese was shipped out from Groote Eylandt, when the archipelago was still under the ministrations of the Anglican Church Missionary Society (CMS) and the Northern Territory administration's Welfare Branch. Translation: Indigenous people were being administered by church and state at the same time, and key decisions were being made on their behalf. The CMS had taken out a permit to both prospect and seek mining titles on the island in 1960 in response to growing interest from international geologists, thus securing the Anglican Church's key role in subsequent negotiations with the mining company BHP. The CMS exchanged its prospecting title for a 1.25 percent ad valorem royalty payment from manganese extraction, to be directed into a Groote Eylandt Aboriginal Trust Fund. A second statutory royalty agreement was also established between BHP and the Australian government, whereby a separate ad valorem 2.5 percent was paid to the Aborigines Benefit Trust Fund (ABTF). These were little amounts, taken in recompense, managed on behalf of Groote Eylandters. It would take until 1973 before a sliver (one-tenth) of the 2.5 percent royalty taken by the Commonwealth for the ABTF would be repatriated back to locals, and even then, it was directed to the earlier church-established trust (Altman 1983). And it would take until 2015 for the Anindilyakwa Land Council to negotiate directly with GEMCO about when and where renewed mining could take place. In the meantime, the notorious profligacy and gangster lifestyles of young men on the archipelago made Groote the exemplary "failed" case within policy circles, with no reference to this wider extractive complex for any kind of context.

The year is 1966, 1973, 2015. The year is every day. Every day since 1966, the highest-quality manganese ore currently available on the planet is ripped and shipped from Groote, for use in every conceivable configuration. Just as most of the world's energy still comes from fossil fuels—propelling trucks, ships, cars, food cooling, storage, freight, the harvest combines that reap food, and the fertilizers that grow them—so too manganese appears everywhere. It is the fourth most used metal per tonnage in global manufacturing, sitting just behind iron, aluminum, and copper (Povinelli 2016b, 32); and 15 percent of the world's supply comes from Groote. It strengthens steel, making it more pliable and able to be manipulated at high temperatures. It bonds railway tracks, safes, rifle barrels, and prison bars. Manganese fills dry-cell batteries, stiffens the more mellow aluminum of soft-drink cans, and forms a violet silicate that cancels the green color of iron, yielding the clear glass we experience as transparency. It appears in pharmaceuticals, in the electric vehicles and "clean" energy technologies of the future, and in the red-hued rock art of the ancient past (Heyes et al. 2014).

It is also listed as a "strategic mineral" for US military operations—defined as an element that is needed to supply the military, industrial, agricultural, and

Figure 12. Ode to manganese. Photograph by Tess Lea.

civilian needs of the US during a national emergency, but that is not found or produced in the US in sufficient quantities to meet this need (Cannon 2014).[3] Manganese is an essential ingredient for making steel pliable, but US manganese is of such poor quality that it cannot do much more than color house bricks red. As Major R. A. Hagerman wrote in his thesis for the US Marine Corps back in 1984:

Without just a few critical minerals, such as cobalt, manganese, chromium and platinum, it would be virtually impossible to produce many defense products such as jet engines, missile components, electronic components, iron, steel, etc. This places the U.S. in a vulnerable position with a direct threat to our defense production capability if the supply of strategic minerals is disrupted by foreign powers. (Hagerman 1984, n.p.)

Since at least World War One, securing supplies of identified strategic minerals is a key aspect of "preparedness" within US foreign policy (Reed 2015), beginning with what is known as the Harbord List of military raw materials, first published in 1921 (Hill 2011, 63–64; Huddle 1976, 654). Writing in *Science*, Franklin P. Huddle, a senior specialist advising the Congressional Research Service, describes the shift in American confidence from a nation certain of its self-sufficiency to one worried about resource shortages (1976, 654). After World War Two, and intensifying following America's expensive involvement in Korea, the list of essential imports climbed—as did pressure to ensure easy global access:

Arkansas bauxite was nearly exhausted. The rich Mesabi iron range was about gone. Imports of materials necessary for U.S. industry were rising generally. . . . And the demands of new technology were enlarging the list of essential imports to include such items as palladium, tantalum, cobalt, hafnium, and especially uranium (Huddle 1976, 655)

Subjacently, securing multinational capitalization of extraction processes became key to Australia's economic policy, just as pressure from civil rights movements domestically and across the globe forced greater recognition of Indigenous cultural rights. How could the state cordon the more subversive elements of demands for land and environmental justice, and still secure multinational and military development interests? The Australian government recast Indigenous policy from one of corralling to one of self-managing, thus retaining the taken-for-granted fundamentals of Euro-American modernity, such as the necessity of wage labor, debt slavery, and alphabetic literacy as key ingredients for a morally worthy, healthy, and "functional" life. Property, extraction, cultural recognition, modernity, social welfare, and so on came as a package. As historian Roxanne Dunbar-Ortiz puts it, revealing the transportable terms of northern hemispheric invasion processes,

The form of colonialism that the Indigenous peoples of North America have experienced was modern from the beginning: the expansion of European corporations, backed by government armies, into foreign areas, with subsequent expropriation of lands and resources. (Dunbar-Ortiz 2016, 6)

To repeat a refrain, my material is Australian, but its tethers can land elsewhere.

The deep imbrication of matters military in geoeconomics

Newly disguised in my hard yakka gear, I was flying to an island where the ability of Indigenous residents to counteract the interferences of wild policies was financed by royalties parsed from manganese mining. I was flying in the military inheritance that is airborne technology (fortified by manganese in its strengthened aluminum carapace) from the US Marine rotation base known as Darwin to an airfield that is owned and managed by the GEMCO mining company, to follow the efforts of islanders to shape the direction of policy-enabled housing and road construction efforts using the steel girders, plant, shipping, and freighting logistics that are also everyday militarized components built into our collective on-grid life. GEMCO owns not only the airport but also the port, the two main mechanisms for conveying food, commodities, essential services, fuel, raw material, equipment, and various forms of policy intervention to this remote island. Mining and military drivers are not the sole machines of everyday consumption, but they are far from incidental.

I ate the mine with every mouthful of locally bought food as I traveled its affordances (cf. Nash 1993 [1979]). When I stop to think about it, I eat the mine all the time, wherever I am. I consume little that has not been delivered through long, complicated networks of extraction and logistics, including the water I might use to nourish any homegrown food. And this, in short, supplies the "no" to the question of whether there can be good Indigenous social policy, even as there can be good efforts to make collateral side effects better. I will return to this point.

What was I in? The drive into and out of the Groote aerodrome crosses a barricaded dirt road, where visitors like me must wait as a steady stream of giant dump trucks and hauling trains rumble past, carrying ore from the island's heavily securitized open-cut mine to the bulk carriers waiting in the harbor, before returning for more. The manganese is shipped from GEMCO's port facilities at Milner Bay on Groote to GEMCO's subsidiary operation, TEMCO (Tasmanian Electro Metallurgical Company), the only manganese alloy smelter in Australia, where it is transformed into ferromanganese. In turn, 90 percent of TEMCO-produced ferromanganese is exported to international customers, along shipping routes that map the economic lifelines of all freight-dependent countries under globalization, heading north to Asia, west to Africa and Europe, and east to the US.[4]

This seagoing commerce flows past colonial posts that are either commercial or military in character, and occasionally both (Peele 1997, 63). Words such as *flow*, *passage*, or *trade route* in turn point to well-mapped trajectories deepened through histories of cross-border exchange, underpinned by a complex network of maritime and overland transport corridors and high-tonnage port facilities (Cowen 2014). These are also protected routes because—catastrophe bonds and disaster derivatives aside—unimpeded passage is consequential for routinized, profitable, transnational commerce (Scheinmann and Cohen 2012).

In the main, containerized and ore-laden ships travel between security "walls," safeguarded via bilateral and multilateral maritime security arrangements. Securing the passage of ships through known chokepoints (long, narrow, and highly trafficked access routes such as the Panama Canal, the Suez Canal, and the Straits of Malacca) is a well-known military priority, authorizing the annexure of land and of sea, of launch pads and of refueling points (Belanger 2018, Vine 2015, Lea and Rollo 2016).

What was I in? An extractive zone, certainly (Gómez-Barris 2017). But this withinness transcends physical proximity, given my complete dependency on the biotechnologies of extractive capitalism. No sentimental words about inclusion or recognition change my exploitative credentials. To admit this dependency is also to admit entanglement with all things militarized, for there is an intimate relation between globalized commerce and the means to defend it, past and present, today and tomorrow. Once acknowledged, the global, febrile, and mutable forms of extraction and extortion enabled by militarized trade and logistics that feed the settler colonial good life immediately become harder to ignore. We are inextricably immersed in a militarized political economy, subtending as it does the wherewithal of everyday life. If, as this book has implied, everything in settler colonial history is about resource and property annexure (Simpson 2014, Wolfe 2007, Tuck and Wayne Yang 2017), then, as the following section will further elaborate, everything about what is stolen, destroyed, extracted, commodified, improved, transformed, or cultivated to feed and sustain sendentized populations in multiple places is also about militarization. I could put this differently. I could join Zoe Todd and Michelle Murphy and talk about petrochemical dependencies, to make a similar point with different taxonomies (Murphy 2017, Todd 2017). As Stuart Rollo has pithily observed, in Australia, "[s]mall European populations had seized control of vast, rich territories from native peoples, and were left with the 'problem' of developing their resources while keeping the wealth for themselves" (Rollo 2018, n.p.). This ongoing "problem" maintains an armory as part of its resolution. Or, as Eve Tuck and K. Wayne Yang put it,

Within settler colonialism, the most important concern is land/water/air/subterranean earth (land, for shorthand . . .). Land is what is most valuable, contested, required. This is both because the settlers make Indigenous land their new home and source of capital, and also because the disruption of Indigenous relationships to land represents a profound epistemic, ontological, cosmological violence. This violence is not temporally contained in the arrival of the settler but is reasserted each day of occupation. (2017, 5)

Within the invisible suturing of intimately conditioned everyday conduct, militarily defended trade shapes Indigenous social policy. I was in policy's ambient conditions of possibility, which are simultaneously always a militarized and extractive life-support system. I am not otherwise separate, but have Indigenous dispossessions redistilled in my enfleshed body and externalized in my capacities to travel between different types of protected shelter. I am part of a proliferating, irrepressible, and continuous metabolic exchange, and, of course, the tolls and benefits are differentially distributed and always relational. Newly aware, we can see that the asking price of legalized Indigenous land repossession makes this differentiated relationality explicit.

July 16, 1945. Two decades before I was born, the first nuclear weapons test was conducted at Alamogordo in New Mexico, and with it began a nuclear arsenal that, like dependencies on other things military and extractive, has become "an (all but invisible) aspect of everyday life" (Masco 2004, 512). After Hiroshima and Nagasaki, with their legacies of genetic mutations and imminent global threat, uranium suddenly became a highly coveted resource. Thought to be rare, sources had to be commandeered. In her studies of African uranium mine workers, nuclear historian Gabrielle Hecht reminds us that the US Atomic Energy Commission deliberately sponsored a frenzied rush to find uranium:

Armed with Geiger counters from the Sears catalog, prospecting handbooks from the AEC, and inspirational pamphlets (with titles like "You Can Find Uranium!"), prospectors combed the deserts and mountains of the Colorado Plateau, often undergoing tremendous hardship. Boomtowns sprouted. Speculators started stock markets. Some people got rich. Most didn't. (Hecht 2012, 176)

As with America, so too Australia. After World War Two, the US held an unparalleled position of global primacy, the power gap between this new hegemonic military empire and any potential rivals being so vast that, for a time, the US economy was larger than those of the rest of the world combined.[5] For a war-weakened British government, the economic benefit of its remnant colonies shriveled as the price of American protection in the war.[6] For a supplicant

Anglophone Australian government, being part of the new nuclear age meant sharing America's new source of projective power, or being left in the pilings. In Hecht's formulation, this was a race in which "Nuclear = colonizer. Non-nuclear = colonized" (2006, 323). Both Britain and its former colony Australia wanted in on nuclear weapons. Both were locked out of American weapons knowhow. Yet Australia has the largest known supply of uranium in the world, and it offered swathes of seemingly unpopulated areas for "producing highly toxic plutonium and for testing the new weapons of mass destruction" (Reynolds 1998, 854).[7] Plus it had a sycophantic prime minister, Robert Menzies, who would do anything for British overlords—including making Australia the only country to voluntarily allow a foreign power to test nuclear weapons within its own borders (see figure 13).

Ernest Titterton, a British nuclear physicist whose voice sounds the hypnotic beat counting down the first nuclear weapon detonation at Alamogordo (and again at Bikini Atoll in the Marshall Islands in the Pacific a year later), was reassigned from his professorial roost at the Australian National University in Canberra to advise the Australian operations. Rest assured, Titterton's reassuringly British accent advised Menzies, "no habitations or living beings will suffer injury to health from the effects of the atomic explosions" (McClelland, Fitch, and Jonas 1985, section 6.1.15, pp. 144–145).

So it was that, just as geologists and hopeful prospectors were fanning out across the rooks and ridges of regional and remote Australia in search of uranium, nuclear weapons were serially detonated inside the Australian continent, a secret to everyone but the Indigenous people, scientists, and military personnel involved. Between 1952 and 1963, the British government conducted nuclear tests at three sites, beginning with the Monte Bello Islands off the Western Australian coast, thence Emu Field and Maralinga Range in South Australia. Deemed unpopulated, these South Australian lands were the homelands of Anangu and Pitjantjatjara people, camels, and other desert critters. These were also the homelands of Yami Lester, original founder of Nganampa Health Council and John Singer's early mentor. Yami had been blinded at the age of ten.[8]

"I was a kid," he later recalled, speaking to the Australian Broadcasting Commission:

I got up early in the morning, I think was 7 o'clock, playing with a homemade toy. We heard the big bomb went off that morning, a loud noise and the ground shook. One big loud and about four or five little ones, sound like: boom, boom, boom, boom, like that. I

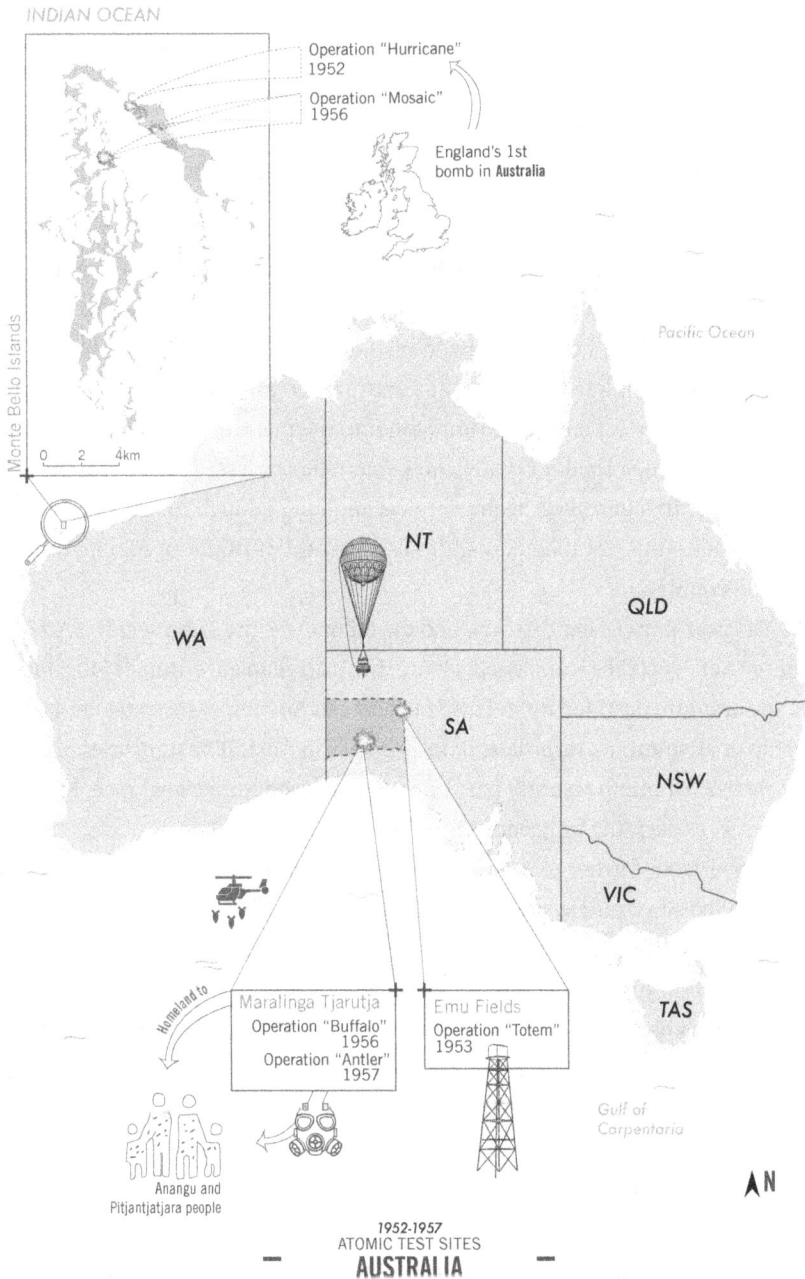

INDIAN OCEAN

Operation "Hurricane"
1952

Operation "Mosaic"
1956

England's 1st
bomb in **Australia**

Monte Bello Islands

0   2   4km

Pacific Ocean

NT

WA

QLD

SA

NSW

VIC

TAS

Homeland to

Maralinga Tjarutja
Operation "Buffalo"
1956
Operation "Antler"
1957

Emu Fields
Operation "Totem"
1953

Gulf of
Carpentaria

Anangu and
Pitjantjatjara people

N

1952-1957
ATOMIC TEST SITES
AUSTRALIA

Figure 13. Atomic test sites. Map by M. Barbagallo.

don't know how long after, we seen this quiet black smoke, oily and shiny, coming across from the south. And the old people knew what it was, saying this is *mamu, mamu*, meaning bad spirit.[9] ... We were scared. Next day ... we had sore eyes, skin rash, diarrhea and vomiting—everybody, old people too. Some of the old people, I don't know how many, they died. And we all had something wrong with our eyes. (Brain 2011)

Yami could not open his eyes for several weeks after witnessing the *puyu pulka*, or black mist, falling over his people's country on the morning of October 15, 1953, Operation Totem day, the first of two atmospheric detonations (Tynan 2016, chap.7). When he finally prized his lids open, his vision was blurred. By 1957, he was completely blind (Brain 2011; Lester 2000, 31–32). He lived long enough to agitate for a royal commission into the nuclear tests; long enough to initiate Nganampa Health Council, now Australia's oldest remote-area Aboriginal community-controlled health service; and long enough to mentor a young John Singer—but not long enough to see the end of uranium mining on Aboriginal country.

The year Yami Lester first watched the fallout was the same year the Atomic Energy Act 1953 (Cth) was passed, giving the Australian government full control of any uranium destined for defense purposes in Australia's six states, and ownership of all uranium, regardless of its purpose, in Australia's territories, including the NT. Uranium was still part of a high-stakes international race. Military drivers were deciding Indigenous fortunes once again.[10]

A year later, further to Australia's north, a uranium operation opened at a place called Rum Jungle, specifically to feed the nuclear arsenals of the Combined Development Agency, a British-American authority (Kay undated, Harris 2011).[11] Rum Jungle uranium mine operated from 1954 to 1971. Today, it is a highly toxic abandoned site, to be returned to its original Kungarakan custodians once long-overdue promised remediation is completed by the Australian government (Mudd and Patterson 2010). At that point, the Kungarakan will get to reassert their sovereignty over spaces of state desertion and military ruination, likely bearing the brunt of future blame for the partiality of what they will be able to wrench out of these toxic policy inheritances. This is the toxic sovereignty that Karrabing films also point to (chapter 4), showing the inequalities still residing in reparative state gestures.

But let's return to the post–World War Two military securing times, when state-funded aerial radiometric surveyors were plying the Alligator Rivers region in Arnhem Land, in a search made urgent by the British and American sprint to grab what was then thought to be rare supplies of a weaponizable ore—until uranium was found to be everywhere, and the imperial hierarchy was instead annexed to keeping the technologies for making weapons as top secret as global racketeering allows.

While uranium was still thought to be rare, the breathless military need to embark on every possible method of uranium discovery in remote and inaccessible areas saw geologists also turn to the rapid reconnaissance tools of the military (Barretto 1981). Drones would be the technology of choice today, with the technologies of military attack used to also locate the mineral resources for military preparedness. Back then, helicopters and fixed-wing planes fitted with gamma-ray spectrometer survey equipment flew back and forth over the escarpment country of what would become the World Heritage–listed Kakadu National Park. Gamma radiation signals dramatically spiked the onboard instruments (I like to imagine the surveyors tapping their dials, as if distrusting the very anomalies they'd come to find), compelling more detailed footwork. On the ground, teams comprising one geologist and two technicians forensically combed thirty-meter-wide grids, their spectrometers set at 1.5 times the background broadband (B.B.) to equalize ambient noise (Rowntree and Mosher 1976, 559, 561).

As the entire area was prospected, "an anomalous anthill located on the scree slope . . . gave broadband readings of 50× background B.B." (Rowntree and Mosher 1976, 561). Termites keep on giving things away in wild policy settings. The scene was set for Aboriginal land to once again be bartered for military-industrial-settler-colonial interests, with four alluring deposit sites (Ranger, Nabarlek, Jabiluka, and Koongarra, all in the East Alligator River region) as targets. Civil rights campaigns in Australia and elsewhere may have made explicit suppression of Indigenous land rights more difficult to sustain, but the price of legal recognition would be clarification of mining access. The East Alligator region was the first test case (Scambary 2013). The uranium operations ushered by Australia's determination to follow Anglo-American nuclear escalation were embedded in subsection 40(6) of the first legislation to recognize Indigenous freehold title, the Aboriginal Land Rights (Northern Territory) Act 1976.

We don't agree

We have clearly said, "No we don't agree to that proposal," and still people keep coming back to us and putting pressure on us. [*Translator's comment: The term used to "put pres-*

sure" literally means to apply the finger to the nose and push backward] . . . Our feeling is that the mining company wants to divide us into two sides, go down the middle, and entice people with large amounts of money and promises of good things. (Commonwealth of Australia 1999, p. 97, §5.80)

To convey what persistent government-enabled mining intrusion on their country feels like, the Mirarr Gundjeihmi clan of Arnhem Land share a metaphor for pain, a nose shoved back into a face. It is no accidental image. Mirarr country was first invaded by cattle let loose from failed soldier and convict/slave settlements in the Coburg peninsula. It was later annexed by Christian missionaries. In the 1970s, it transformed again, when Mirarr lands joined other *bininj* (Aboriginal) clan estates in being annexed within the now iconic Kakadu, opening to hordes of tourists. At the same time, but applying to Mirarr lands exclusively, the Ranger uranium mine, the Jabiluka mineral lease, and the mining town of Jabiru were also approved, all at once (Lawrence 2000, Haynes 2017).

The newly minted Aboriginal Land Rights (Northern Territory) Act 1976 (Cth) originally gave "traditional Aboriginal owners" an unprecedented right to stop mineral exploration and mining on Aboriginal land, except when it conflicts with "the national interest'" (Banerjee 2000). Ranger represented the very first test case in relation to how the act would operate. However, to ensure there could be no obstruction to uranium mining, not even the national interest test needed to apply: the right to veto mining at Ranger was deliberately removed within subsection 40(6) of the act, making uranium mining a fait accompli for Mirarr traditional owners and all their affines.[12] For the Mirarr, the right to veto became the right to put their signatures on an obligatory consent. As an aside to the events at Kakadu, but exemplary of wild policy entailments, identical land rights legislation was meant to apply nationally. Instead, after intense mining industry lobbying, not only were plans for national consistency sunk, but the original NT legislation was also diluted (Libby 1992). The "double veto" over exploration *and* mining was removed, with the consequence that today, mining can only be vetoed by Indigenous groups at the exploration stage—a fact that is not clearly communicated to everyone. A group might allow prospectors in just to look, not realizing that if the outsiders find anything worthwhile, a Pandora's Box is irrevocably opened. In addition, the window for making any new claims for repossessing any land at all under the act was firmly closed in 1997.

An unwanted multinational extraction industry, in the form of the Ranger uranium mine, was loaded onto the Mirarr as the price of land rights for Aboriginal claimants across the NT (O'Brien 2003). In this way, political decisions that were part of the Cold War, led by the US (a country that now had the nuclear capability to level entire cities, having commandeered the resource extraction interests of the former British Empire), quietly but forcefully shaped Australian Indigenous policy. Cue a long, complex, and taxing campaign from 1998 against both Ranger and its authorized extension, Jabiluka, led by the Mirarr, through their royalty-handling organization, the Gundjeihmi Aboriginal Corporation (GAC) (Commonwealth of Australia 1999).

For the Mirarr Gundjeihmi, Ranger was a fait accompli. But Energy Resources Australia (ERA, by now a Rio Tinto subsidiary) had its eye on an even bigger operation at Jabiluka, which it cutely called Ranger II and, sometimes, Ranger North (see figure 14). This second mine, Jabiluka, was likewise presented as a thing accomplished, an irreversible excision. After all, ERA had full license, and the official blessing of former prime minister John Howard, to mine the whole site. ERA had already cleared the land, installed surface infrastructure, and dug a deep incline nearly a mile long to reach the ore body at Jabiluka when the Gundjeihmi's international campaign finally forced all work to stop. In other words, all the infrastructure was in place, aided and abetted by state policing powers, yet still Mirarr opposition prevailed.

I know this telling is too swift. The campaign took year upon exhausting year to wage, yet I must rudely skip to the unheralded new tasks following the Mirarr's victory in stopping Jabiluka.[13] I want to pull away from the geostrategic backstory for land rights, to pay attention to the administrative aftermath, the zone of wild policies, starting with Jabiluka, the mine that never was. Even with fifty thousand tons of waste rock shoveled back down to plug the incline, the boulders of black substrate left behind so distorted the ground temperature that the despoiled site was nearly impossible to revegetate, and certainly not by following the technically vague policy advice relayed by various government agencies. Pallet after pallet of nursery seedlings swiftly died in the strange hot rock forms; animals and birds completely avoided the scarred excision area, further slowing processes of natural seed colonization. These rehabilitation battles are representative studies in the persistence, grit, and resourcefulness required of Indigenous-centered alliances to force policy's black-letter avowals about mining rehabilitation into more than halfway actualities (Lea, Howey, and O'Brien 2018). Indeed, the Gundjeihmi's work is one of insistence in the meso level of wresting benefits out of policy frameworks. Summarizing years

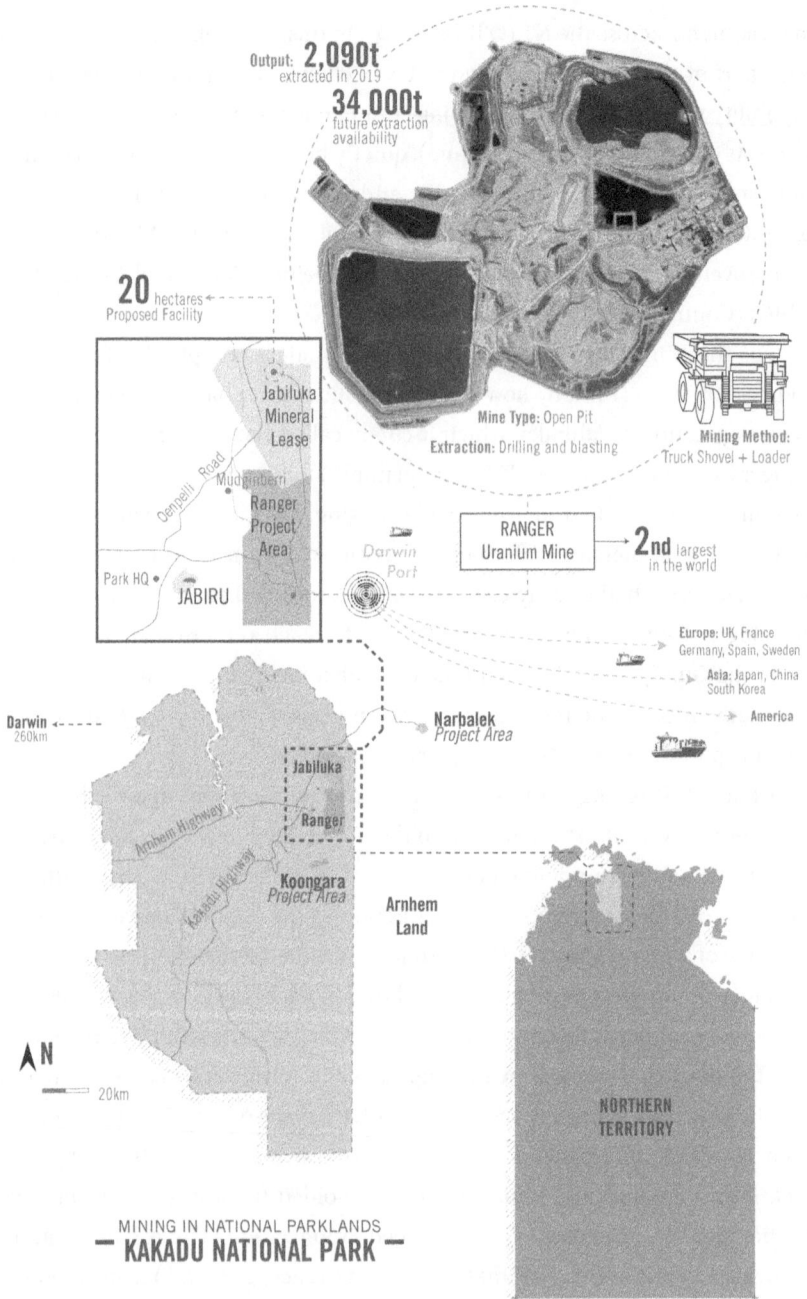

Output: **2,090t** extracted in 2019
34,000t future extraction availability

20 hectares Proposed Facility

Jabiluka Mineral Lease

Oenpelli Road

Mudginberri

Ranger Project Area

Park HQ

JABIRU

Mine Type: Open Pit
Extraction: Drilling and blasting

Mining Method: Truck Shovel + Loader

Darwin Port

RANGER Uranium Mine

2nd largest in the world

Europe: UK, France Germany, Spain, Sweden
Asia: Japan, China South Korea
America

Darwin 260km

Narbalek Project Area

Jabiluka

Ranger

Koongara Project Area

Arnhem Land

Arnhem Highway

Kakadu Highway

N

20km

MINING IN NATIONAL PARKLANDS
— KAKADU NATIONAL PARK —

NORTHERN TERRITORY

Figure 14. Ranger and Jabiluka. Map by M. Barbagallo.

of power struggles with state and industry bodies simply to have mandated re-habilitation guidelines complied with, one GAC member put it this way: "These are not our laws; they are yours: fucking stick by them!"

Like Nganampa Health Council, the Anindilyakwa Land Council, and the Karrabing Film Collective, GAC exemplifies the brokerage and translation slot that Indigenous organizations occupy to extract some use value from ramifying and inherited policies. But here I want to stress that the wild policy legacies that the GAC is grappling with reveal a direct connection between military extrac-tive interests and the formation of Indigenous social policy. Listen to federal Labor senator James Sheehan, a former union organizer, as he speaks in Parlia-ment in 1952 to support amendments to the 1946 Atomic Energy Act:

[B]ecause of the [uranium] deposits in this country, Australia could eventually become the greatest industrial country in the world. Such a development might enable us to hold Australia for the white race instead of being overcome in a possible conflict be-tween those nations which are close to us. . . . I trust that honorable senators . . . will realize that the future of this country is at stake. (Sheehan 1952)[14]

The (very white) state wanted uranium first for nuclear capability, then to gen-erate nuclear power. It arranged the foundational conditions for land repos-session around extractive interests, for mining, clearly; and through section 19 applications under the act, additionally for multiple other forms of industry and enterprise (Howey 2017). The first experiment with land justice was thus also an experiment in enabling militarized mining interests to recognize In-digenous claims, together with an absolute clarification of how extraction and other state-promoted industry desires are to be negotiated. The one came with the other.

Hidden in plain sight

Looked for purposefully, military connections to Indigenous circumstances are everywhere. The manganese ripped and shipped from Groote Eylandt is a strategic military mineral.[15] The desert lands that John Singer tries to pro-tect from disease and death were subject to nuclear bomb tests in the 1950s. Today they are touted as burial sites for Australia's nuclear waste (Power 2016, Morsely 2017). Federal funding for new housing in the NT, the jurisdiction with the highest rates of houselessness and overcrowding in the country, was curi-ously coincidental with the NT government's removal of a moratorium against jurisdiction-wide fracking (Cox 2018, Scientific Inquiry into Hydraulic Fracturing in the Northern Territory 2018). A bridge across the mighty Victoria River in the famed cattle country of Victoria River Downs leads to the armed gates of one the world's largest defense training grounds, the Bradshaw Field Training Area. Bradshaw is used by rotating US Marines as they simulate attacks by Asiatic figures, on acreage that is only two generations away from being the stolen property of gun-wielding pastoralists, their original arsenal also military-issue Martini–Henry rifles left over from the Boer War (Lea 2014a, 127–130, 234–235).

Another connection comes by thinking with the anthropological theorist of nuclear cultures, Joseph Masco. Reflecting on military bodies, he notes, "In a serious way, to be a soldier is to be an experimental subject, one that is not only tested in terms of physical and mental abilities but also subject to the theories, technologies, ambitions, and miscalculations of others" (Masco 2013, n.p.). To be an Indigenous policy subject is to be similarly experimented on: in Australia, the Aboriginal arena is where politics comes to audition (Strakosch 2015).

These examples clearly suggest the hauntings of military interests embedded within Indigenous policy surroundings. I am also arguing that the military-industrial drivers of Indigenous social policy are not restricted to such overt connections. Just as policy presence is not reducible to this or that policy artifact, being simultaneously an ambient existence, so too the militarized dimension of everyday life is one of saturation. Beyond the defended freight delivery systems for year-round trade, military inventions shape everyday life in overlapping ways. Global positioning navigation systems direct my ethnographic rendezvous and reroute our worlds, and digital and aerial photography has reshaped perception itself (Kaplan 2018). The internet drives and delivers unparalleled communication capacities; drones have become Christmas toys and have removed the cost of helicopters from film budgets. As Jennifer Terry (2017) has clearly established, the costs of war are often justified precisely on the promise of life enhancement and "biomedical salvation" (65–67). Improved pain management, burn treatments, new blood clotting products, regeneration of organs from cultured in vitro tissues, neurally integrated prosthetic devices, targeted cancer treatments through nuclear medicine, even practices of infection control and triaging—all are direct military bequests.

An answer to the invisibility of the military political economy in accounts of Indigenous policy (in)effects can be found here, in this overwhelming ubiquity. Yet, as is true with policy ambience, highlighting the everywhereness of militarized economies runs the risk of turning these into totalizing hyperforces, determining everything and diminishing alternatives in the same move. Can there be forms of existence under militarized neoliberal modes of world build-ing through extractive settler capitalism that can be something other than the reproduction of subtractive intrahuman and human–other species inequalities, legalized through state procedures? This convoluted question is, for me, the fuller expression of "Can there be good policy?" As this book has argued, there is a complex hyphenation joining finance–governance–everyday enterprise–sedentarized life (compulsorily and voluntarily entwined). Does the fact that policy so often muddles and spoils what it is intervening in mean that a more logical state of "rightness" exists? Is a state of policy rightness possible, once an ecological approach has been adopted, or is policy simply another actor, as per-manently imperfect as all others? In returning to the question of "good policy," let us insist that there is no necessary equation between acknowledging our total inveiglement in the systems that reproduce and sustain inequality, and total nihilism. Instead, let's return, full circle, to the yes and no of good social policy.

Interlude VI

The following text is pulled from a meeting with John Singer, held over dinner at a Thai restaurant in Alice Springs, July 22, 2019. It maintains its raw transcript form, including redacted material, without the many interruptions for food plating and greetings from passersby. In the full interview, I complain about how much easier it is, writing-wise, to tell the story of atomic bomb detonations in the western desert. Managing the ongoing procedural fallouts of enduring settler administration, John Singer's job, is a harder bombardment to narrate. The transcript version here gives a sense of the negotiations involved, and what we still are not able to say.

Tess: So, John, I wanted to talk with you about the changes we have to make to the *Wild Policy* manuscript. First up. A defamation lawyer looked at our words. There are some things I must redact.

Also, I thought I could write a new Interlude. A final one. It'll describe how we've had to make cuts, to alert readers to the political sensitivities hanging over us. How we can't just say "this happened" even though it did; how we had to consider the administrative payback. Readers will know they've read only part of what could have been said. Am I making sense?

John: *Uwa.* Well, I think there's a reality too. It might be easier for officials to stop funding an organization if you're talking too much. In this environment, you've got to be a bit careful. Because they can easy shut you down.

It's a bit different, talking out now. [Before] If you're a bit outspoken, you was allowed to have a bit of an opinion. Now you can't be too much outside this area [*hands cupped to show a small space*], otherwise it's easier to get classed "Oh, he's a bit of a mouth," or whatever, get punished.

Tess: I want to write about that. How we've had to change the text, *because* this is the risk for Indigenous people now. I have even been told to watch what

I say on Twitter, because certain ministerial staff are keeping watch. Anyway, talking to you about it gives me a chance to catch up on the Coronial Inquiry.

[Announced 1 July 2019, a coronial inquest into the abduction and murder of Gayle Woodford, beloved nurse, wife and mother. Husband Keith hopes this new inquiry will shine a light on SafeWork South Australia's "lip service," stating "we are looking for answers and someone to be held accountable for the lack of security" (Smith 2019).]

John: I worry for staff who worked closely with Gayle. They're still a bit in shock. It's pretty hard to look at.

Maybe this might come out, hopefully, of this Coronial Inquiry. They might start questioning, not just Nganampa, but questioning Corrections. How come this individual was out on the Lands? Why is someone who had been in jail that many times for sexual assaults out in the street walking around, and particularly out in the Lands, and why has there been no police presence at Fregon for over twenty years?

Tess: Could be a good outcome, you reckon, if they ask those questions?

John: Well, some of those areas need to be looked at too. Like you need to look at the bloke, how was he in that place? Should he even have been there?

Tess: Well, I can emphasize it, because it relates to other stories I describe in the book. Remember that one? About the Karrabing families out Belyuen way?

John: Yeah.

Tess: How one night these drunken rampagers, terrorists really, came and killed their dogs, threatening everyone, so they hid in the ceiling until everything quietened down, then crept away. Then they were like homeless refugees living in tents. And the police just said, "Oh well, it's something or other tribal." Hard to imagine that where I am, police just shrugging, "Oh well, that's just how they are on Frangipani Street!"

Anyway, what about that old people's home? Remind me why Nganampa can't run it anymore?

John: You've got to be full-time *in* the business, you've got to be talking to the people in Canberra every day [*table thumped in time*]. Even all them acronyms for new funding proposals, just memorizing *them* is a task, and we got no one [who can specialize like that]. So we had to outsource the management. But we're looking at what are the options for retaining some kind of community control, like we say "Yep, you can come and do it, but know that Nganampa has to have a doctor on the board," or such and such, as part of the governance.

Tess: One of the things I'm trying to emphasize, John, is how hard it is to just run organizations, how much detail and memory work there is. Outsiders make out that Indigenous issues are a "wicked problem," whereas I guess my book's saying No! it's these systems, past and present, that run up against each other, creating a tangle. On the ground, you're trying to neaten it out again, trying to make it work.

John: That's exactly what it is. It's getting so hard to do anything. We know that minister ▇▇ stole Aboriginal dollars from ▇▇ before the election [and diverted this] to ▇▇ for mainstream health services. They reckon too, could be just a rumor, that now the federal and state governments are both the same party, they'll use that South Australian Land Rights power to install their own administrator on the APY Lands, and maybe dump nuclear waste on us.

Tess: The plot thickens. So, to switch the topic a little bit, one of the assessors was dead keen on getting more of your backstory. They said, "I want to know— how did he get from New Guinea to the Lands when he was little?" Do you want to talk about that, or say "It's none of your business"?

John: I was wanting to talk to you about it. It's a little snap between New Guinea and the Lands there. I went three, four years in a place called Murtoa [a wheat district town], in the Wimmera in Victoria, with my stepparents. My adopted dad, he was from around that way. Then when I was about eight, we go to Ceduna [in South Australia]. Maybe that was their intention all along, knowing when they adopted me, that's where my Anangu family's from. I don't know; it might be just a coincidence. Anyway, I ended up in Ceduna, and then from there up Lands. This is how.

When I was in Ceduna I got exposed to that Aboriginal community, and then some family must have been living there, seen me, [and thought] "Hey." I don't know, see, they might be talking sideways, talking, talking, talking, talking, and I don't know, see.

He was a Lutheran minister, that old fella. He was my dad, first, when I was real young. So really, I had two sets of family, two ways to learn the world. Anyway, came back from church one Sunday—and they must have planned it— they [the Lutheran family] were all sitting there in the lounge room.

[*Mimicked surprise*] "Oh!" A knock on the door. "Go open the door there, mate," they tell me.

So, I opened the door, thinking normal, but hello—a couple of old ladies and a couple of young ones standing there.

And I sung out: "There's a couple of people here," and they said, "Oh no, *you* see them, that's your mother." They must have been planning behind, see.

They rocked up, spent about a week there with me, and then they said, "Are you going to come back up with us to the Lands? Go back family?"

Tess: You said yes?

John: Yeah. They my A*n*angu family. And then I always wanted to find out, I suppose. Who I was.

Tess: So, your adopted father, he was happy to let you go?

John: Sad and happy [*nodding*]. I didn't lose touch over the years, because they're important to me. The old man passed away in '92, got a brain tumor, and I keep in touch with my old Mum. I appreciate the role they filled in my life. I believe things happen for a reason. They were meant to be part of my life, and they are here [*head*] and here [*heart*]. But I also needed to find out who I was. And they didn't stand in the way of that, but over the years, as I think about it, I reckon they understood I had to know both ways.

Tess: I should say something about this book process. I sent the whole manuscript in, but before the publishers approved it, they sent it to some other academics, anonymous ones, who read it. Like I said, one person wanted more on you. The second wanted more about different theories. Like, this idea I have, about policies from the past hanging around like malingering ghosts, acting like bureaucratic ancestors—damaging ones, protective ones, all kinds.

I call it "policy hauntology," and I refer to some other writers who helped me work it out, mainly women, ones who think about settler colonialism and engage in different writing experiments to speak about power, race, history, things hidden in plain sight. But this one reader said I should show how this hauntology idea is "intertextual"—meaning, how it connects to stuff written by other theory people: a French philosopher called Jacques Derrida, Karl Marx, one called Bruno Latour, and Giles Deleuze.

There are citational politics involved, but these are all academic dynasties too so . . . anyway. That's my job.

John: Well, for me, I don't really care about that. The only thing really that I want you to do, is just talk a little bit more about how I got back to my family, just that little bit before Ceduna and going to the Lands, just something short. I don't talk about this much, but it is an important part of my story.

Tess: I will. Sitting here with you now, I am thinking I'll either expand that first Interlude, so people get all your chronology in one go, or I'll return to it, so your story works like a bracket. You the manager in between, your life story anchoring either side. I'll see what feels best and show it to you first, like always. Then my conclusions [*swiping hands*]. The end.

John: That's all right. I suppose when I was younger, it was a struggle in here [*pointing to the middle of his forehead*], from when I go back home, a struggle of this family and this family [*one hand, other hand*]. A struggle of when I'm with this family I've got to act this way, white way, that's how they act. But over the years, I got a bit more comfortable with it. It's not like this one's better than this one, whatever, it's just a bit different when you've got two mums, two families, or two dads, one's from an Anglo Saxon thing, one's from a bush traditional thing [*laughing*]. I know *tjungu* [meeting together], inside and out.

I suppose, before this book thing, I haven't had to look at myself and how my life journey has taken me and the impact to me from separation, then being brought up by one loving family, then having to introduce myself back to my natural family. Reflecting on it, I think this in a way, in a small way, is helping my mind and myself to tell my side of life.

All I can say is that all my life experiences and the main people in my life have helped shape who I am.

And that's more just a personal thing I wanted to tell you anyway.

Well, I might get moving then.

Chapter 6

Wild policy manifesto

Wild Policy argues that Indigenous social policy under continuing settler occupation is fundamentally about amelioration, not "cure," because fully expressed Indigenous well-being is irrelevant to state-enabled, militarily-defended, extractivist profiteering. Fights for policy-enabled benefits are thus fights taking place where the outcomes are not vital for militarized capital. I am not offering this as a theory of inevitability or causality. Rather, I am seeking to explain the chaos of policy-related effects within overdetermined fields.

So what are some answers? If we remove the lazy option of calling for "better policy" or of naively assigning responsibility for solving everything onto the shoulders of Indigenous wisdom, creativity, and resistance, what might be done, even so? For me, the resort of decrying the state, then conjuring some place "other" that is magically free of state tentacles, is a failure of intellectual nerve. We have to stay with the state.

Scrutinizing every part of the question "Can there be good Indigenous social policy?" reveals that "good" so often means "the best that can be expected." Indigenous social policy is the best that can be expected given that the full interests of extractive capitalism will always precede, and exceed, the interests of Indigenous people under continuing settler occupation. Herein lies hope. The best that can be expected also spins on expectations of "best"—and expectations not only can be altered but can reroute practices.

There is always policy-enabled extractivism pulsing somewhere in the ambient substrates of our artificially sustained worlds, making contemporary kinds of living possible, fed by state-sanctioned violence and supported through militarized pathways. Still, I will insist, alternatives are possible. By definition, the notion that policy is pulsing within ambient surroundings *distributes* where policy is acting. If policy operations are dispersed and multiple, points for intervention are correspondingly many. That policy is omnipresent, impacting even when it is ostensibly absent, is no reason to be overwhelmed. It is a call to be smarter about tactics for activating possible mutations from within (see also Strakosch 2019). As ordinary people moving through policy-saturated worlds, we all have different capacities to negotiate, moderate, or amplify policy. We do not need to restrict ourselves to artifactual policy domains, or to making entreaties to experts within citadels, to open policy possibilities. Sometimes all it takes is to start doing and expecting, differently.

What follows is a manifesto of sorts, deliberately polemical and unfinished, as an invitation to think about what practices might activate this ever-present potential. The challenge is not really about whether things could be done better, for of course they could. At this point, I want to explicitly put aside the making of policy recommendations as such, configured as a listing of technical prescriptions for how to create good (artifactual) policy. My eclectic recommendations for artifactual policy, should I make them, would include the necessity of honest and beneficial contractual partnerships with community coalitions; primers on listening with humility and responding well to the needs of such coalitions; the importance of ethical, careful project management; investment in housing, water harvesting, and transport designs that factor in the ravages of climate change, accompanied by recurrent funding for quality repair and maintenance regimes that keep infrastructural life supports (in housing, energy, transport, food, and potable water supplies) functioning well; investment in tending and updating legacy infrastructural commons; the necessity of surfacing the true costs of empathetic services and paying for them faithfully; the invention of multiliterate education systems that do more than reproduce class stratification and social compliance; the creation of alternates to carbon economies; and more besides.

Instead, my concern is to develop a theory of action that depends on heroism at neither the top nor the bottom of an imagined chain of policy command, without waiving the possibility for action. It is tentative and unfinished, for what I am describing is unfinishable.

Step one: Stop asking for better policy

The adjacency of extractivism, militarism, and the defense of settler colonial property relations as these are enabled through policy refractions should demand a rethink of what it is we are appealing to when we ask for "better policy." My recommendation, posed as didactically as possible, is that we stop thinking about policy in the singular, or that we at least consider the responsibilities that are displaced by such a blind summons. Stop thinking about policy as if it does not articulate with everything else: other portfolios, other spaces and places, and other times. There is always an a priori policy soakage, both hauntological and three-dimensional. Among other effects, the forces and flows that distribute exposures to toxins and hazards, benefits and opportunities, in unevenly shifting and disparately time-dimensioned ways, disappear with such blasé calls for singular policy.

What do I mean by things disappearing when we pretend policy is not intra-active? Say, for example, that we track precarious immigrant farmworkers in America's Midwest, workers who are forced into abject labor and faced with a constant threat of eviction. Say we track how such workers get overexposed to industrial chemicals, poisoning themselves and the environment alike under the command of increased agricultural productivity and in a chase for their own survival. We will find that the chemical soakage the farmworkers are swamped in is globalized through the leakages and dumpings of agricultural waste into waterways, and through shipping and freighting industries, entering different parts of the trophic system, some residues ending up in the fat of whales and seals and thence into the breast milk of Inuit women and into their breastfeeding infants, who sit at the top of the food chain because of their vulnerable dependence on adult humans for their diet (Mead 2008, Trainor et al. 2010).

As the environmental humanities ecofeminist Astrida Neimanis points out, colonial incursion does not require direct proximity to a colonizer, nor even steady coevality: "Planetary breast milk highlights the uncanny overlap of slow violence (Nixon 2011) and intergenerational violence with the singularity of an infant's hungry yelp that is always insistently now" (Neimanis 2017, 36). With such noncommensurate trails in mind, we might then consider how knowledge of Inuit ecopolitics in turn affects the environmental claims made by groups in Australia, such as the Mirarr Gundjeihmi, where the tactics flow into fights against the past, current, and yet-to-come damages of radioactivity from unwanted uranium mining on their country. We can think of the trauma loads and stress carried in bodies resisting the extraction industry and summoning policy ameliorations (such as money for renal dialysis), to arrive, finally, at a perspective that cannot reduce this or that policy-inflected moment to a matter of good or malignant intent, political will, eponymous act, or historical epoch.

Policy milieus are not single-time events, despite the bracketing attempted with the supply of dates, dollar amounts, authorizers, and proper names. Indigenous people do not encounter policy in the singular. None of us do. Indigenous people are exposed to multiple forms of different policy-inflected institutions and arrangements—to jails, households, hospitals, schools, employment, welfare, transport, policing, commercial food and pharmaceutical supplies, and so on. And on. This multiplicity is never simply about what happened this year or that, under this policy announcement or that political decision alone. Policy is not simply artifactual. It is ambient and hauntological.

Step two: Relieve the burden of being the otherwise

The efforts required to stabilize wild policy unfurlings simply to extract policy benefits or to soften further damage are not minor. Acts of perseverance are exacting. They wear people down, and attempting them as an isolated individual is particularly wearisome. This is also the administrative burden of living "otherwise," a point that may mean more to scholars than to policy practitioners. To briefly elaborate: many critical theorists of the conditions of human-fed climate change and colonial subjectivities suggest that Indigenous lifeworlds offer an alternative, one that teaches humans how to live more attentively in, and more attuned with, the nonhuman universe. Following philosophical traditions, this alter-sphere is sometimes called "the otherwise." Anthropologists Laura McTighe and Megan Raschig expand the liberatory underpinnings of the concept:

[T]he otherwise summons the forms of life that have persisted despite constant and lethal surveillance; it brings forth the possibility for, even the necessity of, abolishing the current order and radically transforming our worlds. (2019, n.p.)

The simple point *Wild Policy* adds is that this otherwise is ever a battleground, never a secure sanctuary (Bessire 2014b; Whyte 2018b). Resistance will remain a struggle, no matter what, for there isn't really an outside. Pure separation under pervasive occupation is increasingly rare. Even prolonging life, and preventing death, rely on militarily-enabled petrochemical ripping and shipping entailments. Indigenous social policy can ameliorate some of the ramifications of this broader political economy, can soften some of the harsher edges, and even, with exhausting backroom toil and sustained campaigning, use policy levers to counteract some of its damages (Lea, Howey, and O'Brien 2018; Lea 2020). This is what living "otherwise" can now mean: being more state than the state in protecting environments and seeking amends for hauntological harms, using the laws of the settler (Simpson 2016). For all that the otherwise might be parasitic and foreign for dominant social orders, Indigenous survivance takes place *within* and in spite of different forms of militarized political economies and their related policy ambience. Who'd have imagined that guerrilla accounting and good bookkeeping from Indigenous organizations would cause an "immunological response" in the settler host (Povinelli 2011a)? That it does suggests some ways forward—but let's not misunderstand the extortionate burden of this hope.

Against any easy nostalgia, let me reiterate the scarring and scattering effects of policy's survivalist instincts pitted against the resilience of Indigenous people on the ground. The burden of both managing service complexity and providing policy continuity editing so often falls on underresourced Indigenous organizations. Often it is an Indigenous conservatism—counteraccounting (tracking), stability, and consistency—that buffers against wild policy fallouts.[1] This is not easy. Demanding services and forcing sense from the insensible extract a greater sacrifice from countermanders than it ever does the state. As I have noted with others elsewhere (Lea, Howey, and O'Brien 2018, 315), it costs an Aboriginal group more to hire and retain staff; more to access expert technical advice; more for the telephony and information communications; more for the office buildings, the heating, cooling, waste management, and vehicle fleets; more for insurance; more for *all* the incidentals than, proportionally, it does a government agency, a ministerial entourage, or a mining company.

Perversely, policy ledgers account for this imbalance inversely, noting the costs confronting the state when it is forced to fund below-scale services. The Commonwealth Grants Commission (the Australian authority charged with redistributing taxation levies to state and territory governments, ostensibly to "equalize" the capacity of each jurisdiction to provide services) refers to "the indivisibility of labour" as a cost that must be borne when it comes to small communities (Commonwealth Grants Commission 2015, 498). Although the size of a school-age population may not warrant a full-time teacher, for instance, primary school education remains compulsory. The costs of providing a teacher to an undersized cohort are begrudgingly accommodated within Grants Commission algorithms as a "disproportionate provision" because the mandated teacher cannot be physically cut up.

This concept of "indivisibility" applies to nonstate actors too, if we consider the cost of being multipurposed while having to respond to inchoate policy forays within limited resources; the price of being stretched membrane-thin over complex matters where key implications are submerged in arcane legalese and buried reportage; the way policy is a nurse wrangling transport for a patient, as much as it is a funding proclamation within parliament. That this indivisibility has a physical as much as a fiscal cost is a point that bears repeating. When "lessons learned"—that familiar refrain of policy development manuals—depend on a material reality of noncommunicative systems and high-turnover positions, on unreadable and unread reports and documents lost to iron-clad archives, continuity editing for policy coherence falls to Indigenous organizations that are not funded for the role. The lessons that Indigenous groups also give, quite concretely, concern the individual and collective tenacity required to force existing policy levers to do any good. The manifesto recommendation here is to stop overloading Indigenous people with the responsibility for curing the world.

Step three: Care for the micro

I have been at pains to point to the pains people go to, the pains people experience, in making policy "work." Within policy ecologies, the opportunity to make little differences sits with everyone all the time across a distributed field. It is always an option for street-level bureaucrats to turn a blind eye, to help translate forms, to bend a rule. Whether someone is favored and argued for, dealt with caringly or with cavalier indifference—all are transacted within these domains of the micropolitical, domains that are never so miniature or isolated once we admit their greater significance.

Policy's cruder, more intrusive modes are more apparent in the lives of disadvantaged or discriminated-against populations, but do not exist only there. For the affluent, policy may seem abstract and benign, or logical and required, sometimes wrongheaded or an undesirable obstruction, but otherwise roughly necessary. For the privileged, it can be an outrage to encounter policy's more chaotic street-level modalities. People registering their frail aged parents into institutional care settings or making a complaint about workplace harassment, or parents with differently abled children, routinely encounter tortured passageways within policy labyrinths, but in the main, such confrontations with policy arbitrariness are more or less manageable or avoidable. Privilege is usually an energy-saving device, making daily life less difficult to transact. (No doubt "less difficult" still feels like more: time slows down when navigating infuriating dead ends and indecipherable processes.)

On the street, at the counter, over the phone, or in a queue—dispositions and attitudes, what is said and the tone it is said in, mark an accumulation of conditions that separate respect from disdain (Sennett 2003). Direct consequences can be shaped by words, manners, interactions, and insistences (Summerson-Carr 2011, Desmond 2016). Care for technical detail also matters. The clues to poor housing design and accelerated degradation lie in recognizing that structures are never stable but are always in states of decomposition (Graham and Thrift 2007; Jackson 2015). Where malfeasance and deregulation are too readily the norm, technically proficient care is essential: care about the design and quality of products used to build houses, care about the rigor of maintaining them, and care about what standards should be met when meeting standards is not really required.

This remains a key insight: microlevel attention and care matter greatly to how policy is enacted and experienced in the everyday. There is a lot that can be done within these interactions; and even while emphasizing issues of unsustainability, stress, toll, and turnover, I have tried to honor the fundamental importance of daily acts of courtesy and ethical expertise. Microlevel care is not restricted to service transactions but can include carpet worlds. The people involved in artifactual policy formulation within policy citadels operate as brokers and translators too. When they nudge wording to limit damage despite being under draconian instructions, they are intervening in their zone of influence. These detailed, contextually encrypted actions might not be readily generalizable as policy recommendations for improvement. They might not be reducible to the kinds of "territorially frail and perverse travelling rationalities" (Craig and Porter 2006, 272) that feed the seductive idea of "best practice," but ethnographically, we can describe their everyday properties and practices. Folk in charge of sites of direct (rather than spectral) policy transaction and encounter should be mindful of how all this works, should be alert to how they can compassionately influence what happens with their artifacts.

However, although ameliorating the harsher edges of policy depends on such attentiveness, it is as unreasonable to place the burden of altering the big drivers of inequality onto the care work of policy formulators and translators as it is to demand that Indigenous people solve climate change and wash away the ills of modernity through the fact of their persistence. It would be better to demand that we all give up the affordances of living in extractive economies. Better, but pointless too. It is a rare person who can exclude herself from such dependencies, without prior accumulated capital, and still be living well. Someone's flourishing within petrochemical militarized political economies remains at the expense of someone else's suffering (see also Povinelli 2008). Here I join Michael Fischer's grim conclusion that what is needed is

a new humanistic politics, open also to the posthuman with its human components, the cyberhuman, and companion species, that will allow us to survive, to live after whatever catastrophes lie in store—climate change, space travel, bodily evolution, farming the Arctic as it warms—and that will counter the widening inequalities and devastations of our current cannibal economies, consuming the lives of some for the luxury of others. (Fischer 2014, 349)

Simply, being a sensitive and indefatigable policy broker armed with ethical principles and a caring heart is essential, but radically insufficient, to sustain the kinds of interventions that might shift disadvantage out of its well-grooved predestinations. Here, the concept of institutional killjoys, adapted by from Sara Ahmed's notion of feminist killjoys, remains highly relevant (Ahmed 2012). Killjoys insist on holding policy promises to account. The fate of killjoys is so often to be shut down or "killed off"; or, as one Indigenous person put it to me (conditional on anonymity), killjoys join the "charcoal institute," blackened by experiencing what black people endure, and burned out because of it. This sounds fatalistic, but again, it is not. Going *athwart wild policy* demands that efforts to countermand structures that shape possibility are better supported, be that through skilled expertise and labor, material resources, a lessening of mad demands . . . whatever one's zone of practice might be.

Even so, microlevel actions and reactions are not, cannot be, sufficient to alter the wider policy ecologies that create relations of inequality. Tilts against the norms of resource rationing and class privileging that are embedded within policy categories are important and matter greatly, but they do not alter (well-defended) institutionalized and societal norms on their own. They might create (deplete and exhaust) institutional killjoys, but they do not change what policy remains part of. To return to housing examples, the daily decisions of housing agents in terms of allocating, caring for, or neglecting Indigenous housing cannot be separated from that which has created the need for Indigenous housing. We might think here of forced sedentism: of being pragmatically clustered in troubled places where food, cash, and services might be accessed, given radically reduced estates; of compulsory school education and the massive adulterations to time, domestic logistics, and mobility that obeying compulsory schooling necessitates; of courts and jails and their locational demands; of depleting disease chronicities and the secret wounds that people carry within their bodies, and the need to access place-tethered and resource-starved health services; to name a few possible influences. And we might think about how settler access to land for agricultural, mining, and construction purposes, fed through globally connected, militarized political economies, is not going to be yielded anytime soon.

Within all this, given the crushing powers of abstractions such as settler colonial extractivism, global profiteering, existential dependency on militarized political economies, and the like, the question of what policy can do, where, or how can feel superfluous. It seems that no amount of adjustment can convert policy—a tool for liberal capitalist extraction activities—into a vehicle of genuine deliverance. If policy is not a singular intervention, changing this or that policy can seem pointless. If forms of administrative violence are embedded within software algorithms and archives, if inequalities reproduce themselves through such ordinary and seemingly unavoidable events as rampant professional turnover and unreturned phone calls, what's the intervention point for a would-be intervener? Answer: let's make this less a labor of individual effort and take advantage of what such an entangled policy wilds might offer. After all, individual efforts are rarely structurally contagious; coalitions, however, are another matter.

Step four: Collectively leverage the meso

The special, demanding achievements of institutional killjoys, or the caregivers, the brokers, and translators who coax outcomes for others, often against the pressures of how they are otherwise expected to operate, sit within what, summoning Isabelle Stengers, we can describe as the mesopolitical, or better, mesopolicy (see also chapter 4). The meso level shimmers between the micro and the macro, structurally speaking. It articulates the detailed care required to wrangle with a funded program to yield some of its potential capacities, without losing a sense of the stickiness or resistances that are simultaneously and uniquely encountered whenever change is attempted.

This is also the aperture for policy possibility, for budging, insisting, creating, maintaining, and building alliances to manipulate interstices and cracks, through coalitions, not singular heroics. The coalitions that, together, undertake local, detailed, complex, and iterative work to release the potential that sits within any milieu, even in the most toxic or seemingly barren of sites, are the emergent grounds for hope. The only way to overcome the big drivers of embedded policy is through collective action. It has ever been thus (INCITE 2017 [fp 2007]). It is interesting to note, then, how much institutional effort has focused on dismantling alliance capacities, with a forcefulness that does not confine itself to the discrediting of unions. Indigenous community-controlled organizations, whether state sanctioned, based on independent fundraising and sponsorship, or established to manage a collective asset (as per land councils), can be a threat *because* of their extrainstitutional alliance formation. Important coalitions can even exist with bureaucratic carpet-worlders—and these too are under pressure.

Encountered ethnographically, today's policy worlds are time poor, media blitzed, sealed off, and occasionally made punch-drunk by an agitated popular mood, fed by a starved media searching for sensational stories that require limited journalistic capacities. The Strategic Indigenous Housing and Infrastructure Program (SIHIP) easily met these criteria (chapter 2). The Department of Prime Minister and Cabinet in Canberra, from whence all national Indigenous policy is meant to be coordinated, has additionally introduced open-plan offices and hot desking, so that relationships between its own officers, let alone between them and any external parties, are perennially disrupted. Officers are warned to avoid being hijacked by too close an allegiance to any particular programs, people, or places, for this threatens their ability to be dispassionate and conceptually agile. Career mobility requires issue skating. This exacerbated distancing and loss of relational ties has made the work of all brokers and translators, wherever they are located, much harder, more discombobulated. But consider this: if there is so much effort to attenuate our attention, to break up relational collectives, imagine reharnessing the power of focused coalitions. In the meantime, let's consider the multiple policy possibilities that surround us and that could be activated through collective leveraging.

Step five: Reject policy normativity
Representing the multidimensional, multitemporal hauntings, ecologies, thickets, unfurlings (my metaphorical tumult reflects the descriptive challenge)

within the everyday contexts of inhabited policy milieus is one way of reconceiving the structural inequalities and privileges that state policy has otherwise been aiding and abetting. Policies infect psyches, making some relationships and forms of well-being feel natural or deserved, cutting into and lacerating others. When we actively confront wild policy's role in structuring life possibilities, we encounter the predicament that every call to improve this or that policy is a call to strengthen the architecture of liberal settler modes of being. Giving wild policy unfurlings a nonnormative vocabulary is essential for "prefiguring the state" (Cooper 2017)—that is, for clarifying what should and could be demanded now and for the future. This requires ethnographic attention to the ways that complex policy surroundings are inhabited. Critique alone will not suffice. There may well come a magical future where the state has decolonized, withered away, or become radically progressive because academics have made vague calls for this, but in the meantime, competent administration must be defended. It is being dismantled and weakened; its protective and regulatory capacities are being wrecked and its subservience to rapacious extraction ambitions deepened. Policy is already unmoored. To be less vague about what we are arguing for, without false disavowals or premature lumping onto an Indigenous otherwise, our analyses must travel dispersed routes too. These are not the last words. Let concrete experimental practices, rather than generalizations, be our guide as we chase the quiet voids that surround spectacular distractions, the better to capture the wounded worlds that policy enters and helps sustain—and perhaps may yet help heal.

Notes

Innterlude I

1. The terms *country* and *on country* are possibly uniquely Australian Indigenous expressions. They represent composite descriptions of sentient sacred sites, lands, and waters toward which a person may have complex ancestral and kinship affiliations and obligations.

2. In this it mimicked the first land repossession legislation, the Aboriginal Land Rights (Northern Territory) Act 1976 (Cth) (ALRA). Under the ALRA, traditional owners in the Northern Territory could make a land claim on unalienated Crown land, which, if successful, resulted in "Aboriginal land" being granted as inalienable freehold title to a land trust "for the benefit of Aboriginals entitled by Aboriginal tradition to the use or occupation of the land concerned" (ALRA s4.1). Traditional Aboriginal owners are defined within s3(1) of the ALRA as "a local descent group of Aboriginals who (a) have common spiritual affiliations to a site on the land, being affiliations that place the group under a primary spiritual responsibility for that site and for the land; and (b) are entitled by Aboriginal traditions to forage as of right over that land." The Native Title Act 1993 operates across Australia and somewhat similarly, although native title is vulnerable to extinguishment and can be directed by other property interests. It is important to note that land rights legislation gives land, not mineral rights, to Indigenous claimants. The wider geostrategic context for the ALRA is examined further in chapter 5.

3. All dollar figures noted are in Australian currency.

Chapter 1

1. There are six states in Australia, each with its own constitution, which divides each state's government into the same divisions of legislature, executive, and judiciary as the federal government (alternately referenced as the national, federal, Australian, or Commonwealth government). There are an additional ten territories, seven of which (Ashmore and Cartier Islands; Australian Antarctic Territory; Christmas Island; Cocos (Keeling) Islands; Coral Sea Islands; Jervis Bay Territory; Territory of Heard Island and McDonald Islands) are entirely legislated for by the Commonwealth government; the two mainland territories—the Australian Capital Territory and the Northern Territory—have quasi-state powers, having each been granted limited rights of self-government under regulation by

the Commonwealth. The tenth territory is Norfolk Island, which runs itself under a regional council model, but otherwise falls under Commonwealth jurisdiction. Few Australians would pass if this account were set as a citizenship test.

2. "Plan to Close More Than 100 Remote Communities Would Have Severe Consequences, Says WA Premier," ABC News, http://www.abc.net.au/news/2014-11-12/indigenous-communities-closures-'will-have-severe-consequences'/5886840.

3. Cris Shore and Susan Wright (1997, 5) note the importance of retrospective policy alignment in their overview of the anthropology of policy; I dedicate a chapter to such infinite readjustments in *Bureaucrats and Bleeding Hearts: Indigenous Health in Northern Australia* (2008, ch.4).

4. I also wanted to write about school-based education and the explosion of regional training centers. I see these as instances of cruel optimism (Berlant 2011); a constant holding of hope for future autonomy through promises of skill and capability building, via substandard and erratically provided education services (see also Spivak 1993, Berlant 2006). But despite years of tilting at the issue in applied and theoretical modes (see, for example, Lea 2010, 2015a), and of wanting to write about education and training anthropologically but not knowing how to do so, I have put down the cudgels—for now.

5. The intertwining of wealth accumulation with forms of (imperial, colonial, and nation-state) labor control through enclosures, measurement of time, control of social reproduction, and state-sponsored assemblies of logistical infrastructures for resource dispossession, assembly, and recirculation—all backed by military actions—has been long commented on. David Harvey (2005a, 2005b) is among the most persistent in calling attention to contemporary forms of accumulation through dispossession, but see also the work of Joan Comaroff and Jean Comaroff (2001), Patricia Seed (2001), Deborah Cowen (2014), Laura Bear (2015), and Sandro Mezzadra and Brett Neilson (2013, 2015).

6. For instance, depending on where they are located and what genealogical bearing they can bring to any rights to negotiate land titles and access within narrow regimes of legal recognition, Aboriginal people have greater or lesser abilities to benefit or be damaged from dredging, drilling, and digging on their country (Povinelli 2002, O'Faircheallaigh 2004).

7. For anthropological accounts of the stabilizing power of myths of statecraft, see Hansen and Stepputat's *States of Imagination: Ethnographic Explorations of the Postcolonial State* (2001). The centralizing metaphors of science are laid out by Gary Downey and Joseph Dumit (1997).

8. The book *Darwin* has enjoyed divergent afterlives. It was taken up both as an example of ethnography-in-action within settler colonial studies and as travel memoir, ideal for Christmas stockings; meanwhile, Karrabing films are shown across the world, but lack a distributor for mainstream cinemas.

9. I borrow this term from Donna Haraway (2008, 31–32), who explains, "Organisms are ecosystems of genomes, consortia, communities, partly digested dinners, mortal boundary formations. Even toy dogs and fat old ladies on city streets are such boundary formations; studying them 'ecologically' would show it."

10. Karen Barad (2012) introduced this term as an antidote to the unitary agents standing behind the word *interact*.

11. I pursue elsewhere the vexed question of repairs and maintenance in contexts where the state is one's landlord (see https://www.hfhincubator.org/). For additional and still relatively rare critical analysis of Indigenous housing policy, see Megan Nethercote (2014, 2015a, b); Louise Crabtree (2013); Peter Phibbs (Habibis, Phillips, and Phibbs 2018; Phibbs and Thompson 2011; Pholeros and Phibbs 2012); and Liam Grealy (2018).

Interlude II

1. http://www.adelaidenow.com.au/news/law-order/gayle-woodford-murder-family-overcome-by-harrowing-sentencing-submissions-for-killer-dudley-davey/news-story/3369f65237fa117ca2dcf14fe5d4b184; https://www.abc.net.au/news/2018-03-05 gayle-woodfords-legacy-for-remote-area-nurses/9499592.

2. *R v. Dudley Davey*, No. SCCRM-17-50, June 8, 2017.

Chapter 2

1. http://www.abc.net.au/lateline/paper-reveals-sexual-abuse-violence-in-nt/1755100.

2. http://www.smh.com.au/news/opinion/a-culture-of-violence-that-must-change/2006/05/17/1147545387118.html.

3. Of note—if only because it usually drops from accounts, being so arcane and difficult to narrate—the federal government had been quietly meddling with the Aboriginal Land Rights (Northern Territory) Act 1976 to introduce township leasing amendments (see chapter 3). For a careful legal parsing of what leasing reforms claimed they were about and what was actually delivered, see Terrill (2016).

4. An alternative view is that different governments had been essentially squatting for thirty years on Aboriginal land, and that land councils used the opportunity presented by the policy change to "secure tenure" during and after the Intervention as leverage to force governments to "pay the rent."

5. The three alliance teams were selected from twenty-four original applicants. None were Indigenous organizations. The government stated that alliances—comprising a head contractor, subcontractor, civil and building designers, and material suppliers, as well as logistics and training organizations—would reduce costs and risks through their capacity to "drive down prices, reduce delivery times, attract larger national companies with capacity to partner with smaller companies with local expertise, use local labor and engage positively with the community" (O'Brien 2011, 67). The method is meant to allow for ongoing troubleshooting in the spirit of shared end goals.

6. SIHIP was in turn replaced by the National Partnership Agreement on Remote Indigenous Housing (NPARIH), which was part of the overall Intervention's second life under a change of government, known as the Stronger Futures Policy. NPARIH also ended abruptly, in July 2018, with housing remaining unfinished business (Commonwealth of Australia 2018). For an electronic archive of Indigenous agreements with other bodies in Australia and overseas, see the invaluable Agreements, Treaties and Negotiated Settle-

ments database, available at http://www.atns.net.au/default.asp.

7. The most significant among the serial reviews are the *Strategic Indigenous Housing and Infrastructure Program—Review of Program Performance—August 2009* (DoFHSCIA and Northern Territory Government 2009); the *Strategic Indigenous Housing Infrastructure Program (SIHIP): Post Review Assessment (PRA)* (FaCSIA 2010); *Review of the Implementation of the NPARIH in the Northern Territory*, Audit Report No. 12 2011–2012 (Australian National Audit Office 2011); the *Report of the Commonwealth Ombudsman into Remote Housing Reforms in the Northern Territory*, Report 03/2012 (Larkins 2012); *National Partnership on Remote Indigenous Housing—Review of Progress (2008–2013)* (FaHCSIA 2013); and, more recently, *Remote Housing Review: A Review of the National Partnership Agreement on Remote Indigenous Housing and the Remote Housing Strategy (2008–2018)* (Commonwealth of Australia 2018).

8. A minimum goal was for Indigenous participants to complete training to Certificate III in building and construction and business administration, with potential candidates to be apprenticed for trade certificate qualifications and provided with support networks (Davidson et al. 2011, 86–87, 96; Fien and Charlesworth 2012, 23).

9. An exact definition of town camps remains difficult to come by, due to their varied genesis as either informal meeting grounds for Indigenous travelers, "cognate spaces to the remote outstations and homelands to which Aboriginal people began moving from more concentrated settlements in the latter half of the 1970s" (Fisher 2015, 153), or as the legacy of administrative fiats, where groups of people were physically forced onto and confined within the fringes of white space. For a list of town camp leases, see Northern Territory National Emergency Response (Town Camps) Declaration 2007 (Cth) (No. 1) and (No. 2). A sixteen-thousand-page Deloitte report on the condition of town camp housing, ostensibly published in 2017, was finally released for public access in 2018 after an eighteen-month delay (Deloitte 2017). This report confirmed ongoing neglect and infrastructural backlogs of overwhelming proportions. It is an ongoing demonstration not only of what Povinelli has described as the economics of abandonment (Povinelli 2011b) but also, as my work argues, of an economics of budgetary gaming.

10. For an elaboration of the arguments against outstations and an ethnographic engagement with their importance as a source of hope and well-being, see Senior et al (2018).

11. Refurbishments at the scale of twenty-five hundred across seventy-two communities were likewise highly unlikely, as the majority of them needed to completely replace the "wet areas" (toilet, bathroom, and kitchen). Such a scope calls for skilled labor, greater regulatory compliance, and expensive materials, and invites the related logistical challenges of delivering on small projects in remote communities with sparse populations (Lea and Pholeros 2010). On-site accommodation is a problem, freight is expensive, and construction time is limited to nonmonsoonal periods in the northern tropical savannah country and to winter in the desert. Such projects seldom achieve the critical mass to warrant having a full complement of skilled construction teams make the arduous journey, and so rely on whoever usually gets the contracts, honest or otherwise.

12. See Jenny Macklin's and Paul Henderson's August 31, 2009 joint media release

"Improving Indigenous Housing in the NT," https://formerministers.dss.gov.au/14469/improving-indigenous-housing-in-the-nt/.

13. Extracts from Balzac's novel *Les employés* are retranslated in Ben Kafka's powerful account of bureaucracy's flourishing in postrevolutionary France (2012, 92).

Interlude III

1. We can imagine this Faustian quality in multiple ways. David Ritter, the former native title lawyer, now CEO of Greenpeace Australia, has written of the separate but related "dispiriting experience of convincing people to stay in town when they would rather be hunting and fishing, in order to prove their traditional relationship to the land" (2009, 26).

Chapter 3

1. There are at least fourteen different clans distributed across Bickerton Island and Groote Eylandt, but there is no term for the people as a whole (Waddy 1988, 47). *Warnindhilyakwa* refers to a key language group spoken by some important family groups, including the Mamarika and Amagula traditional owners. Others prefer to spell this as *Enindhilyakwa* (van Egmond 2012). I retain the more commonplace spelling, as this is also used by the Anindilyakwa Land Council with whom I first negotiated research access.

2. See the BHP Billiton report to the US Securities and Exchange Commission (2011, 147) and the South 32 website, http://www.south32.net/our-operations/australia/gemco.

3. Since the advent of the Aboriginal Land Rights Act in 1976, there are now two main channels for royalty dispensations: the Groote Eylandt Aboriginal Trust, originally established by the Church Missionary Society, and the Anindilyakwa Land Council.

4. See https://www.theguardian.com/australia-news/2015/nov/07/two-killed-in-brawl-involving-spears-and-machetes-on-nts-groote-eylandt; http://www.abc.net.au/news/2015-11-07/groote-eylandt-deaths-machetes-spears-used-in-riot/6921182; and http://www.ntnews.com.au/news/northern-territory/groote-eylandt-man-pleads-guilty-to-spearing-man/news-story/o1b3514b74230c4a23c2560347ded1e5.

5. Many translations phrase this more simply as "The Dreaming." For the anthropologist W.E.H. Stanner, the neologism *everywhen* better captures the idea of always, still now, and to become. He wrote, "One cannot 'fix' The Dreaming *in* time: it was, and is, everywhen" (Stanner 1953, 58).

6. Songlines are memorized and performed encyclopedias of ancestral lore, land knowledge, map references, creation journeys, and how things come to be. If you know the beats, the references, the melodic variations, and more, of a songline, you can navigate unknown territories—no Google maps required. Anthropologist Diana James writes, "The marks of the ancestors' footprints are clear to see for those who have memorised the long song sagas that recount the ancestors' activities at sites along their travelling routes" (2015, 34).

7. This is based on a decision colloquially known as "Blue Mud Bay," after the origins of a high court case (*Northern Territory of Australia v Arnhem Land Aboriginal Land Trust* [2008] High Court of Australia 29 [July 30, 2008]), which determined that traditional own-

ers have exclusive rights to waters that sit over Aboriginal land within the intertidal zone (Brennan 2008).

8. As I discuss further in chapter 5, along with many other communities in receipt of mining royalties, the Anindilyakwa have suffered from their own apparent largesse, for their assumed wealth permits the state to under- and disinvest in services such as roads, clinics, schools, and new and rehabilitated housing (Lea 2012b).

9. For additional insights on tenure changes, see Rosenman and Clunies-Ross (2011).

10. See http://anindilyakwa.com.au/about-us/mission-and-vision.

11. The symptoms of MJD and of overexposure to manganese are remarkably similar, and initially it was thought the two were related (Purdey 2004). When identical diseases turned up in families in the Azores, southern Brazil, and parts of East Asia, genetic predisposition replaced manganese toxicity as the most likely answer. The medical historian Warwick Anderson is researching this switched diagnosis and its implications.

12. This nesting of compromises is neatly captured in the Regional Partnership Agreement evaluation findings: "Some questions that might guide future directions include the following. How can the Anindilyakwa people use the new houses to develop living patterns that will support healthy children and encourage them to attend school and to do homework?" (MacDonald and Browne 2012, 13).

13. At first blush, this can appear as a conflict of interest for the land councils that might, in feverish pursuit of their own income, push for mining on ALRA lands against traditional owner interests. However, the number of mines on ALRA land have not really altered since the 1980s. These include bauxite mining at Gove (now under Aboriginal control), uranium mining at Narbalek and Ranger (one closed, the other about to be), Granites (gold), and Mereenie Oil and Gas. At any rate, in 1984, the right to veto mining as originally enshrined in the ALRA was severely curtailed, so that traditional owners now can only veto exploration. Since township lease amendments in 2006, the floor guarantee of 40 percent of mining royalty equivalents for land councils was also removed. Land council funding is now totally at the discretion of the relevant minister with no guarantees of renewal, placing councils in greater equivalence with other Indigenous-controlled organizations struggling to manage the direction of social policy within threatened grant-dependent budgets.

14. Kirsty Howey's doctoral dissertation, a legal ethnography of the Northern Land Council, shows, among other issues, the backlog of development consent applications the council must churn through, and how impossible it is to superintend the delivery of actual benefits. Povinelli (2002) shows how land rights forced Aboriginal people to reinvent how they spoke about who they were and what their affiliations with their country amounted to, while Vincent (2017) discusses the social conflicts arising from native title legislation in South Australia. Norman (2015) details how New South Wales land rights are a site of contestation and opportunity for the individuals and organizations involved. Ritter (2009) details the business interests at play across the board. Ethnographic work groans with analogous mires across the world as extractivism intensifies. For exemplary accounts of different kinds of inveiglement, see Tanya Li's (2014) account of farmer-led enclosures as the prelude to capitalist inequalities among Indigenous highlanders in Indonesia, and

Lucas Bessire (2014a) on deforestation, anthropological intrusion, and the Ayoreo in South America.

15. The terms of this transition to greater local control of service delivery are set out in the Groote Archipelago Local Decision Making Agreement between the Northern Territory Government and the Anindilyakwa Land Council, signed November 14, 2018. From the time of this agreement, GEMCO's operations will proceed for a further ten years. See https://ldm.nt.gov.au/__data/assets/pdf_file/0005/595796/groote-archipelago-ldm-agreement.pdf. I have written elsewhere about the monumental battles it takes to assert the right to self-govern, when governments assume a priori superiority (see Lea 2012b; 2014b).

16. Early elaborations of Ahmed's complaint work can be found at her blog, https://feministkilljoys.com/.

17. See also *Housing Experience: Post Occupancy Evaluation of Alice Springs Town Camp Housing 2008–2011* (Centre for Appropriate Technology 2013), commissioned by Tangentyere Council, representing town camp housing organizations in Alice Springs, for an analysis of Ritek houses in the arid zones of central Australia.

Interlude IV

1. All information on Australian construction codes can be found at https://ncc.abcb.gov.au/ncc-online/NCC. This is a free, constantly updated resource site, for which a membership registration will be required.

2. ATSIC was established as a statutory authority in 1989 and combined representative and administrative functions for Indigenous groups across the country. It was abolished in 2005, prior to the Intervention. For more on its thwarted potential as a strong form of Indigenous law and governance, see Sanders (2018).

3. http://www.abc.net.au/austory/final-call/9498092.

4. The medical director of the service received threatening emails demanding that he too should resign in disgrace for his callous disregard for nurse safety.

5. As advised by Nganampa Health Council, email January 22, 2018.

Chapter 4

1. Elizabeth Povinelli's work is a far more comprehensive analysis of this encounter over time (Povinelli 1994, 2002, 2011c, 2016b). Her focus is less on policy (although we could argue the toss) than on the claims of late liberalism, as these forces moved through the lives of those whose worlds and spirits she has joined over decades. My account dedicates greater focus to policy workings, the legitimizing vehicle for enabling the forces of late liberalism to enter lives every which way. Policy fodder is recycled into Karrabing films because of its real-life omnipresence. How Povinelli wrecks good Japanese knives cutting magpie geese straight on the kitchen bench is a tale for another time.

2. Films produced to date include the beta version *Karrabing! Low Tide Turning* (2011), which became *When the Dogs Talked* (2014), followed by *Windjarrameru, The Stealing C*nt\$* (2015), *Wutharr: Saltwater Dreams* (2016), *The Jealous One* (2017), *Night Time Go* (2017), *The Mermaids, or Aiden in Wonderland* (2018), and *The Mermaids: Mirror Worlds* (2018).

3. This embrace also helps makes sense of how sites for influencing policy appear to have proliferated with new technologies. People have been forming alliances to change their own and others' circumstances throughout governed history. New technologies make these maneuvering spaces and tactics more visible, which has us believe that technologies are liberating the potential for change. Rather, although the technological means for mobilizing action have changed, the fact of people activating potentials for changing their own policy ecologies is quite ancient.

4. See, for example, the media report "Aboriginal Teens in Remote NT Community Use Hip Hop to Talk about Mental Health," August 22, 2017, http://www.abc.net.au/news/2017-08-23/aboriginal-teens-in-remote-nt-use-hip-hop-to-talk-mental-health/8832026.

5. All Aboriginal sacred sites in the NT are protected by the Northern Territory Aboriginal Sacred Sites Act 1989 and superintended by the Aboriginal Areas Protection Authority (AAPA). As with land rights legislation, AAPA's protective remit is often questioned. The most recent government-commissioned review probed how to "reduce red tape" to "provide certainty and improved processes for economic development" (PricewaterhouseCoopers 2016, 1). Cultural heritage legislation across Australia has been radically weakened to permit easier extraction. The early Karrabing enterprise vision imagined helping AAPA with its underresourced task of registering and monitoring threats to sacred sites; subsequent films refer to the omnipresent nature of such threats.

6. "Rangers" in Australia are not sheriffs, but people paid to superintend wilderness and metropolitan parks and reserves. Monitoring biodiversity and illegal activities is, however, part of their mandate.

7. This would be in contrast to current practices where payments for data inquiries are just as often never offered, even as contributing labor, time, and knowledge is fully expected.

8. This theme of unappeased and vengeful ancestors who refuse to offer protection is elaborated in *Wutharr: Saltwater Dreams* (2016) and *The Mermaids, or Aiden in Wonderland* (2018). Such hauntings are not fictive. As film critic Martha Schwendener (2019) acknowledged of the 2019 Karrabing retrospective showcased at the Museum of Modern Art, New York, "Very little is theoretical about the work of the Karrabing: The history of genocide and discrimination described in their films has been experienced firsthand."

9. For readers familiar with Cox Peninsula land rights arbitration, the brevity of this account is obvious. This is the site of the Kenbi Land Claim (Claim 37), first lodged in March 1979, renowned as the ALRA's longest and most fiercely contentious claim. Agreements were complicated by questions about "with whom" and "with what liabilities," as areas of the land in question were contaminated by previous government activities and military occupations and thus remain in need of funded remediation. What is this if not another policy hauntology?

10. Prepaid mobile phones are also the most expensive. Research conducted in Alice Springs showed that keeping a phone in credit consumes 13.5 percent of income in any week for Indigenous people on unemployment and other welfare payments. (See http://www.clc.org.au/files/pdf/CLC_Tangentyere_Research_Hub_report_on_Mobile_Phone_Use_in_Central_Australia_March_2007.pdf.)

11. Until July 1, 2015, ostensibly "free" calls to 1-800 lines were charged if accessed from mobile (cell) phones, incurring huge costs for callers stuck on hold. Following mid-2015, whether charges are passed on to customers or not depends on the service plan and telecommunications provider. Prepaid plans still fall between the gaps.

12. But see Laura Bear (2015).

13. See also Robinson (2012) and *Aboriginal Areas Protection Authority v OM (Manganese) Ltd* [2013] NTMC 019, https://localcourt.nt.gov.au/sites/default/files/decisions/2013NTMC19.pdf.

14. "OM Holdings Continues as One the [*sic*] ASX's Top Performers," March 22, 2018, http://www.proactiveinvestors.com.au/companies/news/193596/om-holdings-continues-as-one-the-asxs-top-performers-193596.html.

15. Different conceptual genealogies could be offered for the idea of creating change in the interstices. For instance, Giles Deleuze and Felix Guatarri have developed a complex account of the intermediate space between points of (falsely attributed) fixity, where life is always in flux—a point that anthropologist Tim Ingold (2007, 4) elaborates with great clarity in his work on lines.

16. With thanks to Christen Cornell for this insight.

17. Carol Bacchi's "What's the problem?" analytical approach does this exquisitely (2009). Calling on Foucault, Bacchi provides a set of probes analysts might use to uncover how governments selectively whittle issues into problems that can be made amenable to pre-figured government action, narrowing the brackets of possible policy responses.

18. An investigation of the relation between contaminants and childhood development in Australia's oldest continuous lead-mining town of Broken Hill, using test data collected between 2005 and 2008, found that exposed children suffer developmental delays (Dong et. al 2015). The research was partially funded by lawyers acting on behalf of residents. Such independent commissioning was needed. The industry-funded research that regulators had relied on since the mine opened in 1931 had perpetually found zero dangers. It is important to note that living adjacent to a mine has never been listed as a public health risk in accounts of what drives poor health for Indigenous and other exposed groups (but see McMullen, Eastwood, and Ward 2016 for important first steps toward such critical epidemiology).

19. In contemporary theories of Indigenous health, the newly influential concept of epigenetics could take this up, but doesn't, or perhaps cannot. For an overview, see Kowal (2016).

20. A parliamentary committee inquiring into required remediation work notes: "The Commonwealth has utilised 4,750 hectares of land on the Cox Peninsula for maritime, communications and Defence purposes for 70 years, resulting in extensive contamination across a wide area both below and at ground level. Asbestos is widespread and pesticides, heavy metals and polychlorinated biphenyls (PCBs) have been detected above safe levels . . . [presenting] a potential health risk to site users and the local community" (Commonwealth of Australia 2015, 6–7).

Interlude V

1. For a plain English explanation of the modified legislation, see https://www.sa-

health.sa.gov.au/wps/wcm/connect/public+content/sa+health+internet/about+us/
legislation/gayles+law.

2. If health services were classified using the Australian Statistical Geography Standard, places like Ceduna and Kangaroo Island, with their large non-Indigenous populations, would be included. For a useful tool, see https://www.health.gov.au/resources/
apps-and-tools/health-workforce-locator/health-workforce-locator.

3. Andrew "Twiggy" Forrest is an Australian mining magnate who has also enjoyed out-
sized influence on Indigenous policy agendas. In 2006, under Prime Minister Kevin Rudd,
Forrest had boldly promised fifty thousand jobs, by contracting directly with employers,
not job search agencies. In 2014, former prime minister Tony Abbott commissioned Forrest
to report on ways forward with Indigenous employment programs. John Singer is referring
to the report's hyperemphasis on market forces (to wit, "only employers and the market
can deliver real jobs" [Forrest 2014, 5]) and to Forrest's original fifty thousand jobs promise
(misremembered by Singer as five hundred promised jobs). Forrest's actual model involves
quasi-private Vocational Training and Employment Centres being allocated federal funding to essentially pay businesses to subcontract Indigenous workers.

4. For more information on the Remote and Aboriginal and Torres Strait Islander Aged
Care Service Development Assistance Panel and the responsibilities of panel members, see
https://agedcare.health.gov.au/programs/flexible-care/information-for-panel-members
(consulted December 24, 2018).

Chapter 5

1. Increasing attention is being paid to military and anthropological connections, as
the encyclopedic work of David Price (2016) makes clear. Although there were also direct
relations between anthropologists, warfare, and strategic military research in Australia
(Thomas and Neale 2011, Thomson 1983), my arguments draw more on feminist and critical military studies perspectives to reconsider the everyday militarism imbuing ambient
policy.

2. Gravel extraction and cement production ownership belongs to a shadowland of
construction monopolies across Australia, which not only preclude Indigenous people operating local enterprises but re-award large firms and their associated kinship networks.
GCC was attempting to enter a heavily protected business enclave from a very unequal
starting point.

3. US Department of Defense (2009), *Reconfiguration of the National Defense Stockpile
Report to Congress*, Appendix F-6, available at http://www.acq.osd.mil/mibp/docs/nds_
reconfiguration_report_to_congress.pdf; see also http://www.usgs.gov/blogs/features/
usgs_top_story/going-critical-being-strategic-with-our-mineral-resources/.

4. For a sense of the scale of manganese as a commodity traded across the globe, I
recommend the Chatham House Resource Trade Database, available online as https://re-
sourcetrade.earth. To visualize global maritime trade, see the University College London
Energy Institute's interactive map, available at www.shipmap.org.

5. Even as its global economic and sociocultural influence wanes, America remains

the world's largest military empire, using a network of overseas bases and sovereign-controlled territory plus a variety of trade arrangements to furnish military access for global power projection—including from my hometown of Darwin (Lea 2014a, Vine 2015).

6. America's Lend-Lease Agreement of 1943, ostensibly designed to give Britain and its allies the "sinews of war" (cf. Mackenzie 1999), required that Britain remove any discrimination against US imports and relinquish its system of imperial preferencing in imports and exports. Australia and other colonial dominions were thereby rapidly opened to US commodities, and America could exert extraordinary influence over the shape of postwar global economics and policy emphasis.

7. The US government separately secured uranium supplies in Canada, preventing Britain from invoking Commonwealth ties in their other former colony to realize their atomic ambitions (van Wyck 2011).

8. Yami was not the only person whose eyes suffered, as Eve Vincent's analysis further reveals: "We got up in the morning from the tent. . . . The smoke caught us—it came over us. We tried to open our eyes in the morning, but we couldn't. . . . We had red eyes and tongues and our coughing was getting worse. . . . There were no doctors, only the station bosses. All day we sat in the tent with our eyes closed. Our eyes were sore, red and shut. We couldn't open them. . . . All people got sick right up to Oodnadatta . . . we all got sick" (Eileen Kampakuta Brown in Vincent 2007, 158).

9. See Eickelkamp (2014, 57) on the "'soul-destroying, devouring, malignant power called *Mamu*."

10. By the end of the secret nuclear testing program, "Maralinga had been the site for seven major trials of nuclear weapons and about 580 minor trials[, which] left the Range contaminated by radioactive and toxic materials" (McClelland, Fitch, and Jonas 1985, 527).

11. The name Rum Jungle apparently comes from the region's earlier radical transformation from land belonging to the Kungarakan people into gold diggings. This is the story according to Bill Beatty, a journalist writing about whimsical settler place names. Sometime in the late nineteenth century, prospectors at the John Bull gold mine were carrying a find of 750 ounces of gold when they met a teamster who generously plied them with rum. When they returned to consciousness, their gold, their horses, and the teamster had disappeared. "Every man in the district began a search which lasted for months until the thieving teamster and the gold were found" (Beatty 1947, 6). Hence the name Rum Jungle. The Rum Jungle uranium mine operated from 1954 to 1971, with Australia exporting its uranium pursuant to a sales contract with the Combined Development Agency, a UK-US authority established to purchase uranium for those countries' nuclear arsenals. Today, it is a contaminated region renowned for its abject rehabilitation failure (Mudd and Patterson 2010).

12. Section 41(1) of the Aboriginal Land Rights (Northern Territory) Act 1976 provided that traditional Aboriginal owners, through the Northern Land Council (NLC), had the right to veto mining and exploration on Aboriginal land. However, pursuant to section 41(2) of the same act, the veto did not apply to the Ranger project area. Instead, the NLC (on behalf of traditional Aboriginal owners) and the Commonwealth had to—as in, were mandatorily required to—make an agreement before uranium mining activities could

take place (s44(2)). If there was a stalemate in negotiations, the minister could appoint an arbitrator to determine the terms and conditions of the agreement and then enter into the agreement on the NLC's behalf instead (s46).

13. Just how the Mirarr Gundjeihmi stopped Jabiluka from proceeding is told elsewhere (see especially O'Brien 2003; Lawrence and Sweeney 2019). It is a story the world should know, representing the only instance to date of an Indigenous group successfully halting live uranium operations.

14. With thanks to Stuart Rollo for drawing the passionate pro-uranium stance of earlier politicians to my attention.

15. I could make similar points about bauxite, another mineral of great military and domestic application (Sheller 2014, 16–17; 180–183).

Chapter 6

1. Patrick Sullivan has separately documented the inveiglement of Indigenous incorporated bodies within public sector arrangements, which, with their mimicry of commercial operations, create labyrinthine regimes, fragmented through outsourcing and the recruitment of NGOs (Sullivan 2011). Abdication of policy to NGOs in the form of contracting with audit companies is another piece of the puzzle, as early chapters have hinted.

References

Agamben, Giorgio. 1999. *Remnants of Auschwitz: The Witness and the Archive*. Translated by Daniel Heller-Roazen. Cambridge, MA: Zone Books, the MIT Press.

Ahmed, Sara. 2012. *On Being Included: Racism and Diversity in Institutional Life*. Durham and London: Duke University Press.

Akman, Amos. 2016. "Community Leaders Want Overhaul of 'Resented' Township Leases." *The Australian*, April 18, 2016. http://www.theaustralian.com.au/national-affairs/indigenous/community-leaders-want-overhaul-of-resented-township-leases/news-story/58715b93c114869a53ddaaedaf620421.

Akhbari, Rouzbeh. 2017. "Petro-Violence: Merging Militarism and Corporate Secrecy." *Environment and Planning D: Society and Space*. Forum on Investigating Infrastructures, October 10, 2017. https://www.societyandspace.otg/articles/petro-violence-merging-militarism-and-corporate-secrecy.

Altman, Jon. 1983. *Aborigines and Mining Royalties in the Northern Territory*. Canberra: Australian Institute of Aboriginal Studies.

———. 2005. "Economic Futures on Aboriginal Land in Remote and Very Remote Australia: Hybrid Economies and Joint Ventures." In *Culture, Economy and Governance in Aboriginal Australia*, edited by Diane Austin-Broos and Gaynor Macdonald, 121–134. Sydney: University of Sydney Press.

———. 2009. "Indigenous Communities, Miners and the State in Australia." In *Power, Culture, Economy: Indigenous Australians and Mining*, edited by Jon Altman and David Martin, 17–49. Canberra: ANU Press.

Altman, Jon, and Melinda Hinkson, eds. 2007. *Coercive Reconciliation: Normalise, Stabilise, Exit Aboriginal Australia*. Melbourne: Arena Publications.

Altman, Jon, and Susie Russell. 2012. "Too Much 'Dreaming': Evaluations of the Northern Territory National Emergency Response Intervention 2007–2012." *Evidence Base* 3:1–24.

Australian Bureau of Statistics. 2016. *4714.0 - National Aboriginal and Torres Strait Islander Social Survey, 2014-15*. Canberra: Australian Bureau of Statistics.

Australian National Audit Office. 2011. *Implementation of the National Partnership Agreement on Remote Indigenous Housing in the Northern Territory*. Canberra: Australian National Audit Office.

Anderson, Alison. 2009. "Full Statement Released by Alison Anderson on Her Resignation."

Sydney Morning Herald, August 4, 2009. https://www.smh.com.au/national/full-statement-released-by-alison-anderson-20090804-e85y.html.

Angelo, Bonnie, and Toni Morrison. 1989. "The Pain of Being Black." *TIME* 133 (21):120.

Bacchi, Carol. 2009. *Analysing Policy: What's the Problem Represented to Be?* Frenchs Forest: Pearson Education.

Ball, Stephen J. 1993. "What Is Policy? Texts, Trajectories and Toolboxes." *Discourse* 13 (2):10–17.

Banerjee, Subhabrata Bobby. 2000. "Whose Land Is It Anyway? National Interest, Indigenous Stakeholders and Colonial Discourses: The Case of the Jabiluka Uranium Mine." *Organization & Environment* 13 (1):3–38.

Barad, Karen. 2012. "Nature's Queer Performativity (the Authorized Version)." *Kvinder, Køn og Forskning* 1–2:25–53.

Barker, Anne. 2007. "Aboriginal Communities Abundant with Child Abuse: Report." *World Today*. Australian Broadcasting Commission. June 15, 2007. http://www.abc.net.au/worldtoday/content/2007/s1952348.htm.

Barretto, Paulo M. 1981. "Recent Developments in Uranium Exploration." *IAEA Bulletin* 23 (2): 15–20.

Batty, Phillip. 2005. "Private Politics, Public Strategies: White Advisers and Their Aboriginal Subjects." *Oceania* 75 (3):209–221.

Bear, Laura. 2015. *Navigating Austerity? Currents of Debt along a South Asian River*. Stanford: Stanford University Press.

Beatty, Bill. 1947. "There's Drama and Tragedy in Place Names." *Sydney Morning Herald*, August 2, 1947:6–7.

Belanger, Pierre, ed. 2018. *Extraction Empire 2017–1217*. Cambridge, MA: MIT Press.

Belanger, Pierre, and Alexander Arroyo. 2016. *Ecologies of Power: Countermapping the Logistical Landscapes and Military Geographies of the U.S. Department of Defense*. Cambridge, MA: MIT Press.

Berlant, Lauren. 2006. "Cruel Optimism." *Differences: A Journal of Feminist Cultural Studies* 17 (3):20–36.

———. 2011. *Cruel Optimism*. Durham and London: Duke University Press.

Bessire, Lucas. 2014a. *Behold the Black Caiman: A Chronicle of Ayoreo Life*. Chicago: University of Chicago Press.

———. 2014b. "The Rise of Indigenous Hypermarginality: Native Culture as a Neoliberal Politics of Life." *Current Anthropology* 55 (3):276–295.

Bessire, Lucas, and David Bond. 2014. "Ontological Anthropology and the Deferral of Critique." *American Ethnologist* 41 (3):440–456.

BHP Billiton. 2011. *BHP Billiton 20-F 2011 Annual Report Pursuant to Section 13 or 15d of the Securities Exchange Act of 1934 for the Fiscal Year Ended June 2011*. Washington DC: US Securities and Exchange Commission.

Biddle, Jennifer. 2000. "Writing without Ink: Literacy, Methodology and Cultural Difference." In *Culture and Text: Discourse and Methodology in Social Research and Cultural Studies*, edited by Alison Lee and Carol Poynton, 170–187. St. Leonards, NSW: Allen and Unwin.

————. 2016. *Remote Avant-Garde: Aboriginal Art under Occupation*. Durham: Duke University Press.

Biddle, Jennifer, and Tess Lea. 2018. "Faking It with the Truth." *Visual Anthropology Review* 34 (1):5–25.

Bolton, Katrina. 2009. "Head Rolls over Indigenous Housing Wrangle." Australian Broadcasting Commission. August 18, 2009. https://www.abc.net.au/news/2009-08-18/head-rolls-over-indigenous-housing-wrangle/1395246.

Brain, Caddie. 2011. *55 Years since Maralinga Atomic Bombs*. Australian Broadcasting Commission, ABC Rural. September 27, 2011. Sound recording available at https://www.abc.net.au/news/2011-09-27/yami-lester/6178744.

Brennan, Sean. 2008. "Wet or Dry, It's Aboriginal Land: The Blue Mud Bay Decision on the Intertidal Zone." *Indigenous Law Bulletin* 7 (7):6–9.

Brough, Mal. 2007. *Northern Territory National Emergency Response Bill 2007—Second Reading Speech*. House of Representatives, Commonwealth Parliamentary Debates. https://formerministers.dss.gov.au/2929/northern-territory-national-emergency-response-bill-2007-second-reading-speech/.

Brown, Anthony. 2003. "Prisoner of the Monsoon: Matthew Flinders in the Gulf of Carpentaria." *Australian Heritage* 9 (2):33–40.

Butterly, Lauren, and Rachel Pepper. 2017. "Are Courts Colourblind to Country? Indigenous Cultural Heritage, Environmental Law and the Australian Judicial System." *UNSW Law Journal* 40 (4):1313–1335.

Callon, Michel. 1986. "Some Elements of a Sociology of Translation: Domestication of the Scallops and Fishermen of St Brieuc Bay." In *Power, Action and Belief: A New Sociology of Knowledge?* edited by John Law, 196–233. London: Routledge and Kegan Paul.

Cannon, William F. 2014. *Manganese—It Turns Iron into Steel (and Does So Much More)*. US Department of the Interior, Geological Survey Mineral Resources Program. https://pubs.usgs.gov/fs/2014/3087/pdf/fs2014-3087.pdf.

Carrington, Kerry, Russell Hogg, Alison McIntosh, and John Scott. 2012. "Crime Talk, FIFO Workers and Cultural Conflict on the Mining Boom Frontier." *Australian Humanities Review* 53 (17). http://australianhumanitiesreview.org/2012/11/01/crime-talk-fifo-workers-and-cultural-conflict-on-the-mining-boom-frontier/.

Carrington, Kerry, Alison McIntosh, and John Scott. 2010. "Globalisation, Frontier Masculinities and Violence: Booze, Blokes and Brawl." *British Journal of Criminology* 50 (3):393–413.

Carrington, Kerry, and John Scott. 2008. "Masculinity, Rurality and Violence." *British Journal of Criminology* 48:641–666.

Castro-Klaren, Sara. 1998. "Literacy, Conquest and Interpretation: Breaking New Ground on the Records of the Past." *Social History* 23 (2):133–145.

Centre for Appropriate Technology. 2013. *Housing Experience: Post Occupancy Evaluation of Alice Springs Town Camp Housing 2008–2011*. Alice Springs, NT: Centre for Appropriate Technology, for Tangentyere Council.

Chaloupka, George. 1999. *Journey in Time: The World's Longest Continuing Art Tradition*. Sydney: Reed New Holland.

Comaroff, Jean, and John L. Comaroff, eds. 2001. *Millennial Capitalism and the Culture of Neoliberalism*. Durham: Duke University Press.

Commonwealth Grants Commission. 2015. *Report on GST Revenue Sharing Relativities 2015 Review—Volume 2—Assessment of State Fiscal Capacities*. Canberra: Commonwealth of Australia.

Commonwealth of Australia. 1999. "Jabiluka: The Undermining of Process: Inquiry into the Jabiluka Uranium Mine Project." In *Report of the Senate Environment, Communications, Information Technology and the Arts References Committee*. Canberra: Senate Inquiry under the Environment Protection (Impact of Proposals) Act 1974.

———. 2015. *The Cox Peninsula Remediation Project: Report 4/2015: Referrals Made December 2014 and March 2015*. Canberra: Parliamentary Standing Committee on Public Works.

———. 2018. *Remote Housing Review: A Review of the National Partnership Agreement on Remote Indigenous Housing and the Remote Housing Strategy (2008–2018)*. Canberra: Department of the Prime Minister and Cabinet.

Cooper, Davina. 2017. "Prefiguring the State." *Antipode*. 49 (2):335–356.

Cooper, Melinda. 2018. "Money as Punishment: Neoliberal Budgetary Politics and the Fine." *Australian Feminist Studies*. 33 (96):187–208.

Cowen, Deborah. 2014. *The Deadly Life of Logistics: Mapping the Violence of Global Trade*. Minneapolis: University of Minnesota Press.

Cowlishaw, Gillian. 1999. *Rednecks, Eggheads and Blackfellas: A Study of Racial Power and Intimacy in Australia*. St Leonards, NSW: Allen and Unwin.

———. 2003. "Disappointing Indigenous People: Violence and the Refusal of Help." *Public Culture* 15 (1):103–125.

Cox, Lisa. 2018. "Not Safe, Not Wanted': Is the End of NT Fracking Ban a Taste of Things to Come?" *Guardian*, June 18, 2018. https://www.theguardian.com/environment/2018/jun/18/not-safe-not-wanted-is-the-end-of-nt-fracking-ban-a-taste-of-things-to-come.

Crabtree, Louise. 2013. "Decolonising Property: Exploring Ethics, Land, and Time, through Housing Interventions in Contemporary Australia." *Environment and Planning D: Society and Space* 31:99–115.

Craig, David Alan, and Doug Porter. 2006. *Development beyond Neoliberalism? Governance, Poverty Reduction and Political Economy*. London: Routledge.

Davidson, James, Paul Memmott, Carroll Go-Sam, and Elizabeth Grant. 2011. *Remote Indigenous Housing Procurement: A Comparative Study AHURI Final Report No.167*. Melbourne: Australian Housing and Urban Research Institute.

Deloitte. 2017. *Living on the Edge: Northern Territory Town Camps Review*. Darwin: Northern Territory Department of Housing and Community Development.

Derrida, Jacques. 1994. *Specters of Marx: The State of the Debt, the Work of Mourning and the New International*. Translated by Peggy Kamuf. New York: Routledge.

Desmond, Matthew. 2016. *Evicted: Poverty and Profit in the American City*. New York: Crown Publishing Group.

DoFHSCIA and Northern Territory Government. 2009. *Strategic Indigenous Housing and*

Infrastructure Program—Review of Program Performance. Canberra: Department of Families, Housing, Community Services and Indigenous Affairs.

Dombrowski, Kirk. 2007. "Subsistence Livelihood, Native Identity and Internal Differentiation in Southeast Alaska." *Anthropologica* 49 (2):211–229.

———. 2010. "The White Hand of Capitalism and the End of Indigenism as We Know It." *Australian Journal of Anthropology* 21 (1):129–140.

Dong, Chenyin, Mark Patrick Taylor, Louise Jane Kristensen, and Sammy Zahran. 2015. "Environmental Contamination in an Australian Mining Community and Potential Influences on Early Childhood Health and Behavioural Outcomes." *Environmental Pollution* 207:345–356.

Douglas, Josie. 2015. "Kin and Knowledge: The Meaning and Acquisition of Indigenous Ecological Knowledge in the Lives of Young Aboriginal People in Central Australia." PhD diss., Charles Darwin University.

Downey, Gary Lee, and Joseph Dumit, eds. 1997. *Cyborgs and Citadels: Anthropological Interventions in Emerging Sciences and Technologies.* Santa Fe: School of American Research Press.

Dunbar-Ortiz, Roxanne. 2016. *An Indigenous People's History of the United States.* Boston: Beacon Press.

Eickelkamp, Ute. 2014. "Specters of Reality: *Mamu* in the Eastern Western Desert of Australia." In *Monster Anthropology in Australasia and Beyond,* edited by Yasmine Musharbash and Geir H. Presterudstuen, 57–73. New York: Palgrave Macmillan.

FaCSIA. 2010. *Strategic Indigenous Housing Infrastructure Program (SIHIP): Post Review Assessment (PRA).* Canberra: Department of Families, Community Services and Indigenous Affairs.

FaHCSIA. 2013. *National Partnership on Remote Indigenous Housing—Progress Review (2008–2013).* Canberra: Department of Families, Housing, Community Services and Indigenous Affairs.

Fenech, Katherine. 2010. "WA Mine Sites 'the Worst' for Fly-In, Fly-Out Violence: Study." *Sydney Morning Herald,* December 6, 2010. https://www.smh.com.au/national/western-australia/wa-mine-sites-the-worst-for-flyin-flyout-violence-study-20101206–18mm1.html.

Ferguson, James. 1990. *The Anti-Politics Machine. "Development," Depoliticization, and Bureaucratic Power in Lesotho.* Cambridge, UK: Cambridge University Press.

Fien, John, and Esther Charlesworth. 2012. "'Why Isn't It Solved?' Factors Affecting Improvements in Housing Outcomes in Remote Indigenous Communities in Australia." *Habitat International* 36:20–25.

Findlay, Elisabeth. 1988. *Arcadian Quest: William Westall's Australian Sketches.* Canberra: National Library of Australia.

Fischer, Michael M. J. 2014. "The Lightness of Existence and the Origami of 'French' Anthropology: Latour, Descola, Viveiros de Castro, Meillassoux, and Their So-Called Ontological Turn." *HAU: Journal of Ethnographic Theory* 4 (1):331–355.

Fisher, Daniel. 2015. "An Urban Frontier: Respatializing Government in Remote Northern Australia." *Cultural Anthropology* 30 (1):139–168.

———. 2018. "A Subject Deferred: Exposure and Erasure in an Ethnographic Archive." *Oceania* 88 (3):292–304.

Flinders, Matthew. 1814. "Voyage to Terra Australis Undertaken for the Purpose of Completing the Discovery of That Vast Country, and Prosecuted in the Years 1801, 1802 and 1803, in Majesty's Ship *The Investigator*, and Subsequently in the Armed Vessel Porpoise and Cumberland Schooner." http://gutenberg.net.au/ebooks/e00049.html.

———. 2015. *Australia Circumnavigated: The Voyage of Matthew Flinders in HMS Investigator, 1801–1803*. Edited by Kenneth Morgan. Farnham, Surrey, and Burlington, VT: Ashgate for the Hakluyt Society.

Forrest, Andrew. 2014. *The Forrest Review: Creating Parity*. Canberra: Commonwealth of Australia. https://www.pmc.gov.au/sites/default/files/publications/Forrest-Review.pdf.

Froud, Julie, Sukhdev Johal, Michael Mora, and Karen Williams. 2017. "Outsourcing the State: New Sources of Elite Power." *Theory, Culture & Society* 34 (5–6):77–101.

Garneau, David. 2014. "Extra-Rational Aesthetic Action and Cultural Decolonization." *FUSE* 36 (4):13–21.

Garnett, Stephen T., Beverley Sithole, Peter J. Whitehead, Chris Burgess, Faye Johnston, and Tess Lea. 2009. "Healthy Country, Healthy People: Policy Implications of Links between Indigenous Human Health and Environmental Condition in Tropical Australia." *Australian Journal of Public Administration* 68 (1):53–66.

Gibson, Jano. 2009. "Macklin Blamed for Indigenous Housing Wrangle." *ABC News*, August 9, 2009. https://www.abc.net.au/news/2009-08-19/macklin-blamed-for-indigenous-housing-wrangle/1396706.

Gieryn, Thomas F. 2002. "What Buildings Do." *Theory and Society* 31 (1):35–74.

Gómez-Barris, Macarena. 2017. *The Extractive Zone: Social Ecologies and Decolonial Perspectives*. Durham: Duke University Press.

Gordon, Avery. 2008. *Ghostly Matters: Haunting and the Sociological Imagination*. Minneapolis: University of Minnesota Press.

Graeber, David. 2011. *Debt: The First Five Thousand Years*. New York: Melville House.

———. 2012. "Dead Zones of the Imagination: On Violence, Bureaucracy and Interpretive Labour." *HAU: Journal of Ethnographic Theory* 2 (2):102–128.

———. 2015. *The Utopia of Rules: On Technology, Stupidity and the Secret Joys of Bureaucracy*. Kindle Edition. Brooklyn and London: Melville House.

Graham, Stephen. 2010. "When Infrastructures Fail." In *Disrupted Cities: When Infrastructure Fails*, edited by Stephen Graham, 1–26. New York: Routledge.

Graham, Stephen, and Nigel Thrift. 2007. "Out of Order: Understanding Repair and Maintenance." *Theory, Culture & Society* 24 (1):1–25.

Grealy, Liam. 2018. "States of Deferral: Securing Housing in Borroloola, NT." *Crikey*. https://blogs.crikey.com.au/northern/2018/11/09/states-of-deferral-securing-housing-in-borroloola-nt/.

Gregg, Melissa. 2018. *Counterproductive: Time Management in the Knowledge Economy*. Durham and London: Duke University Press.

Gupta, Akhil. 2012. *Red Tape: Bureaucracy, Structural Violence, and Poverty in India*. Durham and London: Duke University Press.

Gusterson, Hugh. 2007. "Anthropology and Militarism." *Annual Review of Anthropology* 36:155–175.

Habibis, Daphne, Rhonda Phillips, and Peter Phibbs. 2018. "Housing Policy in Remote Indigenous Communities: How Politics Obstructs Good Policy." *Housing Studies* 34 (2):252–271.

Hage, Ghassan. 2016. "État de Siège: A Dying Domesticating Colonialism?" *American Ethnology* 43 (1):38–49.

———. 2017. *Is Racism an Environmental Threat?* Cambridge, UK: Polity Press.

Hagerman, R. A. 1984. *U.S. Reliance on Africa for Strategic Minerals*. CSC 1984. GlobalSecurity.org. https://www.globalsecurity.org/military/library/report/1984/HRA.htm.

Hall, Lex. 2010. "NT Indigenous Housing Builder Earth Connect Alliance Axed from SIHIP Program." *The Australian*, March 18, 2010. http://www.theaustralian.com.au/news/nation/nt-indigenous-housing-builder-earth-connect-alliance-axed-from-sihip-program/news-story/a198652ca4171582c06c008f71a7d021.

Hansen Bailey. 2015. *Groote Eylandt Mining Company (GEMCO) Eastern Leases Project Draft Environmental Impact Statement*. https://www.south32.net/docs/default-source/gemco/draft-environmental-impact-statement-2015/executive-summary.pdf?sfvrsn=750d5d8c_3.

Hansen, Thomas Blom, and Finn Stepputat, eds. 2001. *States of Imagination: Ethnographic Explorations of the Postcolonial State*. Durham and London: Duke University Press.

Haraway, Donna. 2008. *When Species Meet*. Minneapolis and London: University of Minnesota Press.

———. 2016. *Staying with the Trouble: Making Kin in the Chthulucene*. Durham: Duke University Press.

Harris, Marty. 2011. *The Origins of Australia's Uranium Export Policy*. Parliamentary Library Background Paper. Canberra: Department of Parliamentary Services, Parliament of Australia.

Harvey, David. 2005a. *A Brief History of Neoliberalism*. Oxford and New York: Oxford University Press.

———. 2005b. *The New Imperialism*. Oxford and New York: Oxford University Press.

Haynes, Chris. 2017. "The Value of Work and 'Common Discourse' in the Joint Management of Kakadu National Park." *Australian Journal of Anthropology* 28 (1):72–87.

Hecht, Gabrielle. 2006. "Nuclear Ontologies." *Constellations* 13 (3):320–331.

———. 2012. *Being Nuclear: Africans and the Global Uranium Trade*. Cambridge, MA: MIT Press.

Hetherington, Kregg. 2011. *Guerrilla Auditors: The Politics of Transparency in Neoliberal Paraguay*. Durham: Duke University Press.

Heyes, Peter J., Konstantinos Anastasakis, Wiebren de Jong, Annelies van Hoesel, Wil Roebroeks, and Marie Soressi. 2014. "Selection and Use of Manganese Dioxide by Neanderthals." *Scientific Reports* 6 (22159):1–9.

Hill, Callum. 2011. *An Introduction to Sustainable Resource Use*. Abingdon, UK: Earthscan.

Horne, Ralph, Andrew Martel, Paula Arcari, Denise Foster, and Audrey McCormack. 2013. *Living Change: Adaptive Housing Response to Climate Change in the Town Camps of Alice Springs*. Gold Coast, Qld: National Climate Change Adaptation Research Facility. https://www.nccarf.edu.au/sites/default/files/attached_files_publications/Horne_2013_Living_change.pdf.

Howey, Kirsty. 2017. "The Northern Territory's Environmental Assessment Laws: Development, Land Rights and the Entanglements of History." *Australian Environment Review* 32 (1):9–14.

Huddle, Franklin P. 1976. "The Evolving National Policy for Materials." *Science* 191 (4228):654–659.

Hull, Matthew S. 2012. *Government of Paper: The Materiality of Bureaucracy in Urban Pakistan*. Berkeley: University of California Press.

INCITE. 2017 (fp 2007). *The Revolution Will Not Be Funded: Beyond the Non-Profit Industrial Complex*. Durham: Duke University Press.

Ingold, Tim. 2007. *Lines: A Brief History*. London: Routledge.

———. 2010. *Bringing Things to Life: Creative Entanglements in a World of Materials* (Working Paper No. 15). Vital Signs 2: Engaging Research Imaginations, University of Manchester, Manchester UK, September 7–9, 2010. http://eprints.ncrm.ac.uk/1306/1/0510_creative_entanglements.pdf.

Jackson, Steven. 2015. "Repair." Theorizing the Contemporary, *Cultural Anthropology*, September 24, 2015. https://culanth.org/fieldsights/repair.

James, Diana. 2015. "Tjukurpa Time." In *Long History, Deep Time: Deepening Histories of Place*, edited by Ann McGrath and Mary Ann Jebb, 33–45. Canberra: ANU Press.

James, Melinda. 2009. "Indigenous Housing Bill to 'Blow Out to $1b." *ABC News*, August 18, 2009. https://www.abc.net.au/news/2009-08-19/indigenous-housing-bill-to-blow-out-to-1b/1396326.

Jefferies, Marcus, Adam Schubert, and Ramsey Awad. 2011. "A Project Alliance Approach for the Procurement of Indigenous Social Housing in Australia." COBRA 2011: RICS International Research Conference: Legal Research Symposium, Salford, UK, September 12–13, 2011.

Jones, Tony. 2006. "Crown Prosecutor Speaks Out about Abuse in Central Australia." *ABC Lateline*, May 16, 2006, Australian Broadcasting Corporation. https://www.abc.net.au/lateline/nannette-rogers-spoke-with-tony-jones/1755090.

Kafka, Ben. 2012. *The Demon of Writing: Powers and Failures of Paperwork*. New York: Zone Books.

Kaplan, Caren. 2018. *Aerial Aftermaths: Wartime from Above*. Durham and London: Duke University Press.

Kay, Paul. n.d. *Australia's Uranium Mines Past and Present*. Canberra: Science, Technology, Environment and Resource Group, Parliamentary Library.

Klare, Michael T. 2012. *The Race for What's Left: The Global Scramble for the World's Last Resources*. New York: Metropolitan Books.

Kowal, Emma. 2015. *Trapped in the Gap: Doing Good in Indigenous Australia*. New York and Oxford: Berghahn.

———. 2016. "The Promise of Indigenous Epigenetics." *Discover Society*, October 4, 2016. https://discoversociety.org/2016/10/04/the-promise-of-indigenous-epigenetics/.

Kristensen, Louise Jane, and Mark Patrick Taylor. 2016. "Unravelling a 'Miner's Myth' That Environmental Contamination in Mining Towns Is Naturally Occurring." *Environmental Geochemistry and Health* 38 (4):1015–1027.

Larkins, Alison. 2012. *Remote Housing Reforms in the Northern Territory*. Canberra: Commonwealth Ombudsman.

Latour, Bruno. 2005. *Reassembling the Social: An Introduction to Actor-Network-Theory.* London: Oxford University Press.

Lattas, Andrew, and Barry Morris. 2010. "Embedded Anthropology and the Intervention." *Arena* 107:15–20.

Lawrence, David. 2000. *Kakadu: The Making of a National Park*. Melbourne: Melbourne University Press.

Lawrence, Rebecca, and David Sweeney. 2019. *Unfinished Business: Rehabilitating the Ranger Uranium Mine*. Sydney: Sydney Environment Institute and Australian Conservation Foundation.

Lea, Tess. 2008. *Bureaucrats and Bleeding Hearts: Indigenous Health in Northern Australia*. Sydney: UNSW Press.

———. 2010. "Indigenous Education and Training: What Are We Here For?" In *Culture Crisis: Anthropology and Politics in Remote Aboriginal Australia*, edited by Jon Altman and Melinda Hinkson, 195–211. Sydney: UNSW Press.

———. 2012a. "Contemporary Anthropologies of Indigenous Australia." *Annual Review of Anthropology* 41:187–202.

———. 2012b. Housing, Mines and Infrastructure on Groote Eylandt. *Australian Humanities Review* 53. http://australianhumanitiesreview.org/2012/11/01/ecologies-of-development-on-groote-eylandt/.

———. 2014a. *Darwin*. Sydney: NewSouth Books.

———. 2014b. "From Little Things, Big Things Grow": The Unfurling of Wild Policy. *e-flux journal* 58 (10). https://www.e-flux.com/journal/58/61174/from-little-things-big-things-grow-the-unfurling-of-wild-policy/.

———. 2015a. "Educating for Inequality: Indigenous Schooling in Northern Australia." In *Cultural Pedagogies and Human Conduct*, edited by Megan Watkins, Greg Noble, and Catherine Driscoll, 144–157. London and New York: Routledge.

———. 2015b. "What's Water Got to Do with It? Indigenous Public Housing and Australian Settler Colonial Relations." *Settler Colonial Studies* 5 (4):375–386.

———. 2016. "Infrastructure Reform in Indigenous Australia: From Mud to Mining to Military Empires." In *Infrastructures and Social Complexity: A Companion*, edited by Penny Harvey, Casper Bruun Jensen, and Atsuro Morita, 62–75. New York: Routledge.

Lea, Tess, Kirsty Howey, and Justin O'Brien. 2018. "Waging Paperfare: Subverting the Damage of Extractive Capitalism in Kakadu." *Oceania* 18 (3):305–319.

Lea, Tess, and Paul Pholeros. 2010. "This Is Not a Pipe: The Treacheries of Indigenous Housing." *Public Culture* 22 (1):187–209.

Lea, Tess, and Elizabeth Povinelli. 2018. "Karrabing: An Essay in Keywords." *Visual Anthropology Review* 34 (1):36–46.

Lea, Tess, and Stuart Rollo. 2016. "A Servant Is Not Greater Than His Master: American Primacy in Australian Security." In *Hearts and Minds: US Cultural Management in 21st Century Foreign Relations*, edited by Matthew Chambers, 17–42. Bern: Peter Lang.

Leigh Star, Susan. 1999. "The Ethnography of Infrastructure." *American Behavioral Scientist* 43 (3):377–391.

Lester, Yami. 2000. *Yami: The Autobiography of Yami Lester*. Alice Springs, NT: IAD Press.

Li, Tanya. 2014. *Land's End: Capitalist Relations on an Indigenous Frontier*. Durham and London: Duke University Press.

Libby, Ronald T. 1992. *Hawke's Law: The Politics of Mining and Aboriginal Land Rights in Australia*. University Park: Penn State Press.

Lipsky, Michael. 1980. *Street Level Bureaucracy: Dilemmas of the Individual in Public Services*. New York: Russell Sage Foundation.

Lutz, Catherine. 2014. "Cars and Transport: The Car-Made City." In *Companion to Urban Anthropology*, edited by Donald M. Nonini, 142–153. Hoboken: Wiley.

MacDonald, Margaret, and Margaret Browne. 2012. *Groote Eylandt and Bickerton Island Regional Partnership Agreement Progress Evaluation, February 2012*. Tempo Strategies. https://www.dss.gov.au/sites/default/files/documents/09_2012/evaluation_of_the_rpa_0.pdf.

Mackenzie, Hector. 1999. "Sinews of War and Peace: The Politics of Economic Aid to Britain, 1939–1945." *International Journal* 54 (4):648–670.

Macknight, Campbell C. 1976. *Voyage to Marege: Macassan Trepangers in North Australia*. Melbourne: Melbourne University Press.

Macoun, Alissa. 2011. "Aboriginality and the Northern Territory Intervention." *Australian Journal of Political Science* 46 (3):519–534.

Madden, Aodhan. 2015. "Making Batteries: Conversation with the Karrabing Film Collective." *Un* 9 (2). http://unprojects.org.au/magazine/issues/issue-9-2/making-batteries/.

Markham, Francis, and Bruce Doran. 2015. "Equity, Discrimination and Remote Policy: Investigating the Centralization of Remote Service Delivery in the Northern Territory." *Applied Geography* 58:105–115.

Masco, Joseph. 2004. "Mutant Ecologies: Radioactive Life in Post–Cold War New Mexico." *Cultural Anthropology* 19 (4):517–550.

———. 2013. "Atomic Soldiers." In *Soldier Exposure and Technical Publics: A Collaborative Visual Essay*, edited by Zoë Wool. Public Books.org. Available at http://www.public-books.org/soldier-exposures-and-technical-publics/.

McClelland, J. R., J. Fitch, and W.J.A. Jonas. 1985. *The Report of the Royal Commission into British Nuclear Tests in Australia*. Canberra: Royal Commission into British Nuclear Tests in Australia, Australian Government Publishing Service.

McKee, Martin. 2017. "Grenfell Tower Fire: Why We Cannot Ignore the Political Determinants of Health." *British Medical Journal* 357 (8111):j2966.

McMullen, Cheryl, Ashley Eastwood, and Jeannette Ward. 2016. "Environmental Attributable Fractions in Remote Australia: The Potential of a New Approach for Local Public Health Action." *Australian and New Zealand Journal of Public Health* 40 (2):174–180.

McTighe, Laura, and Megan Raschig. 2019. "An Otherwise Anthropology." Theorizing the Contemporary, *Cultural Anthropology*, July 31, 2019. https://culanth.org/fieldsights/series/an-otherwise-anthropology.

Mead, M. Nathaniel. 2008. "Contaminants in Human Milk: Weighing the Risks against the Benefits of Breastfeeding." *Environmental Health Perspectives* 116 (10):A426–A434.

Mezzadra, Sandro, and Brett Neilson. 2013. *Border as Method, or the Multiplication of Labor.* Durham and London: Duke University Press.

———. 2015. "Operations of Capital." *South Atlantic Quarterly* 114 (1):1–9.

Michel, Thomas. 2015. "The Special Case of Reform in the Northern Territory: What Are the Lessons?" In *Perspectives on Australian Local Government Reform*, edited by Ian Tiley and Brian Dollery, 102–116 Sydney: Federation Press.

Michel, Thomas, and Andrew Taylor. 2012. "Death by a Thousand Grants? The Challenge of Grant Funding Reliance for Local Government Councils in the Northern Territory of Australia." *Local Government Studies* 38 (4):485–500.

Mignolo, Walter D. 1992. "The Darker Side of the Renaissance: Colonization and the Discontinuity of the Classical Tradition." *Renaissance Quarterly* 45 (4):808–828.

Mignolo, Walter D., and Arturo Escobar, eds. 2010. *Globalization and the Decolonial Option.* London and New York: Routledge.

Moreton-Robinson, Aileen. 2015. *The White Possessive: Property, Power and Indigenous Sovereignty*. Minneapolis: University of Minnesota Press.

Morsely, Angela. 2017. "Protecting Authority, Burying Dissent: An Analysis of Australian Nuclear Waste Law." *Macquarie Law Journal* 17:55–81.

Mosse, David. 2004. "Is Good Policy Unimplementable? Reflections on the Ethnography of Aid Policy and Practice." *Development and Change* 35 (4):639–671.

Mudd, Gavin M., and James Patterson. 2010. "Continuing Pollution from the Rum Jungle U–Cu Project: A Critical Evaluation of Environmental Monitoring and Rehabilitation." *Environmental Pollution* 158 (5):1252–1260.

Murphy, Michelle. 2017. "Afterlife and Decolonial Chemical Relations." *Cultural Anthropology* 32 (4):494–503.

Musharbash, Yasmine 2009. *Yuendumu Everyday: Contemporary Life in Remote Aboriginal Australia*. Canberra: Aboriginal Studies Press.

Nash, June. 1993 [1979]. *We Eat the Mines and the Mines Eat Us: Dependency and Exploitation in Bolivian Tin Mines*. New York: Columbia University Press.

Neale, Timothy. 2017. *Wild Articulations: Environmentalism and Indigeneity in Northern Australia*. Honolulu: University of Hawaii Press.

Neimanis, Astrida. 2017. *Bodies of Water: Posthuman Feminist Phenomenology*. London: Bloomsbury.

Nethercote, Megan. 2014. "Reconciling Policy Tensions on the Frontlines of Indigenous Housing Provision in Australia: Reflexivity, Resistance and Hybridity." *Housing Studies* 29 (8):1045–1072.

———. 2015a. "Neoliberal Welfare, Minorities and Tenancy Support." *Social Policy and Society* 16 (1):15–32.

———. 2015b. "Operationalizing a Responsibility Agenda in Australia's Indigenous Communities: Confused, Doubtful and Subversive Public Housing Tenants." *Housing, Theory and Society* 32 (2):171–195.

———. 2019. "Kemeny Revisited: The New Homeownership-Welfare Dynamics." *Housing Studies* 34 (2):226–251.

Neu, Dean. 2000. "Accounting and Accountability Relations: Colonization, Genocide and Canada's First Nations." *Accounting, Auditing & Accountability Journal* 13 (3):268–288.

Norman, Heidi. 2015. *What Do We Want? A Political History of Aboriginal Land Rights in New South Wales.* Sydney: NewSouth Books.

Northern Territory Government. 2017. *Northern Territory Correctional Services and Youth Justice Annual Statistics 2015–2016.* Darwin: Department of the Attorney-General and Justice.

O'Brien, David. 2011. "Home to Own: Potential for Indigenous Housing by Indigenous People." *Australian Aboriginal Studies* 1:65–80.

O'Brien, Justin. 2003. "Canberra Yellowcake: The Politics of Uranium and How Aboriginal Land Rights Failed the Mirarr People." *Journal of Northern Territory History* 14:79–91.

O'Faircheallaigh, Ciaran. 2004. "Denying Citizens Their Rights? Indigenous People, Mining Payments and Service Provision." *Australian Journal of Public Administration* 63 (2):42–50.

Pasternak, Shiri, and Tia Dafnos. 2018. "How Does a Settler State Secure the Circuitry of Capital?" *Environment and Planning D: Society and Space* 36 (4):739–757.

Peele, Reynolds B. 1997. "The Importance of Maritime Chokepoints." *Parameters* 27 (2):61–74.

Phibbs, Peter, and Susan Thompson. 2011. *The Health Impacts of Housing: Toward a Policy-Relevant Research Agenda.* Melbourne: Australian Housing and Urban Research Institute.

Pholeros, Paul, and Peter Phibbs. 2012. *Constructing and Maintaining Houses. Resource Sheet no. 13.* Closing the Gap Clearinghouse. Canberra and Melbourne: Australian Institute of Health and Welfare and Australian Institute of Family Studies.

Pignarre, Philippe, and Isabelle Stengers. 2011. *Capitalist Sorcery: Breaking the Spell.* Translated by Andrew Goffey. New York: Palgrave MacMillan.

Povinelli, Elizabeth A. 1994. *Labor's Lot: The Culture, History and Power of Aboriginal Action.* Chicago: University of Chicago Press.

———. 2002. *The Cunning of Recognition: Indigenous Alterities and the Making of Australian Multiculturalism.* Durham and London: Duke University Press.

———. 2008. "The Child in the Broom Closet: States of Killing and Letting Die." *South Atlantic Quarterly* 107 (3):509–530.

———. 2011a. "Routes/Worlds." *e-flux* 27. https://www.e-flux.com/journal/27/67991/routes-worlds/.

———. 2011b. *Economies of Abandonment: Social Belonging and Endurance in Late Liberalism.* Durham: Duke University Press.

———. 2011c. "The Part That Has No Part: Enjoyment, Law and Loss." *GLQ: A Journal of Lesbian and Gay Studies* 17 (2–3):287–307.

———. 2012. "The Will to Be Otherwise/The Effort of Endurance." *South Atlantic Quarterly* 111 (3):453–475.

———. 2015a. "Transgender Creeks and the Three Figures of Power in Late Liberalism." *Differences: A Journal of Feminist Cultural Studies* 26 (1):168–187.

———. 2015b. "Windjarrameru, the Stealing C*nts." *e-flux* 65. http://supercommunity.e-flux.com/texts/windjarrameru-the-stealing-c-nts/.

———. 2016a. "Dear Attorney General So-and-So, Correspondence Series #2." *Hearings: The Online Journal of Contour Biennale*, May 19, 2016. http://hearings.contour8.be/2016/05/19/dear-attorney-general-soandso/.

———. 2016b. *Geontologies: A Requiem to Late Liberalism*. Durham: Duke University Press.

Powell, Alan. 1988 (fp 1982). *Far Country: A Short History of the Northern Territory*. Carlton, Vic: Melbourne University Press.

Power, Sophie. 2016. *Radioactive Waste Management*. Canberra: Australian Parliamentary Library. https://www.aph.gov.au/About_Parliament/Parliamentary_Departments/Parliamentary_Library/pubs/BriefingBook45p/RadioactiveWaste.

Price, David H. 2016. *Cold War Anthropology*. Durham: Duke University Press.

PricewaterhouseCoopers. 2016. *Sacred Sites Processes and Outcomes Review*. https://dcm.nt.gov.au/__data/assets/pdf_file/0004/297148/sacred-sites-review.pdf.

Proudfoot, Fiona, and Daphne Habibis. 2015. "Separate Worlds: A Discourse Analysis of Mainstream and Aboriginal Populist Media Accounts of the Northern Territory Emergency Response in 2007." *Journal of Sociology* 15 (2):170–188.

Purdey, Mark. 2004. "The Pathogenesis of Machado Joseph Disease: A High Manganese/Low Magnesium Initiated CAG Expansion Mutation in Susceptible Genotypes?" *Journal of the American College of Nutrition* 23 (6):715S–729S.

Reed, David, ed. 2015. *In Pursuit of Prosperity: U.S Foreign Policy in an Era of Natural Resource Scarcity*. New York: Routledge.

Reynolds, Wayne. 1998. "Rethinking the Joint Project: Australia's Bid for Nuclear Weapons, 1945–1960." *Historical Journal* 41 (3):853–873.

Ritter, David. 2009. *The Native Title Market*. Perth: University of Western Australia Press.

Ritvo, Harriet. 2014. "Back Story: Invasion, Migration and Assimilation in the Nineteenth Century." In *Rethinking Invasion Ecologies from the Environmental Humanities*, edited by Jodi Frawley and Iain McCalman, 17–30. London and New York: Routledge.

Robinson, Natasha. 2009. "Slice of Pie for Building Is Shrinking by the Day." *The Australian*, August 20, 2009. https://www.theaustralian.com.au/opinion/slice-of-pie-for-building-is-shrinking-by-the-day/news-story/2d022d5e68fa6298797ca5e4f4f42089.

———. 2012. "Mining Firm Accused of Blowing Up Aboriginal Sacred Site." *The Australian*, April 9, 2012:1. https://www.theaustralian.com.au/national-affairs/indigenous/mining-firm-accused-of-blowing-up-aboriginal-sacred-site/news-story/db7ba0d49d521969d85a4aeded605ea4.

Robinson, Natasha, Tony Koch, and Michael Owen. 2009. "Failure of Indigenous Housing Policy in the Northern Territory." *The Australian*, August 15, 2009. https://www.theaustralian.com.au/news/investigations/refugees-in-their-own-land/news-story/6460e0804d68cf6b4fa958f2ca12c66e.

Rollo, Stuart. 2018. "The 'Asia Threat' in the US–Australia Relationship: Then and Now." *International Relations of the Asia-Pacific* 19. https://doi.org/10.1093/irap/lcz009.

Rose, Deborah Bird, Sharon D'Amico, Nancy Daiyi, Margaret Daiyi, Kathy Deveraux, Linda Ford, and April Bright. 2011. *Country of the Heart—An Indigenous Homeland*. Canberra: Aboriginal Studies Press.

Rosenman, Nadia, and Alex Clunies-Ross. 2011. "The New Tenancy Framework for Remote Aboriginal Communities in the Northern Territory." *Indigenous Law Bulletin* 7 (24):11–16.

Rothwell, Nicolas. 2017. "Colonial Turbulence in the North." *Arena* 148:11–17.

Rowntree, J. C., and D. K. Mosher. 1976. "Case History of the Discovery of Jabiluka Uranium Deposits, East Alligator River Region, Northern Territory of Australia." In *Exploration for Uranium Ore Deposits*, edited by IAEA editorial staff, 551–574. Vienna: International Atomic Energy Agency.

Russell, Denise. 2004. "Aboriginal–Makassan interactions in the Eighteenth and Nineteenth Centuries in Northern Australia and Contemporary Sea Rights Claims." *Australian Aboriginal Studies* 1:3–17.

Sanders, Will. 2018. "Missing ATSIC: Australia's Need for a Strong Indigenous Representative Body." In *The Neoliberal State, Recognition and Indigenous Rights: New Paternalism to New Imaginings*, edited by Deirdre Howard-Wagner, Maria Bargh, and Isabel Altamirano-Jiménez, 113–130. Canberra: ANU Press.

Scambary, Benedict. 2013. *My Country, Mine Country: Indigenous People, Mining and Development Contestation in Remote Australia*. Canberra: ANU E Press.

Scheinmann, Gabriel M., and Raphael Cohen. 2012. "The Myth of 'Securing the Commons.'" *Washington Quarterly* 35 (1):115–128.

Schlunke, Katrina. 2016. "Burnt Houses and the Haunted Home: Reconfiguring the Ruin in Australia." In *Housing and Home Unbound: Intersections in Economics, Environment and Politics in Australia*, edited by Nicole Cook, Aidan Davison, and Louise Crabtree, 218–231. London: Routledge.

Schwendener, Martha. "Karrabing Film Collective Reflects a Disturbing Reality at MoMA PS1." *New York Times*, May 16, 2019. https://www.nytimes.com/2019/05/15/arts/design/karrabing-film-collective-moma-ps1.html.

Scientific Inquiry into Hydraulic Fracturing in the Northern Territory. 2018. *Final Report*. Darwin: Northern Territory Government. https://frackinginquiry.nt.gov.au/inquiry-reports?a=494286.

Scott, James C. 1998. *Seeing Like a State: Why Certain Schemes to Improve the Human Condition Have Failed*. New Haven: Yale University Press.

———. 2009. *The Art of Not Being Governed: An Anarchist History of Southeast Asia*. New Haven: Yale University Press.

Seed, Patricia. 2001. *American Pentimento: The Invention of Indians and the Pursuit of Riches*. Minneapolis and London: University of Minnesota Press.

Seigel, Monica. (2014). "Hypothecation." *Transition* 114:134–145.

———. 2018. "Violence Work: Policing and Power." *Race & Class* 59 (4):15–33.

Senior, Kate, Richard Chenhall, Julie Hall, and Daphne Daniels. 2018. "Re-Thinking the Health Benefits of Outstations in Remote Indigenous Australia." *Health & Place* 52:1–7.

Sennett, Richard. 2003. *Respect in a World of Inequality*. New York: Norton.

SGS Economics and Planning. 2009. *A Baseline Community Profile of the Groote Eylandt and Bickerton Island Communities of Angurugu, Umbakumba and Milyakburra*. Canberra: Department of Families, Houses, Community Services and Indigenous Affairs.

Sheehan, James. 1952. Speech given June 3 in the 20th Parliament Senate Debate, Atomic Energy (Control of Materials) Bill 1952. Canberra: Australian Parliament. https://historichansard.net/senate/1952/19520603_senate_20_217/#debate-29-s5.

Sheller, Mimi. 2014. *Aluminum Dreams: The Making of Light Modernity*. Cambridge, MA: MIT Press.

Shore, Cris, and Susan Wright. 1997. "Policy: A New Field of Anthropology." In *Anthropology of Policy: Critical Perspectives on Governance and Power*, edited by Chris Shore and Susan Wright, 3–39. London and New York: Routledge.

Sider, Gerald. 2014. *Skin for Skin: Death and Life for Inuit and Innu*. Durham: Duke University Press.

Sikka, Prem. 2001. "Regulation of Accountancy and the Power of Capital: Some Observations." *Critical Perspectives on Accounting* 12 (2):199–211.

Sikka, Prem, and Glen Lehman. 2015. "The Supply-Side of Corruption and Limits to Preventing Corruption within Government Procurement and Constructing Ethical Subjects." *Critical Perspectives on Accounting* 28:62–70.

Simpson, Audra. 2014. *Mohawk Interruptus: Political Life across the Borders of Settler States*. Durham: Duke University Press.

———. 2016. "Consent's Revenge." *Cultural Anthropology* 31 (3):326–333.

Siza, Álvaro, and Antonio Angelillo. 1997. *Álvaro Siza: Writings on Architecture*. London: Thames & Hudson.

Skelton, Russell. 2006. "Sex Abuse 'Rife' in NT Communities." *The Age*, May 16, 2006. https://www.theage.com.au/national/sex-abuse-rife-in-nt-communities-20060516-ge2bla.html.

Smee, Ben. 2018. "Sacked NT Minister Ken Vowles Accuses Government of 'Ripping Off' Indigenous People." *Guardian*, December 23, 2018. https://www.theguardian.com/australia-news/2018/dec/24/sacked-nt-minister-ken-vowles-accuses-government-ripping-off-indigenous-people.

Smith, Diane. 2008. "Cultures of Governance and the Governance of Culture: Transforming and Containing Indigenous Institutions in West Arnhem Land." In *Contested Governance: Culture, Power and Institutions in Indigenous Australia*, edited by Janet Hunt, Diane Smith, Stephanie Garling, and Will Sanders, 75–111. Canberra: ANU E-Press.

Smith, Matt. 2019. "Coronial Inquiry into Murder of Gayle Woodford in APY Lands." *The*

Advertiser, July 1, 2019. https://www.adelaidenow.com.au/news/law-order/coronial-inquiry-into-murder-of-gayle-woodford-in-apy-lands/news-story/13c562706e63cbc9326a6d200341ef2c.

Spivak, Gayatry. 1993. *Outside in the Teaching Machine*. London: Routledge.

Stanner, W.E.H. 1953. "The Dreaming." In *The Dreaming and Other Essays*, edited by Robert Manne, 57–72. Collingwood, Vic: Black Inc. Agenda.

———. 1968. *The Boyer Lectures 1968: After the Dreaming*. Sydney: Australian Broadcasting Commission.

Stengers, Isabelle. 2009. "History through the Middle: Between Macro and Mesopolitics." *Inflexions: A Journal for Research Creation* 3:183–275.

———. 2012. Reclaiming Animism. *e-flux* 36. https://www.e-flux.com/journal/36/61245/reclaiming-animism/

———. 2017. *Another Science Is Possible: A Manifesto for Slow Science*. Translated by Stephen Muecke. Cambridge, UK: Polity Press.

Stoler, Ann Laura. 2008a. *Along the Archival Grain: Epistemic Anxieties and Colonial Common Sense*. Princeton: Princeton University Press.

———. 2008b. "Imperial Debris: Reflections on Ruins and Ruination." *Cultural Anthropology* 23 (2):191–219.

———. 2013. "Introduction: 'The Rot Remains': From Ruins to Ruination." In *Imperial Debris: On Ruins and Ruination*, edited by Ann Laura Stoler, 1–38. Durham and London: Duke University Press.

Strakosch, Elizabeth. 2015. *Neoliberal Indigenous Policy: Settler Colonialism and the "Post-Welfare" State*. Basingstoke and New York: Palgrave MacMillan.

———. 2019. "The Technical Is Political: Settler Colonialism and the Australian Indigenous Policy System." *Australian Journal of Political Science* (54) 1:114–130.

Stringer, Rebecca. 2007. "A Nightmare of the Neocolonial Kind: Politics of Suffering in Howard's Northern Territory Intervention." *Borderlands e-journal* 6 (2). http://borderlands.net.au/vol6no2_2007/stringer_intervention.htm.

Sullivan, Patrick. 2008. "Bureaucratic Process as Morris Dance: An Ethnographic Approach to the Culture of Bureaucracy in Australian Aboriginal Affairs Administration." *Critical Perspectives on International Business* 4 (2/3):127–141.

———. 2009. "Reciprocal Accountability: Assessing the Accountability Environment in Australian Aboriginal Affairs Policy." *International Journal of Public Sector Management* 22 (1):57–72.

———. 2011. *Belonging Together: Dealing with the Politics of Disenchantment in Australian Indigenous Policy*. Canberra: Aboriginal Studies Press.

Summerson-Carr, E. 2011. *Scripting Addiction: The Politics of Therapeutic Talk and American Sobriety*. Princeton: Princeton University Press.

Sutherland, Heather. 2000. "Trepang and Wangkang: The China Trade of Eighteenth-Century Makassar c. 1720s–1840s." *Bijdragen tot de Taal-, Land- en Volkenkunde* 156 (3), Authority and Enterprise among the Peoples of South Sulawesi:451–472.

Taussig, Michael. 2012. *Beauty and the Beast: The Monstrous Side of Plastic Surgery*. Chicago: Chicago University Press.

Terrill, Leon. 2016. *Beyond Communal and Individual Ownership: Indigenous Land Reform in Australia*. Abingdon, Oxon, and New York: Routledge.

Terry, Jennifer. 2017. *Attachments to War: Biomedical Logics and Violence in Twenty-First-Century America*. Durham and London: Duke University Press.

Tew, Kara, Judy You, and Sabine Pircher. 2008. *Validation of Patient Demographic Data: Northern Territory Hospitals, 2008*. Darwin: Northern Territory Department of Health and Families. https://digitallibrary.health.nt.gov.au/prodjspui/bitstream/10137/295/1/validation_report_001%2021Nov.pdf.

Thomas, Martin, and Margo Neale, eds. 2011. *Exploring the Legacy of the 1948 Arnhem Land Expedition*. Canberra: ANU E Press.

Thomson, Donald. 1983. *Donald Thomson in Arnhem Land*. Edited by Nicolas Peterson. South Yarra, Vic: Curry O'Neil.

Todd, Zoe. 2017. "Fish, Kin and Hope: Tending to Water Violations in *amiskwaciwâskahikan* and Treaty Six Territory." *Afterall: A Journal of Art, Context and Enquiry* 43 (Spring/Summer 2017):102–107.

Toohey, Paul. 2011. "Hard Times: Life after the Intervention." *The Monthly*, March 2011. https://www.themonthly.com.au/issue/2011/march/1300237168/paul-toohey/hard-times.

———. 2017. "Fight for a Place to Call Home." *Northern Territory News*, August 19, 2017:20.

Trainor, Sarah Fleisher, Anna Godduhn, Lawrence K. Duffy, F. Stuart Chapin III, David C. Natcher, Gary Kofinas, and Henry P. Huntington. 2010. "Environmental Injustice in the Canadian Far North: Persistent Organic Pollutants and Arctic Climate Impacts." In *Speaking for Ourselves: Environmental Justice in Canada*, edited by Julian Agyeman, Peter Cole, Randolph Haluza-DeLay, and Pat O'Riley, 144–162. Vancouver and Toronto: University of British Columbia Press.

Tuck, Eve, and C. Ree. 2013. "A Glossary of Haunting." In *Handbook of Autoethnography*, edited by Stacey Holman Jones, Tony E. Adams, and Carolyn Ellis, 639–658. London and New York: Left Coast Press, Routledge.

Tuck, Eve, and K. Wayne Yang. 2017. "Decolonization Is Not a Metaphor." *Decolonization: Indigeneity, Education & Society* 1 (1):1–40.

Tynan, Elizabeth. 2016. *Atomic Thunder: The Maralinga Story*. Sydney: NewSouth Books.

van Egmond, Marie-Elaine. 2012. "Enindhilyakwa Phonology, Morphosyntax and Genetic Position." PhD diss., University of Sydney.

van Wyck, Peter C. 2011. *Highway of the Atom: The Surprising Story of the Atomic Bomb's Origins in Canada's North*. Montreal: McGill-Queen's University Press.

Vincent, Eve. 2007. "Knowing the Country." *Cultural Studies Review* 13 (2):156–165.

———. 2017. *Against Native Title: Conflict and Creativity in Outback Australia*. Canberra: Aboriginal Studies Press.

Vine, David. 2015. *Base Nation: How U.S. Military Bases Abroad Harm America and the World*. New York: Metropolitan Books.

Vismann, Cornelia. 2008. *Files: Law and Media Technology*. Translated by Geoffrey Winthrop-Young. Stanford: Stanford University Press.

Vizenor, Gerald. 2008a. "Aesthetics of Survivance: Literary Theory and Practice." In *Survivance: Narratives of Native Presence*, edited by Gerald Vizenor, 1–24. Lincoln: University of Nebraska Press.

Vizenor, Gerald, ed. 2008b. *Survivance: Narratives of Native Presence*. Lincoln: University of Nebraska Press.

Waddy, Julie-Ann. 1988. *Classification of Plants and Animals from a Groote Eylandt Aboriginal Point of View*. North Australian Research Unit Monograph. Darwin: Australian National University.

Watson, Irene. 2009. "In the Northern Territory Intervention: What Is Saved or Rescued and at What Cost?" *Cultural Studies Review* 15 (2):45–60.

Weszkalnys, Gina. 2017. "Infrastructure as Gesture." In *Infrastructures and Social Complexity: A Companion*, edited by Penny Harvey, Casper Bruun Jensen, and Atsuro Morita, 284–295. Abingdon, Oxon, and New York: Routledge.

Whyte, Kyle P. 2018a. "Is It Colonial Déjà Vu? Indigenous Peoples and Climate Injustice." In *Humanities for the Environment: Integrating Knowledges, Forging New Constellations of Practice*, edited by Joni Adamson and Michael Davis, 88–104. London and New York: Routledge.

———. 2018b. "Indigenous Science (Fiction) for the Anthropocene: Ancestral Dystopias and Fantasies of Climate Change Crises." *Environment and Planning E: Nature and Space* 1 (1–2):224–242.

Wild, Rex, and Pat Anderson. 2007. *Ampe Akelyernemane Meke Mekarle: "Little Children Are Sacred": Report of the Northern Territory Board of Inquiry into the Protection of Aboriginal Children from Sexual Abuse*. Darwin: Northern Territory Government.

Wolfe, Patrick. 2007. "Settler Colonialism and the Elimination of the Native." *Journal of Genocidal Research* 8 (4):387–409.

Wright, Alexis. 2016. "What Happens When You Tell Somebody Else's Story?" *Meanjin* 75 (4):58–76.

Yale, Elizabeth. 2015. "The History of Archives: The State of the Discipline." *Book History* 18:332–359

Index

Page numbers in italics refer to figures

Anthropology of Policy

Cris Shore and Susan Wright, editors

The authorized representative in the EU for product safety and compliance is:
Mare Nostrum Group
B.V Doelen 72
4831 GR Breda
The Netherlands

www.ingramcontent.com/pod-product-compliance
Lightning Source LLC
Chambersburg PA
CBHW030818270326
41928CB00007B/793